BUILDERS OF LATIN AMERICA

BUILDERS OF
LATIN AMERICA

WATT STEWART
New York State College for Teachers,
Albany, New York

AND

HAROLD F. PETERSON
State Teachers College
Buffalo, New York

HARPER & BROTHERS PUBLISHERS
New York and London

CONTENTS

v

CONTENTS

Part Four: Toward a Better Future!

ILLUSTRATIONS

ILLUSTRATIONS

PREFACE

The peoples of the Western Hemisphere have recently become aware of a dangerous menace to their general security and common welfare. To resist that threat the people and government of the United States have revealed a deepening desire to be "good neighbors" to the other American republics. Similarly, the nations of Latin America have shown a growing willingness to accept the neighborly gestures of the United States. The future welfare of all Americans seems to depend in great measure on the extent to which they can coöperate in the defense of common interests.

The people of Latin America and their fascinating history have been largely unknown to young students in the United States. To them, therefore, this recently-created interest opens a new field of knowledge, fresh in its appeal and rich in its new materials for study. Only as they gain a comprehension of the spirit and traditions of the Latin-Americans can true inter-American understanding develop and flourish.

In this volume we have tried to fill a gap in the historical literature of scholars of the earlier high-school years. We have sought to attract them to the history of Latin America by introducing them to typical and engaging individuals. The individual has been made the center of interest in the belief that young students are more readily interested in a person than in an idea, a process, or an impersonal fact. But at the

same time, the leading features of a period or an institution
are presented, though incidentally.

We have divided the four and a half centuries of Latin-
American life into four major stages of development, and a
section of the book is devoted to each. In a concise introduction to each section, lending unity to the separate chapters,
we have summarized Latin-American growth in that stage.
To illustrate each stage we have described the lives and contributions of five or six personalities. We have selected little
known as well as famous persons; evil as well as good; scholars and reformers as well as generals and politicians. We have
given representation to as many of the twenty republics as
possible, in any case to every geographical region. Each person is typical of an age, a country, a movement, or an institution, sometimes of all four. Considered together, these biog-
raphies comprise a reasonably complete introduction to the
history of Latin America.

In every possible instance, we have sought to correlate the
history of Latin America with the history of the United States
by emphasizing similarities and differences in their development. Attention has been given to geographic, economic, and
cultural influences, as well as to the political and military.
Current trends, especially in international affairs, social reform, and modern scholarship, have not been overlooked. In
every phase, we have searched for the typical, not the rare,
and the colorful, not the sensational.

Many of the chapters have been used experimentally in
the Milne High School, New York State College for Teachers, Albany, and the Practice School, State Teachers College,
Buffalo, New York. For valued assistance in these experiments
we are indebted to Dr. Wallace W. Taylor, Supervisor of
Social Studies, and Miss Helena McShane, Milne High

School, State College for Teachers, Albany, and Miss Marguerite Stockberger, Practice School, State Teachers College, Buffalo, New York. Miss Eileen Mulholland, Assistant Professor of English, State Teachers College, Buffalo, has read much of the manuscript with fine critical helpfulness. For aid with the Pronouncing Glossary we are indebted to Dr. James Wesley Childers, of the Spanish Department, State College for Teachers, Albany. Our decision to prepare the book was the result of the suggestion of Dr. Donnal V. Smith, head of the Department of History, State College for Teachers, Albany. But the plan of the work and any errors which may have crept into its writing are our own.

W. S.

H. F. P.

PART ONE

FOUNDATIONS

INDIAN CULTURE
- Aztecs and Mayas
- Incas
- Araucanians
- Tupis and Guaranis
- Caribs

UNITED STATES

MEXICO
Vera Cruz
MEXICO CITY
Santiago
CORTES
CARIBBEAN SEA
CENTRAL AMERICA
Panama
ATLANTIC OCEAN

PACIFIC

OCEAN
Tumbez
Cajamarca
PIZARRO
CUZCO
VALDIVIA
La Serena
Concepción
Valdivia

Amazon
TUPIS
SOUTH
GUARANIS
AMERICA
Uruguay
Rio de la Plata

0   500   1,000 MILES

INTRODUCTION

Colonial Latin America was a region of immense extent at
a time when English America was but a narrow strip, hug-
ging the irregular shores of the Atlantic from Maine to
Florida. Latin America—controlled by Spain and Portugal—
embraced the whole of South America, Central America,
Mexico, the West Indies, Florida, and most of North
America west of the Mississippi River. It was a truly imperial
domain.

At the end of the fifteenth century Spain and Portugal
were well prepared for colonial ventures. After many centuries of struggle they had conquered the invading Moors in
the Hispanic Peninsula. The kings had succeeded in forming
strong governments through which they exercised broad and
effective control of their people. Foreign trade and domestic
activities provided many Spaniards and Portuguese with the
money needed for equipping and sending out expeditions of
exploration and colonization. It was to the advantage of the
Hispanic peoples, moreover, that for still another century
England and France were to be disturbed and weakened by
religious and political conflicts. Too, a new spirit of curiosity
and confidence was rousing the people of Western Europe in
general. Thus Columbus' accidental discovery of the Americas
came at an opportune time, and both Spain and Portugal
were quick to take advantage of it.

As early as the grade school, every American youth learns

3

something about Columbus, Cortés, Pizarro, De Soto, Balboa, and Coronado. Not so many are introduced to Valdivia, Benalcázar, Orellana, Martim Affonso de Souza, and scores of others whose activities were of great importance in exploring, subduing, or colonizing Latin America. They were men like John Smith, Henry Hudson, Lewis and Clark, and many of our own explorers and pioneers. The history of all these men is one of bravery and daring, and sometimes of self-sacrifice and Christian zeal.

French explorers entered the interior of North America by the great avenue of the St. Lawrence River and the Great Lakes. The English, to gain the same region, had to cross the Appalachian Mountains, although they were not very high nor were they arid and barren. Spaniards in North America were not so fortunate. To reach the great central plateau of Mexico they climbed ranges of ten thousand feet. From that plateau northward, the way led through desert or semi-arid country where life was hard. In South America, the Portuguese, coming in from the east, found low-lying mountains such as those the English encountered. But beyond, instead of finding in a temperate climate one of the richest valleys of the world, they found a matted jungle. There life was a constant struggle with too-opulent nature, with ferocious animals and poisonous insects. From the Pacific coast, either deserts or soaring mountains received the would-be Spanish settler. And beyond, again there was the forbidding jungle. Only in the southern regions of South America, both east and west, were the early comers welcomed by a land where, with reasonable effort, they could develop the normal civilized life to which they had been accustomed. Argentine *pampas* and Chilean valleys were hospitable to European cereals and European animals. It is common to speak of the hardships of frontier life as our ancestors lived it, but in many parts of Latin America frontier life was far more difficult, as well as quite different.

In comparing the life of these two groups of settlers, English and Spanish-Portuguese, the Indian factor must be borne in mind. English and French settlers found Indians of low development and in small numbers. One of our pious early settlers rejoiced that "God had seen fit to send a plague to destroy the Indians" on a certain portion of the Atlantic coast, and thus to prepare the ground for English settlers. Perhaps it could be said that God was just as good to the Spaniards (at that time few persons seemed to think that God had any thought for the Indian), though in a different fashion. In Mexico and Peru, the greatest early centers of Spanish colonization and civilization, the Spaniards found Indians of relatively high development, who had stored up much treasure which the Spaniards could seize. More important, there were many millions of them, enough to furnish an inexhaustible labor supply for the development of the new regions. This was a "blessing" decidedly different from that of the English colonizers. Moreover, these Mexican and Peruvian Indians were not of the fierce, warlike type of the Forest and Plains Indians of North America, and thus, despite their large numbers, they were more readily subdued.

Whereas the Englishman solved the problem of the Indians by killing them or driving them back, the Spaniard found it essential to "get along" with his Indians. From this necessity he developed the mission as a great agency of Christianizing and civilizing. Because few Spanish women came to the Americas in the early years, the Spaniard intermarried with the Indian, and soon developed a class of mixed-bloods, the *mestizo*, a class which is now of much importance in many of the Latin-American nations. The Portuguese, on the other hand, did not encounter Indians in such numbers nor of such high attainments as did the Spaniard. But the Portuguese, like the Spaniard, generally settled the Indian problem by intermarriage and civilizing. These contrasts in numbers and types of Indians encountered furnish some of the basic differences in the history of English and of Spanish-Portuguese colonization.

In England, since the drawing of the Magna Carta in 1215, political development had been toward greater participation of the people in their government. This was decidedly not the case in Spain and Portugal, where kings ruled "by divine right" and with absolute control. In English America the colonies from the first enjoyed some degree of self-government. In Latin America no self-government existed until the wars of independence against Spain. This, of course, is another factor of the first importance in understanding differences between Latin-Americans and Anglo-Americans. The latter had training in self-government; the former did not.

In economic matters Spanish colonial history differed only in degree from English colonial history. Insofar as it was possible, England maintained a monopoly of trade and manufacturing, a monopoly which the liberty-loving English colonists struggled to destroy. For a much longer time and to a greater degree Spain and Portugal were successful in controlling colonial trade. Legally, no Spanish or Portuguese colony could trade with foreigners. Nevertheless, because neither Spain nor Portugal was able to supply its colonies with all the manufactured goods they needed, from early times the smuggler found a "happy hunting ground" in Latin America. Over the vast extent of territory that was Latin America it was impossible to enforce trade regulations. Yet, in an effort to do so and to protect the trade from foreign attack, Spain organized a system of merchant fleets. At stated times each year, great fleets, convoyed by warships, sailed from the Spanish peninsula to the "Spanish Main," as the Caribbean was called. Though it operated with considerable success for a time, it was finally abandoned. In the long run, this economic repression was one of the strongest reasons for discontent among the Spanish colonists in America.

With the passage of time a complex social life was built up in the Latin Americas. In Spanish America, Indians had already gathered much wealth in gold and silver. The Spaniards early discovered rich gold and silver mines which they worked industriously—with the labor of the enslaved Indians. Spanish colonists, therefore, had a surplus of wealth with which to support schools and to import those civilizing elements which they believed made life worth living. Mexico City and Lima, Peru, became great cultural centers. The first two universities of the Western Hemisphere were founded in those cities in 1551, more than three-quarters of a century before Harvard University was thought of. Mining and other technical schools were founded. Art schools flourished; artists and writers did excellent work. Already, by 1607, when Jamestown was settled, these cities and many others in Latin America were important centers of European culture. Santa Fe, a distant outpost in what is now New Mexico, was founded by pioneers from Mexico City at about the time that colonists from England were settling Jamestown.

Portugal lagged behind Spain in developing social life in the New World, because in Brazil there was a lack of ready money and of those materials which could be quickly converted into money. Even there, however, in the cities, European civilization was to be found in a rather high stage of development. To such an extent had Spain and Portugal got into the American colonizing field and profited by their century's start over England and France.

In general, the luxuries and the graces of life in the Latin-American colonies were for the ruling classes, the Spaniards and the Portuguese. Indians lived in poverty, perhaps in many cases worse than that existing before the conquest. The *mestizo* was in somewhat better case, though he was looked down upon by the pure-blood white and made to feel his inferior position. But even for these the dreariness of existence was relieved by numerous religious fiestas, cockfights, and, in some sections, bullfights. The rich had their beautiful palaces, their fine horses and carriages, their gorgeous dresses from Spain and Portugal, and their hosts of servants to do the actual work. To some extent the rich patronized artists and actors. In the courts of the colonial viceroys the forms of Spanish and Portuguese court life were carefully observed. For the people of the upper classes, therefore, it appears to have been a grand life.

Though there are some grounds for criticism, the colonial systems of Spain and Portugal in the Americas cannot be condemned out of hand. They held their colonies for more than three hundred years, almost twice as long as did England. And in that period they achieved a great work of colonizing and civilizing. The history of colonial Latin America has many elements that are worth study, both for their interest and for the lessons that may be gained from them.

CHAPTER I

HERNANDO CORTÉS: CONQUEROR OF MEXICO

The Spaniard, Hernando Cortés, contemplated in wonder the Valley of Mexico. With him were the four hundred Spanish warriors who had climbed and fought their way up the mountains from the Gulf of Mexico. Now, as they scaled a crest in the sierras, they suddenly saw, stretched out below them, Tenochtitlán, capital of the Aztecs. Weary from three months of hard marching and fighting, the invaders could now refresh themselves on the magnificent panorama which unrolled before them. They beheld a gorgeous landscape of woods, lakes, and meadows, flanked by towering mountains. Fields of Indian corn and the flowers of orchards and gardens added gay tones to the solemn greens of the forest. Here and there, clinging to the lakes or reposing on the plains, were villages of crude, white homes. Most impressive of all, on an island in the center of the largest lake, like a gem in a silver setting, sat the shining capital city of Mexico. With its massive temples, its luxurious palaces, and its enchanting gardens, it was a kind of "Venice in America."

The Aztec chief who ruled his people from this palatial city was Moctezuma II. During seventeen years before the appearance of Cortés in 1519 he had held sway over the Indians of the valley and the surrounding mountains. Centuries before, his ancestors had first invaded this area, streaming in from the lands to the north. After years of wandering and fighting, in 1325 they had settled down on the shores of Lake Texcoco. This place they had chosen because there, poised on the branch of a thorny cactus, they had beheld a magnificent eagle, a serpent in its claws, its wings stretched for flight. Legend says that the Indians accepted this spectacle as a divine command to build there the capital of their kingdom. They called the place Tenochtitlán, although the rest of the world has come to know it as Mexico, after the Aztec war god, Mexitli. The eagle, serpent, and cactus are familiar to modern Mexicans in the coat of arms of the republic.

The Aztecs prospered in Tenochtitlán, soon replaced their first crude buildings with fine stone ones, and spread their population over the surrounding valley. Capable chieftains developed powerful armies, and by conquest and plunder brought neighboring tribes under their control. Speedily Aztec lands and those of Indians subject to them stretched over the mountains and down to the plains, east and west. By 1500 they controlled or collected tribute from tribes who lived from the Atlantic to the Pacific and as far south as present-day Guatemala. Treasure of great value was brought back to the capital to beautify their city, to enrich the chiefs, or to increase their power. Tenochtitlán grew to be a city of several hundred thousand persons, with two stone aqueducts to furnish drinking water and with three concrete causeways to connect the city with the mainland. Hospitals, great palaces, floating gardens, and a zoo contributed to the comfort and pleasure of the nobles.

The ruler of this "Rome-like" empire was chosen by a small committee of nobles and installed with the pomp and ceremony of an Egyptian monarch. Once in office, the chief ruled with all the powers of an autocrat. He made and administered the laws, respecting the lives and property of the rank and file only when he saw fit. Garrisons were stationed at key points to enforce the royal will. The communication system was so effective that fresh fish could be carried the two hundred miles from the Gulf of Mexico to the royal table in twenty-four hours. The Aztecs, it is clear, were far more advanced than the wandering Indians of North America, such as the Mohawks, the Blackfeet, or the Seminoles.

Still, in another respect, the Aztecs were astonishingly barbarous, for, in their religion, they practiced human sacrifice and cannibalism. Although they believed in a Supreme Creator of the universe, they worshiped numerous deities, thirteen principal ones and several hundred others. Almost every day or week in the year was devoted to the honor of one of the gods. In the capital city alone there were more than forty temples, one of which maintained a staff of five thousand priests. The most important of the temples was a huge pyramid of earth and stone, four or five stories high, which covered at least two acres. On this pyramid, captives taken in battle were sacrificed. Here, six priests, clad in robes of sable, stretched out the victim on the sacrificial stone and, to appease their gods, cut the heart from the living body. Then the body of the prisoner was turned over to the soldier who had taken him in battle, so that, with appropriate drink and food, he might entertain his friends at dinner. All of this was done, not in sheer barbarity, but as a part of a sacred ritual. It is said that sometimes as many as twenty thousand victims were sacrificed in a single year. It was a curious mixture of the civilized and the inhuman.

It was, Cortés said, to rid Mexico of these inhuman practices that he invaded Tenochtitlán in the early part of November, 1519. However, before we witness his entry into

the city and his dramatic meeting with Moctezuma II, we
need to explain his sudden appearance on the heights above
the valley. By what strange daring were Cortés and a few
hundred countrymen able to march into the heart of powerful
Tenochtitlán? What promise of reward had persuaded these
adventurous *conquistadores* (conquerors) from faraway Spain
to invade the New World?

Only twenty-seven years before Cortés invaded Mexico,
Christopher Columbus had discovered the "Indies." In the
meantime, Spanish adventurers of all types—penniless noble-
men, soldiers of fortune, crusading friars, debtors and
criminals, substantial citizens—flocked to the Caribbean in
search of fame, fortune, or fleeting adventure. Once the West
Indies were well subdued, the more daring *conquistadores*
penetrated the mainland of North and South America. Within
half a century after Columbus' first voyage, Spain brought
under its yoke all those parts of the Western Hemisphere
now inhabited by Spanish-speaking peoples. Daring, ruthless
sons created an empire for "God, gold, and glory!" They
brought the God of the Old World to the natives of the
New World, but the gold and glory they took for their
king—and for themselves.

Of all the great commanders who conquered an empire for
Spain—Balboa, Magellan, Pizarro, Valdivia, De Soto, Coronado, and dozens of others—none was greater than Hernando
Cortés. In 1504, at the age of nineteen, he first landed on
the island of Haiti, happy to escape from a life of idleness in
his Spanish home, eager to search for the mystery and
romance, the glory and gold, of the New World. Soon after
his arrival Cortés received a grant of land and a group of
Indians to work it and, had he chosen, might have settled
down to the life of a prosperous planter. The monotonous life

was not for him, however, and soon he was engaging in duels over love-affairs, in studying the methods of Indian warfare, and in learning the acts of cruelty that he was to use—too often—in his conquest of Mexico.

When, in 1511, the opportunity came to participate in the subjugation of Cuba, Cortés eagerly joined. His courage and good-humor won the respect and favor of the new governor of the island, for whom he became a secretary. Still craving action, however, the young adventurer was not ready to settle down. With other young "hotheads" he conspired against the governor. He was twice imprisoned, but escaped on both occasions. He was reconciled with the governor, received another grant of land and Indians, and returned to the life of a cattle-raiser. Then, with a wife, with increasing income from his plantation and his gold mines, and as an official in his town, Cortés was apparently resigned to enjoying the life of a contented citizen.

This life of repose, however, was abruptly interrupted in 1518 by fantastic tales of new conquests and new sources of riches in Mexico. The governor of Cuba, searching for a commander to lead a new expedition and to help finance it, made Cortés captain-general of the fleet. This was the great object for which the young *conquistador* had come to the New World fifteen years before. Now he was free to throw off the monotony of life on the islands and to satisfy the ambition that had been gnawing within him—the ambition to discover, to explore, and to conquer. His whole fortune, together with funds from his friends, went to the outfitting of vessels, to the purchase of arms and provisions, and to the recruiting of men. His instructions were broad. He was to convert the Indians, survey the coasts, and report on the products, people, and progress of the country—all in the name of his God and his king.

On February 18, 1519, Cortés sailed from Cuba with the strongest force he was able to collect—eleven vessels, seven hundred men, and sixteen horses. His banner of black velvet, embroidered with a brilliant red cross, bore, in Latin, this motto· "Friends, let us follow the Cross; and under this sign, if we have faith, we shall conquer." W. H. Prescott, the great American historian, says that, at this time, Cortés

was thirty-three, or perhaps thirty-four years of age. In stature he was rather above the middle size. His complexion was pale; and his large dark eye gave an expression of gravity to his countenance, not to have been expected in one of his cheerful temperament. His figure was slender, at least until later life; but his chest was deep, his shoulders broad, his frame muscular and well proportioned. It presented the union of agility and vigor which qualified him to excel in fencing, horsemanship, and the other generous exercises of chivalry. In his diet he was temperate, careless of what he ate, and drinking little; while to toil and privation he seemed perfectly indifferent. His dress . . . was such as to set off his handsome person to advantage; neither gaudy nor striking but rich. He wore few ornaments, and usually the same; but those were of great price. His manners, frank and soldierlike, concealed a most cool and calculating spirit. With his gayest humor there mingled a settled air of resolution, which made those who approached him feel they must obey; and which infused something like awe into the attachment of his most devoted followers. Such a combination, in which love was tempered by authority, was the one probably best calculated to inspire devotion in the rough and turbulent spirits among whom his lot was to be cast.'

[1] *History of the Conquest of Mexico* (First Modern Library edition, New York, 1936), pp. 142-43.

Thus began for Cortés the career of conquests that was to lead him up the mountains of Mexico and up the peaks of fame in the history of the Americas. The army first landed in Yucatán, then moved on to Tabasco on the Gulf of Campeche. In both places, as indeed, everywhere he went, Cortés undertook the conquest of the Indians, then their conversion to Christianity. These first two conquests were chiefly important because they brought to Cortés two persons who were to prove invaluable to him during the next two years—two interpreters, a man and a girl. The first was Aguilar, a Spaniard who had been shipwrecked on the coasts of Yucatán eight years before and who had learned to speak the language of the Maya Indians of that region. The second was a bright Indian maiden, who was given to Cortés along with a number of female slaves. Called Malinche by her people, she was christened Doña Marina by the Spaniards. She was able to speak the languages of both the Mayas and the Aztecs. Therefore, Cortés could speak to Aguilar in Spanish, Aguilar to Malinche in Mayan, and Malinche to the Mexican chiefs in Aztec.

Malinche soon made herself indispensable to Cortés. First only his interpreter, she soon became his comrade, his adviser, and mother of his child. Her admiration for the manly Cortés changed to devotion, and she quickly learned Spanish in order that she might speak directly to her lover. Her charm and sympathy, her knowledge of the languages and the habits of the Indians, and her loyalty to the Spaniards made her as essential to Cortés as any one of his most trusted lieutenants. The name of Malinche, or Marina, became known far and wide throughout Mexico and even in Spain.

From these interpreters Cortés learned of the wealth and power of the Aztecs, and he determined to set about their conquest. Moving his fleet northward along the coast of Mexico, he founded the town of Villa Rica de Vera Cruz (Rich City of the True Cross). This spot, where the army landed on April 21, 1519, Good Friday, was to become one of the greatest ports of Spain in the New World and is today one of the chief cities of Mexico. Here, on Easter Sunday, Cortés received special messengers from Moctezuma, who brought gifts of richly colored feather work and finely carved gold ornaments. From these and other Indians who came to visit him from time to time, Cortés learned more and more of Moctezuma and his kingdom. He learned that the Aztec chief ruled by the power of his army, and that many of the tribes were obedient to him only because they were forced to be. The conqueror was wise enough in the ways of men to see that this was a source of weakness in the Aztec empire; he readily saw the possibility of weaning these disloyal tribes from Moctezuma and using them as allies against the chief. Cortés also learned that Quetzalcoatl, the chief god of the Aztecs, was believed to have white skin and a long beard. He was also thought to have left Mexico at an earlier day for a voyage across the Atlantic, with the promise to return at some future time. This belief, too, Cortés could use to good advantage. He would pretend to be that fair white god. He was white, wore a long beard, and, riding his horse, might appear as something divine. This was all the more possible, since the Indians had never before seen a horse.

Cortés now began to prepare for the march to the capital city of the Aztecs. He ordered the destruction of all but one of the vessels in the harbor of Vera Cruz so that there might be no turning back. The little band of four hundred warriors was now completely on its own, without means of escape, planning to march into a country of hundreds of thousands of hostile Indians. With their few horses, seven field guns, thirteen hundred Indian warriors, and a thousand baggage-carriers, on August 16, 1519, they set out.

The army marched the first day over the hot, sandy coastal section of Mexico—the land of vanilla and cacao, of bright flowers and sweet fruits, of tropical birds and insects, of burning heat, heavy rains, and malaria. Then they began to climb the mountains through narrow passes and dense forests, into clearer air and more temperate climate. By the end of the third day they had reached the tablelands, seven thousand feet high, where great trees and fields of corn and cactus were common. As they proceeded, they passed more frequently through Indian villages, where the natives marveled at the horses and dogs, the huge guns, and the strange dress of the white men. Here and there the commander halted to rest his men and animals or to treat with the Indians. Always the invaders must be on their guard against ambush, sleeping with their weapons at their sides. Always there were difficulties to cope with: changing climate, illness, ferocious enemies, treachery within the ranks.

Before Cortés could enter Tenochtitlán itself, there were two powerful groups of Indians who must be subdued—those who resided in the cities of Tlascala and Cholula. By the massacre of thousands, the conqueror was able to subdue them, and by appeal to their hatred of Moctezuma, he won them as allies for the march on the capital. Thousands of the Tlascalans joined the Spaniards for the march up to the plateau of Mexico, past one of the highest volcanoes in North America, Popocatepetl (the mountain that smokes). Slowly and carefully, the enlarged army crept up into the area of cold winds, snow, and sleet, where cotton clothing provided inadequate warmth for their tired bodies. Early in November, they reached the mountain heights above Tenochtitlán, where we first observed them at the beginning of this sketch.

Now there occurred one of the most dramatic incidents in all history—the march of four hundred Spaniards into the heart of a city of two or three hundred thousand hostile Indians. It was a moment from which an ordinary man would have shrunk in panic, but Cortés was not an ordinary man. He marched his little army straight into the villages that lay about the lakes surrounding the capital city, villages so lovely that the soldiers could scarcely believe their eyes. One of them, Bernal Díaz, described the sight as follows:

. . . To many of us it appeared doubtful whether we were asleep or awake; nor is the manner in which I express myself to be wondered at, for it must be considered, that never yet did man see, hear, or dream of any thing equal to the spectacle which appeared to our eyes on this day.

When we approached Iztapalapa, we were received by several great lords of that country, relations of Montezuma, who conducted us to our lodgings there, in palaces magnificently built of stone, and the timber of which was cedar, with spacious courts, and apartments furnished with canopies of the finest cotton. After having contemplated these noble edifices we walked through the gardens, which were admirable to behold from the variety of beautiful and aromatic plants, and the numerous alleys filled with fruit trees, roses, and various flowers. Here was also a lake of the clearest water, which communicated with the grand lake of Mexico by a channel cut for the purpose, and capable of admitting the largest canoes. The whole was ornamented with works of art, painted, and admirably plaistered and whitened, and it was rendered more delightful by numbers of beautiful birds.

A view of two Mexican volcanoes, Popocatepetl (left) and Ixtaccihuatl. From the sulphur of Popocatepetl, the mountain that smokes, Cortés manufactured gun powder with which to attack the Aztecs.

These "plumed serpents" are at the base of Pyramid Temple of Quetzalcoatl, chief god of the Aztecs. The Aztecs believed the god had white skin and a long beard—a belief which Cortés used to advantage when he invaded Tenochtítlan, the Aztec capital.

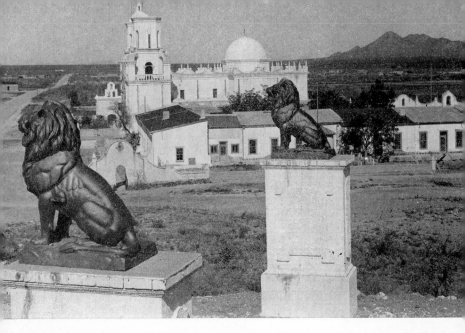

The Mission of San Xavier del Bac, Tucson, Arizona, founded by Father Kino. This was one of his largest and most influential missions, and is still in use today.

Some Navajo woven blankets recently displayed at the Museum of Modern Art, in New York City. This collection illustrates characteristic Navajo designs—striping, squares, diamonds, terraced borders, zigzagging.

When I beheld the scenes that were around me, I thought within myself that this was the garden of the world![2]

As the army left the mainland, it was obliged to follow a narrow causeway, four or five miles in length and only a few feet wide, which led to the island city. On either side thousands of Indians paddled hundreds of canoes, with the hope of catching sight of the curious invaders. From the causeway the Spaniards marched on to the island of Moctezuma, wondering what fate awaited them. Would Cortés be greeted as the returning white god? Would the chief receive them in friendliness? Would they ever leave the island alive? Sobering thoughts must have been in their minds as Moctezuma, regal in his embroidered cloak and precious stones, came forward. There was a brief interview, during which Cortés placed a chain of sparkling stones about Moctezuma's neck. The Aztec chief greeted the Spaniard as the *representative* of Quetzalcoatl and invited him and his men to rest in one of the royal palaces.

During the next few days, the Spaniards were shown the sights of the city. They visited the public buildings, chapels, and temples. On top of one of the temples, built in the form of a pyramid, a Spanish soldier spent many hours counting the skulls of the victims who had been sacrificed to the gods. There were more than one hundred and thirty-six thousand. All these experiences were, of course, fascinating to the Spaniards, but Cortés had come to Mexico as a conqueror, not as a sightseer. His mind was growing restless; he must be about his business. After consulting his officers he decided to make a prisoner of Moctezuma and hold him as a hostage. Within

[2] Captain Bernal Díaz del Castillo, *The True History of the Conquest of Mexico* (New York, Robert M. McBride & Company, 1927), I, 160-61.

a week, the Aztec chief was seized, then forced to see his highest officials burned alive and to acknowledge the king of Spain as his master. Moreover, great amounts of treasure were exacted. Finally, the Aztecs were obliged to cease their practice of human sacrifice. Cortés could now feel that he had conquered Mexico.

The Spaniards had been in the city of Mexico about six months when bad news was brought up from the coast—the news that Pánfilo de Narváez had come to Vera Cruz to undertake the suppression of Cortés. The governor of Cuba who had commissioned Cortés was by now jealous of his success and accused him of rebellion. The governor's agent, De Narváez, was sent to punish Cortés. This was a threat which the conqueror of Mexico could not ignore. Leaving his aide, Pedro de Alvarado, with one hundred and forty men, in charge of the city, Cortés marched off to deal with De Narváez. With little difficulty, stout Cortés defeated the army of De Narváez and put his enemy in chains. This was late in May, 1520.

No sooner had Cortés crushed the danger from his own countrymen than bad news again reached him, this time from Tenochtitlán. The Indians of the capital had revolted and were besieging Alvarado and his little band in their own quarters. Immediately, with some hundreds of fresh Spanish soldiers in his ranks, Cortés marched again up to the plateau. This time the Spaniards entered a city of sinister quietness. There were no canoes, no curious spectators, no chiefs to greet them, nothing of the formal welcome that had been theirs only seven months before. From Alvarado, Cortés soon learned the cause of this stillness. During a religious festival some weeks before, Alvarado and his men, in cold blood, had slain six hundred high-ranking nobles of the Aztec empire. He said he had learned of a conspiracy among them. Within a few minutes, the dancing, chanting chiefs, without means of defense, had been butchered. Almost to a man, the Aztecs rose against this insult to their religion and to their leaders, and now, as Cortés returned, the Indians were waiting until thirst and famine should force the surrender of Alvarado's murderers. The conqueror was furious at the action of his aide. "You have done badly," he said to him. "You have been false to your trust. Your conduct has been that of a madman!"

But the damage was done. The angered Aztecs now rose up in all their native ferocity to attack the Spaniards. For a week the fighting raged, as wave after wave of the Indians moved on the quarters of the Spaniards, only to be mowed down by the artillery. Even the appearance of Moctezuma himself was not enough to quiet the Indian hordes. They hurled stones at their king with such force that one killed him. Now, the last great advantage of Cortés over the Aztecs was gone; no longer could he hold the chief as a pledge against the violence of the Indians. Moreover, food and water were running low in the Spanish camp. There was now no doubt as to the course to be pursued. Cortés must flee the city.

The Spaniards determined to make a run for it at midnight. A cold rain was falling, when Cortés, with his Spanish and native warriors, ventured forth. The city slept, but not the Aztec sentinels. Their cries of alarm rang through the streets, and quickly the city was alive with warriors. The Spaniards sought to flee over one of the causeways leading to the mainland. Everywhere along the way, Indians in canoes were ready to pull the Spaniards down into the waters of the lake, where, laden with golden treasure, their bodies sank to the chilly depths. Three breaches in the causeway had to be crossed, two of them without bridges. Wagons, guns, booty, and the bodies of men and horses piled up in the breaks until the last to come could climb over them. Cortés and his leaders tried to rally the men, but there was only confusion. It was every man for himself, only the shattered remains of the army crossing safely. This was the awful night of June 30, 1520, that has come to be known as *la noche triste*, "the sad night."

It was, indeed, a sad night for Cortés. As morning came, he could contemplate only losses and sorrow. He had lost four or five hundred of his men, many of his Indian allies, most of the treasure, many of the horses, and every gun. Of the women, only the faithful Malinche and two others remained. Most damaging of all, the conqueror had lost Tenochtitlán. With only their swords and what was left of their courage remaining, the battered Spaniards dragged themselves to Tlascala, there to rest among their Indian friends.

The star of Cortés had sunk very low, but it had certainly not set. The conqueror was still determined to have Mexico. Step by step, in the city of the friendly Tlascalans, he prepared for one final assault on the home of the Aztecs. He secured more men, more horses, and more guns from Spanish ships which had stopped at Vera Cruz. He manufactured powder with sulphur taken from inside the crater of the smoking Popocatapetl. With timber and pitch from nearby woods and iron from Vera Cruz, he directed the construction of thirteen sailing vessels. These were taken apart, transported piece by piece on the backs of thousands of Indian allies sixty miles to the lakes of Tenochtitlán, and there rebuilt. There, too, he assembled every man, every gun, every horse he could muster. By the end of May, 1521, he was ready to attack the waiting Aztecs.

For nearly three months the city lay besieged. Spanish ships drove the Indian canoes from the lakes. Many of the temples and palaces and most of the homes were destroyed. The natives ate grass and the bark of trees to sustain life. One hundred thousand, perhaps many more, died from wounds, famine, or disease. Finally, unable to hold out longer, the city surrendered, and the remaining defenders, feeble and stricken, were permitted to straggle out into the countryside. The Aztecs, once the proud rulers of a mighty empire, had come to their end—their chiefs dead, their army wiped out, and their capital destroyed. Cortés, at last, had conquered Mexico.

Yes, Cortés was a conqueror—and a destroyer. With a handful of men he had conquered one of the two largest empires in the Western Hemisphere and destroyed its civilization. Still, he was a builder too. Upon the ruins of the city he had destroyed he began the construction of a new capital, the capital of "New Spain." Swarms of Indians built new homes, new market places, and new gardens. There was a new temple as well, a great Christian cathedral, where human sacrifice would not be practiced. Spanish settlers were brought in, and, with them, the most important European grains, fruits, and vegetables. The countryside began to prosper anew, with the oranges, peaches, vines, and olives of the Old World. Horses, cattle, sheep, and hogs began to graze for the first time in the meadows of the Valley of Mexico. New Spain, soon to be the greatest Spanish colony, had been founded. Unfortunately, however, hundreds of thousands of the defeated Indians were reduced to practical slavery by the Spaniards and were forced to labor on public works, in the mines, or on the large estates. Only in the last twenty-five years have the Indians of Mexico begun to regain some of their lost pride and dignity.

Meanwhile, Cortés continued his conquests and explora-

tions. South he went into Guatemala and Honduras and west
to the Pacific, winning new lands for the Spanish crown. On
one of these expeditions, Malinche, his loyal companion for
years, was turned over to one of his friends who became her
lawful husband. In 1528, for the first time, Cortés returned
to his native Spain to receive thanks and gifts from his king.
He was given the title of Marquess of the Valley of Oaxaca,
together with huge grants of land in Mexico and control over
twenty-three thousand Indian vassals. In spite of these great
gifts, however, Cortés was disappointed that he received no
position in the government of the colony he had founded. Two
years later, he returned to take charge of his vast estates in
Mexico, where he lived actively, but unhappily, until 1540.
Then he returned again to Spain. There, old, poor, and almost
forgotten, he lived until his death in 1547.

CHAPTER II

ATAHUALPA: LAST OF THE INCAS

A huge oil painting hangs on a wall of the National Museum in Lima, Peru. A work of the Peruvian artist, Montero, it is called "The Funeral of Atahualpa." The scene represents the great, shadowy interior of the church of San Fernando—a pagan temple converted into a place of Christian worship. Slightly removed from the center of the canvas, appearing serene and noble in death, lies the body of the Inca emperor, Atahualpa. In the immediate foreground, handsome, bronze-skinned, dressed in brilliant colors, are several wives of the dead emperor. The shining armor of a number of Spanish officers and soldiers highlights the painting and contrasts strikingly with the somber background and the gaudy dress of the women. The faces of the Indian women are distorted with grief and rage as they struggle in the hands of the Spaniards. The struggle—so unexpected and so unseemly in the presence of death and in a Christian church—is taking place because the widows are attempting to commit suicide and accompany their lord on his journey into the Unknown. What is the origin of this scene? Why is the emperor dead? How does it happen that these warriors from across the ocean are witnesses of and participants in this barbaric incident? The explanation is found in the story of the conquest of Peru by the Spaniard, Francisco Pizarro. And to understand that

25

story one must know something of the Indians whom Pizarro encountered when he entered Peru in 1532.

The empire of the Incas[1] was the most completely, and perhaps the most wisely, organized of all the native governments which the Spaniards found when they came to the Americas. It was also the largest. *Tahuantinsuyo* (four quarters of the world), as the Indians called it, at its greatest extent, included present Ecuador, Peru, Bolivia, the greater part of Chile, much of Northwestern Argentina, and parts of Western Brazil. It contained probably ten to fifteen million inhabitants. All of this immense empire was ruled from the capital, Cuzco. This city, still existing, though with no more than thirty thousand inhabitants, deserves special attention.

Cuzco is called by the Peruvians, and quite justly, "the archeological capital of South America." It lies at the center of Peru in the Andes at an elevation of eleven thousand feet. Some authorities estimate that its population once numbered two hundred thousand. At any rate, it was a large city and, considering that those who built it were only high-stage barbarians, it was a city at which to marvel. The houses of most of the inhabitants were of mud or other unsubstantial materials, but the residences of the Inca and the nobles and the many buildings for religious uses were constructed of stone. The perfection of that stonework may be observed today, for some of the streets of Cuzco display on both sides walls of Inca construction. The great Temple of the Sun in Cuzco was the most magnificent structure in the Americas, and, in its richness of decoration, the Spaniards thought it worthy of comparison with any building in Europe. The fine stonework

---

[1] The word "Inca," properly used, is applied to the ruler himself, but by usage it has been extended as well to the people whom he ruled.

of this temple can still be judged by examining certain portions of the church of Santo Domingo, Cuzco's finest showpiece. The ancient Peruvians were master masons. Any doubt on that score must be removed when one examines the ruins of Sacsahuamán, a strong fortress that crowned a hill which rises eight hundred feet above the city. Some of the stones of those walls measure thirty-eight by eighteen by six feet. And they were brought to the spot from quarries some miles distant. It is to be doubted that the Egyptians did anything more difficult when they built the famous pyramids.

Cuzco was the capital of the empire of the Incas. Thence all lines of power went out. And those lines were very numerous. The government was a despotism, though a somewhat mild one. Every person's life was completely planned and controlled by the Inca and his officers. One couldn't even *enjoy* himself in his own fashion, for all picnics and celebrations were planned by the government and supervised by it. The people were organized into groups of ten families, each with an official who was responsible for order and for proper performance of duties. Ten groups of ten families made up the next higher unit, also with its superior officer. Ten of these— or a thousand families—constituted another unit; and so on to the top where the four great divisions of the entire empire were. Over each of these was a lieutenant of the Inca, directly responsible to him.

The Inca was thought to be a child of the sun. As such he was not only respected as the head of the political government, but he was also venerated as a blood-relative of the great Sun God. Even the highest officer always removed his shoes before he entered the presence of the Inca and bore a small burden on his back in token of humility. There could be no thought of disrespect for the emperor nor of disobedience to his command.

Everything in the empire belonged to the Inca. The land in any given section was divided into three parts. One was devoted to the support of the Inca and his government; one was for the gods; the third was for the people. A redistribution of land took place every year, though it is probable that the same plot was returned to a family more or less regularly. The law determined the order in which the people should work these three classes of land. First, that of the gods was cared for. The people next worked their own fields. Last, they tilled the lands of the emperor. The third operation was accompanied by feasting and singing to show respect for the emperor and to demonstrate their happiness in serving him. Not all of the common people worked in the fields. Special groups manufactured the many necessities other than food— tools, pottery, weapons, textiles. The ancient Peruvians were particularly skilled in making fine cloth, beautifully colored and woven. Cloth made from the wool of the vicuña (a wild cousin of the llama and the alpaca, all cousins of the camel) was finest; it could be worn only by the Inca and his family. Every man's task was assigned him, and usually the son followed the occupation of his father, the daughter that of her mother. Each village specialized in some particular craft. Distribution of the products of all this labor was made regularly, each family getting what was needed for its support. The portion for the gods was turned over to the priests for use or storage. The share of the Inca was placed in storehouses distributed about the empire. Wherever the army or the Inca happened to be, there would be found ample stores of food and equipment. It is clear that the system did not provide for idleness. To be idle was to be criminal.

The family was the social unit. An interesting feature of family life was the manner in which it was begun. At a given time each year a great wedding festival was held. The young men and women of marriageable age were paired, according to their own wishes—if they had a special wish—or by an official. Then the marriage ceremony was performed, the wedding feast was celebrated, and everyone went back to work. There were no honeymoon trips. In this fashion, work was not disorganized. The newlyweds were apportioned a plot of land (to be increased with the birth of each child). Bachelors and old maids were exceedingly rare among the ancient Peruvians.

There was little education for the masses except that which was immediately practical. They were instructed in the operations of farming and the care of stock—that is, of the llama and the alpaca which were the only domesticated animals. Those chosen for specialized occupations were taught their craft, usually by the parents. Sons of the Inca and the nobles received a special type of training. They, of course, were prepared for holding office. This higher instruction was given by the priests. As the Incas had no system of writing, the youngsters spent no time in the painful process of learning to spell and to read. However, they did have to learn to make knots in strings—the means by which records were kept.

For all except the ruling class, life among these people was rather limited. The common people were not permitted to travel about. However, whole villages, if the Inca decided it was desirable, might be picked up and moved to form a colony in a newly-conquered region. Yet no one could starve. There was a perfect system of old-age pensions. There were no beggars among the Incas. And, for evident reasons, there were few thieves. A stick set across the doorway was sufficient to keep everyone out; when the stick was there, the door was presumed to be "locked." The great criticism, from our point of view, is that there was no room for ambition, for personal advancement. One did not advance; he remained where he was born. Not every boy could, as with us, hope some day to be the Inca. Even among the more intelligent upper class, there was little **opportunity** for developing or exercising initiative. That is perhaps one of the reasons why the Spaniards so readily conquered the Peruvians.

Huayna Capac, the father of Atahualpa, was one of the greatest of the Incas. He ruled his empire with wisdom and extended its bounds. The greatest extension was in the conquest of Quito, now Ecuador. In Quito the Inca found a beautiful princess whom he added to his harem. This woman became the mother of Huayna Capac's son, Atahualpa. In his later years, the Inca spent much time in Quito, and he became very fond of this intelligent, handsome, and energetic son. He took him on military campaigns and taught him everything that a young man in his station was expected to know. The Inca Huayna Capac had many other sons, but the only one that need be mentioned was Huascar. Huascar's mother was the Inca's sister and, according to Inca custom, this son was the legal successor to the throne. However, when Huayna Capac saw the end of his life approaching, he did a strange thing, something that none of his predecessors had ever done: he decreed that on his death the empire should be divided between Huascar and Atahualpa. Huascar was to have the southern part with the capital at Cuzco. Atahualpa was to have for his domain the northern section, including Quito, the land of his mother.

The death of Huayna Capac and the division of the empire occurred only a few years before the Spaniards came to Peru.

In the meantime, some unfortunate developments took place. Huascar, inclined toward a peaceful life, accepted his father's will in good faith. Atahualpa, however, was ambitious. He was not content to rule his part of the empire, but encroached upon the territories of his brother. Huascar resented this unfairness, and soon the brothers were engaged in a bloody war. Atahualpa was the better leader and had two excellent generals whom he sent to take Huascar's capital. The old city and the fortress nearby were the scenes of some fierce fighting, but they fell to Atahualpa's forces. Huascar was captured and taken with the troops when they returned northward. He was imprisoned at Jauja, some two hundred miles south of the city of Cajamarca, where for a time Atahualpa had his headquarters. It was at this juncture that Pizarro arrived with his tiny band of rapacious, but fearless, Spaniards.

Francisco Pizarro was an unlettered Spaniard of humble birth, who had come to the Isthmus of Panama to seek his fortune. About 1525, having heard reports of a rich land to the south, he conceived the idea of leading an expedition in that direction. Perhaps he could find another native people as rich as the Mexicans, whom Cortés had just conquered, and from whom he was taking much gold. With the assistance of another adventurer and gold-seeker, Diego de Almagro, and a priest, Hernando de Luque, he made several attempts to reach Peru. The partners had many misfortunes and made only slight progress for some years.

One of the most famous episodes of this period occurred on the little Island of Gallo, off the coast of Ecuador, only two degrees north of the equator. On one of his expeditions down the Pacific, Pizarro had stopped there with half a hundred men while Almagro returned to Panama for more men and supplies. Food ran low, the torrid climate was atrocious, and tropical insects made life miserable. The men became discouraged and threatened to quit the project. In the midst of their grumblings, Pizarro called them together. With his sword he drew a line in the sand from east to west. Then turning toward the south he said:

Friends and comrades, on that side are toil, hunger, nakedness, the drenching storm, desertion, and death; on this side, ease and pleasure. There lies Peru with its riches; here Panama and its poverty. Choose each man what best becomes a brave Castilian. For my part, I go to the south.[2]

Pizarro then stepped across the line. He was followed by thirteen of his party. The thirteen continued with Pizarro. The others were permitted to return to Panama where they no doubt bitterly bewailed their lack of courage. A leader who possesses as fearless a spirit as Pizarro displayed under these circumstances seldom fails in his projects. At last, early in 1532, after many additional discouragements, Pizarro found himself on shore in Northern Peru, not far from the present port of Paita.

What a ridiculous venture it seemed—less than two hundred Spaniards setting out to take an empire of more than ten million! But strangely enough, they succeeded. Pizarro learned that the Inca was at Cajamarca, so he set out for that place, sending ahead a messenger to announce his coming. The party had some very rough country to cover. Cajamarca lies inland two hundred miles or so beyond one of the ranges of the Andes. The Spaniards had to ascend ten or twelve thousand feet before they could go down to the tableland on which Cajamarca is seated. As they proceeded, they were met

[2] Wm. H. Prescott, *History of the Conquest of Peru* (Home Library ed.), I, 200.

by messengers from Atahualpa, bearing friendly greetings and presents of llamas (a welcome addition to the menu) and an invitation to visit the Inca. After many hardships, the crossing was made. As the party approached Cajamarca, they were appalled by the sight of the encampment of the Peruvians spread out on the slopes near the city. The Indians appeared countless.

When the Spaniards reached the city, they found it deserted—to make room for the guests, the Inca later explained. They established themselves in the chief square of the town in quarters which were, apparently, intended originally for the Inca and his soldiers. Then Pizarro sent Hernando de Soto with fifteen horsemen to call on the emperor and learn, if possible, how matters stood. Atahualpa received them somewhat silently, explaining that he was engaged in a religious fast. He promised, however, to come to Cajamarca the following day. Though the Spaniards on their horses were strange sights to the Peruvians and some were frightened by them, Atahualpa exhibited no concern.

When De Soto returned and reported, the Spaniards began to take stock of their situation. It would be extremely desperate if the Inca should prove hostile. And though his expressions had been friendly, it was feared that he was planning treachery. Pizarro had persevered too long in his project to be scared out at this point. The situation called for desperate measures, and such were those decided upon. They would seize Atahualpa! With the emperor in their power, they might be able to control his subjects. So all arrangements were made to that end, and the Spaniards lay down to sleep—if they could.

The following day (it was November 16, 1532), soon after noon, the Inca with a large retinue and a considerable body of troops was seen approaching. Pizarro had already placed his forces in the buildings around the square in which he was going to receive Atahualpa. The rooms were large with wide doorways opening on the square. In two of these rooms he placed bodies of horsemen, in another all the foot soldiers except a few who were to man two small cannon placed nearby and twenty who were to be with him. All except Pizarro and his twenty were to remain under cover until the sound of a gun, when they were to dash out and seize Atahualpa and fall upon his men. Then the little group said mass. At this point in his description of the scene, Prescott exclaims, "One might have supposed them a company of martyrs, about to lay down their lives in defense of their faith, instead of a licentious band of adventurers, meditating one of the most atrocious acts of perfidy on the record of history!"

The Inca approached, borne on a litter on the shoulders of his most eminent nobles. He was seated on a throne of massive gold. The litter was decorated with brilliant feathers and shining plates of gold and silver. Altogether it was a gorgeous spectacle, which must have made the eyes of the covetous Spaniards glisten with desire. After the Inca was borne into the plaza, he was treated to a sermon by a friar, Vicente de Valverde. The sermon must have been pretty hard for the eminent visitor to understand. It included the doctrine of the Trinity, the story of the creation of man, his fall, his redemption, the crucifixion of Christ, and many other things. Valverde at the end signified to the monarch that he was to acknowledge the supremacy of the Spanish king. When Atahualpa understood what was being demanded of him, he was looking at a Bible that the friar had placed in his hands. He became indignant and threw the book to the ground. This seemed the

This scene in modern Cuzco shows how the Spanish built their fashionable homes on the foundation stones of Incan buildings.

The ruins of Sacsahuamán, Incan fortress above Cuzco. The huge stones used were brought from quarries miles away.

Lower wall of the Inca Temple of the Sun at Cuzco, Peru, now part of the wall of the Church of Santo Domingo. Made of rounded blocks fitted together without any cement, the wall has been in this position at least five centuries.

Statue of Francisco Pizarro, in front of the Cathedral of Lima, Peru. Pizarro, in conquering Peru for Spain, destroyed the civilization of the Inca Empire, with all its wealth of art and culture.

proper time for action. So Pizarro blew a whistle, a gun was fired, and the men rushed from their concealment and fell upon the emperor and his courtiers. As all of the Peruvians in the plaza were unarmed, they had no defense. When they endeavored heroically to protect the Inca, they were slaughtered. Atahualpa was taken, though with some difficulty, and the horsemen dashed from the plaza and fell upon the Indians outside, who were seized by panic. The terrible suddenness of the attack, the sound of firearms, and the horses in action prevented their taking any adequate means of protection. They fled, pursued by the Spaniards, who slew them without mercy. Estimates of the number killed in the massacre vary from two thousand to ten thousand.

Pizarro's stratagem had succeeded perfectly and with no loss of life among his men. The only wound was one which he himself received as he threw out his arm to protect Atahualpa from a Spanish blow. Holding the Inca they were, for the time at any rate, safe. Pizarro hoped the Indians would be disorganized and uncertain for a period long enough for help to come from Panama. Almagro was already gathering reinforcements and supplies there, when Pizarro started inland.

Atahualpa was greatly shocked by what had happened. His station all his life had been so far above most other human beings that he could hardly have believed that such a thing as this could befall him. However, he conducted himself like a monarch and was treated as such by the Spaniards. The people of his household were permitted to serve him; he was allowed to have visitors.

The Inca soon noticed how much his captors liked gold, and an idea occurred to him. He bargained with Pizarro for his freedom in exchange for a golden ransom. He declared that, given two months' time, he would fill the room in which he was sitting (a room seventeen by twenty-two feet) with gold as high as he could reach (about nine feet) if Pizarro would release him. He would also fill a smaller adjoining room twice over with silver. Pizarro agreed—it was a fine way to collect the gold and silver without trouble to himself! The notary drew up the contract. Then Atahualpa sent out his couriers all over the empire to order the precious metals brought in. (It should also be said that he ordered the execution of his brother, Huascar, lest he escape and reëstablish himself in his former position.) After several weeks had passed, the amount of gold and silver collected was still not equal to that agreed upon. However, the Spaniards decided that they would declare it sufficient and melt it down. The task of guarding the metal was proving burdensome. Besides, they feared that all of that gold might prove too great a temptation to the Indians. They would divide it, and then each person would be responsible for his portion. When the gold was melted down (think of the beautiful pieces of craftmanship that were destroyed!) and weighed for distribution, it was found to represent a value equal in our money to more than fifteen million dollars. This estimate was worked out more than a hundred years ago. Today it would probably be worth much more than that.

But alas for Atahualpa! Though the ransom had been paid, he was not released. Pizarro felt that his position was too desperate to permit his fulfilling his promise. If Atahualpa were at large, it was only natural to believe that he would organize his people against the Spaniards, particularly considering the way they had used him. So he was held. But he was a liability. He couldn't be released; it was dangerous to hold him longer. The alternative was plain, at least to the Spaniards. A long list of charges—all of them rather childish—was brought against him and he was tried. He was, of course, found guilty. And immediately he was executed—by being choked to death. The decision to try the Inca, the drawing of the charges, the trial, the verdict, and the execution, all were a matter of less than one day—an action as unjust as it was speedy.

Before his execution Atahualpa begged Pizarro to care for his children and requested that his body be sent to Quito for burial. History is silent about what happened to the children, but it is recorded that the body was buried there in Cajamarca. And the incident shown in the painting did actually occur in the course of the burial service. Later, however, the Indians secured permission to remove the body to Quito.

To anyone who may be critical of the treatment that Pizarro and his lieutenants meted out to Atahualpa and his people, it is a matter of satisfaction to know that in the course of a few years every one of the Spaniards met a violent death —the result not of quarrels with the Indians but with one another. The only one who did not suffer this fate was Hernando de Soto. He was absent from Cajamarca when Atahualpa was condemned and executed, and when he returned he was exceedingly angry and critical of the act. He frankly told Pizarro so. Everyone knows, of course, that De Soto lived to return to North America, where he was buried in the muddy waters of the Mississippi he explored.

Before Atahualpa was executed, reinforcements had arrived from Panama under command of Almagro. By such means as those above described, and by later strengthening of his forces, Pizarro was able to take the city of Cuzco and eventually the whole of Peru. But many years passed before a government was established that could control the Spaniards and reorganize the life of the native Peruvians. The sight of scores of beggars on the streets of Lima today affords distressing basis of comparison between the present and the past in the ancient Land of the Incas.

CHAPTER III

PEDRO DE VALDIVIA: FOUNDER OF CHILE

The twelfth day of February, 1941, was a memorable one in the history of Chile. On that day the country's five million people celebrated with high enthusiasm and impressive ceremony the four hundredth anniversary of the founding of their capital city, Santiago. It was the first city established by the Spaniards in that southern nation.

Chile is a museum of geography. Though it is only slightly larger than our state of Texas, it exhibits almost every type of geographic feature. It has lofty mountains, barren deserts, fertile agricultural sections, wonderful grazing country, extensive forests, and frigid wastes. Its climate taxes the thermometer, ranging from the oppressive heat of the northern deserts to the intense cold of the mountain peaks and the far South. The country is remarkable in form. It is almost twenty-eight hundred miles long, though it averages less than two hundred miles in width—well deserving the name, "the shoestring republic," which is sometimes applied to it. It might be compared to a steeply sloping, irregular roof with its upper edge attached to the crest of the Andes Mountains and the lower resting, far below, in the waves of the Pacific Ocean. Chile is, moreover, unique in its geographic isolation. At the north is a desert more than six hundred miles long; at the east is one of the highest mountain ranges in the world; to the west lies

39

the widest ocean of the globe; while the southernmost point at Cape Horn is fifteen hundred miles nearer the South Pole than the southern tip of the continent of Africa.

The country's products are almost as varied as its geography. They comprise immense deposits of minerals, of which nitrates and copper are the most important, almost every type of agricultural and pastoral product, and an infinite variety of foods furnished by the generous Pacific. Though its population is a million less than that of Texas, it is one of the strongest and most advanced of the Latin-American nations. In many respects, Chile is a remarkable country with a remarkable history.

In the course of the four hundredth anniversary, the name of Pedro de Valdivia, founder of the nation and its capital, was often spoken. However, Valdivia was not the first Spaniard to enter Chile. That honor belongs to Diego de Almagro, partner of Pizarro in the conquest of Peru. Almagro spent a large fortune (his share of the ransom of Atahualpa) in organizing and carrying out his expedition to Chile. He and his men suffered tremendous hardships in traversing the wild country between Cuzco, Peru, and the central region of Chile. Many died of cold while attempting to cross the Andes. Others died of thirst in the deserts of Northern Chile. And then, after enduring all of these hardships, the survivors found only hostile Indians and, as it seemed to them, an inhospitable country. To Spaniards of that era, a country that lacked gold lacked hospitality. Almagro and his men returned to Peru with their thirst for gold unsatisfied and with very damaging reports on the land they had visited. It is no wonder that five years passed before another band of Spaniards entered Chile. The wonder is that they went so soon.

Pedro de Valdivia organized and led the second expedition. All of the Spanish conquerors were remarkable for their courage; some of them for additional reasons. Valdivia was remarkable because he did not thirst for gold. Almagro's report had shown quite clearly that riches in gold were not to be found in Chile. What Valdivia sought was glory. To occupy Chile would be a difficult, but a great, undertaking. All the more honor then would be due the man who should do it. Success might gain for him much credit with the Spanish king. Power and position might be the reward.

Valdivia was born at the beginning of the sixteenth century in the Spanish province of Extremadura. He had served with Spanish armies in Italy before he decided to seek his fortune in America. Departing, he left his wife in Spain, as did many of the *conquistadores*. At that time the Spanish gentlewoman did not consider America a desirable place of residence. Besides, most of the Spaniards expected to make their fortunes and return to Spain to enjoy their riches in peace and comfort. (Señora de Valdivia did at length go to Chile, but she arrived after the death of her husband.) Valdivia fought against the Indians in Venezuela, and was with Pizarro in Peru. As a reward for his services, Pizarro had given him a silver mine together with an allotment of Indians to work it. However, Valdivia appears not to have profited a great deal from his mining operations, for when he set about organizing his Chilean venture, he could raise only nine thousand dollars. As that was far from enough, he had to borrow an equal amount from a merchant recently arrived from Spain.

It was very hard to enlist men for this project. Because of Almagro's adverse report, Chile had a bad reputation in Peru. No one was attracted by the prospect of freezing to death or dying of thirst merely to occupy a poor land, half desert. But

Valdivia persevered. He finally got together a dozen Spaniards and a thousand Indians. With this small group, he left Cuzco in January, 1540. He had arranged with a subordinate to follow within four months with more men and supplies and two ships. Chilean historians state that with the advance party went a certain Inés Suárez, a comely and courageous Spanish woman who was in love with Valdivia.

Valdivia did not follow the trail which Almagro had pioneered through Northwest Argentina and across the Andes. Instead, he struck southward along the ocean and crossed the terrible deserts of North Chile. This route was somewhat shorter than Almagro's, and it avoided the perils of the Andean cold. However, it involved much more desert travel. The northern part of this desert is now called Tarapacá, the southern, Atacama. While his party was crossing Tarapacá, Valdivia was fortunate in being overtaken by a party of sixty Europeans. Other small groups caught up later, until the number of whites was raised to one hundred and fifty. These were important additions, but the party was still perilously small. However, Valdivia advanced and, toward the end of December, arrived at the Mapocho River. This march can justly be compared with those made by some of our pioneers when they were moving from the Mississippi across the Great West —with its deserts and its Indians—and occupying the Pacific coastal region. The dangers encountered in the two cases were much alike.

There was, it is true, little gold in Chile. But the Spaniards could have rejoiced, had they but known the future, that all about them lay the stuff of riches—the fertile soil which has always been the most important source of the country's wealth. They were in the middle of the Valley of Chile. This valley is another of Chile's extraordinary features. It stretches north-south in the center of the country for a distance of three hundred miles. Its width, while irregular, averages seventy-five miles. Always visible to the east are the snows of the Andes, while toward the ocean is a lower coastal range. The valley's elevation above sea level is about two thousand feet. Its climate is splendid. Its southern section has abundant rainfall, while the northern portion can be, and is, irrigated by water from the ocean-flowing mountain streams. As the valley's climate ranges from semi-tropical to temperate, an infinite variety of grains and fruits is produced. In the heyday of the settlement of California, dozens of ships laden with potatoes and wheat—and migrating Chileans—made the long voyage to San Francisco. Today its grapes and wines are famous, and in our winter season (which is Chile's summer) many shiploads of delicious Chilean melons, nectarines, and other fruits find their way to our markets. Yes, truly, the Valley of Chile is a rich agricultural mine.

But Valdivia's people could not see all of this. They saw a valley covered with short trees—with *bosques* (woods), they said. It was only slightly cultivated in that day, for the Indian population was scant. Still they arrived at the future site of Santiago in midsummer and could well have been delighted with the climate. At the point where there is a fork in the Mapocho River they found a small Indian settlement and some crops that were a welcome addition to their supplies.

Lying closely within the fork of the river is a great rock, perhaps three hundred yards long, a hundred or more wide and, at its apex, four hundred feet high. Tradition says that for safety Valdivia made his camp on the elevated portion of this rock. That verdure-covered rock is now the park of Santa Lucía, surely one of the loveliest and most unusual city parks in all the world. One can stand at its highest point and, turning slowly about, see spread below him, perfectly visible on a clear day, the entire great Chilean capital with its million people. Not far away is the hill of San Cristóbal, several hundred feet higher and crowned by an immense statue of the Virgin (electrically illuminated at night), while there are always the Andes and the coastal range, and the vast reaches of the Vale of Chile. It is a magnificent site for a modern city.

The virtues of the site were apparent to Valdivia, and he decided to make his settlement there. The official act of founding the city took place on February 12, 1541. On a terrace of Santa Lucía is a lovely little square with fountain, flowers, and tiled seats and walks. At its center stands a marble statue, the heroic figure of the *conquistador*, Pedro de Valdivia, in full armor and looking very much the conqueror. On the four sides of the base are inscribed the names of the original band of Spaniards who founded the city along with the date of that foundation.

Already Valdivia had named the country Nueva Extremadura (New Estremadura), after his home province in Spain. The name was chosen in part, perhaps, from homesickness, in part because of natural similarities between the two regions. The city which he founded at the base of Santa Lucía he baptized Santiago de Nueva Extremadura, after St. James (Santiago), the national patron of Spain. When the name Chile was later adopted for the region, the city became Santiago de Chile. Within Chile, of course, it is called merely Santiago. The town was laid out in the usual Spanish style— streets crossing at right angles with a vacant square or plaza left in the center. Around this plaza were grouped the governor's palace, the market, the cathedral, and dwellings of some of the leading men. In the earliest days the plaza was often used for drilling soldiers; hence this chief square in

Spanish-American cities is frequently called the Plaza de Armas. That is the case in Santiago.

The native inhabitants of the place were forced to acknowledge the lordship of the Spanish king. Soon the natives were divided among the Spaniards and compelled to work the fields for them. Each Spaniard was allotted a tract of land for his use. As time passed such allotments became very large, in part through new grants and in part through the action of the individual himself in securing land from natives who had been left in possession of it. In such manner developed one of Chile's fundamental institutions—even to the present day —the *hacienda*. In colonial times these early land grants were called *encomiendas*. The *encomienda*, or the *hacienda*, may be compared to one of our large southern plantations of the pre-Civil War period. In Chile, in colonial times, the *hacienda* was worked by the Indians. Gradually, as intermarriage continued between Indian and white, the worker on the *hacienda* became a man of mixed blood, now often called a *roto*. There are many great *haciendas* in Chile (the late president, Pedro Aguirre Cerda, owned one) and tens of thousands of agricultural workers, peons, underpaid and underprivileged. The existence of the *hacienda* means, of course, that there is not enough land for distribution to the agricultural workers. It is a problem which has received a great deal of attention in Chile for more than a hundred years, but which is not yet satisfactorily solved.

The first years in Chile were very difficult ones. Peru was the nearest source of supplies and new colonists. The trip by land was a matter of many weeks. The distance by sea was some fifteen hundred miles, and in the ships of those days the voyage required weeks. Even today, by passenger steamer, the trip from Valparaíso to Callao requires six days. And added to the slowness of communications was the distressing fact that, until the first bad period had been weathered successfully, nobody really wanted to go to Chile.

One of the first crises of the young colony was a rebellion of the natives in the immediate vicinity of Santiago. They had been greatly embittered, quite naturally, by the seizure of their lands and houses. In September of the first year, when Valdivia was absent from the town, they rose and attacked the fifty Spaniards and some hundreds of Peruvian Indians who remained. The town was taken and the public and private buildings burned; clothing, utensils, foodstuffs were destroyed. The fight lasted the whole day. All of the Spaniards were wounded and perhaps would have been killed if the Indians had not given up the attack at nightfall. The chroniclers declare that the retreat of the Indians was owing to "the happy daring of Inés Suárez, who conceived the plan, immediately put into execution, of cutting off the heads of the Indian chiefs who were held as prisoners because of a former attempt." At the next counter-attack the Indians fled, and the day was saved—or at any rate, partly saved.

A very serious result of this attack was the destruction of domestic animals and seed grain. Only three milk goats, a hen and a rooster, and a few handfuls of wheat escaped the fury and fire of the Indians. Fifteen horses were killed—and horses under the circumstances were worth almost their weight in gold. From these scant remainders, herds, flocks, and field crops had to be slowly rebuilt. The seriousness of this situation is fully appreciated only when it is remembered that for a number of years there was practically no communication with Peru or aid from that colony. It is interesting to reflect on the possible importance to a nation of a few goats and a hen and a rooster! At once Valdivia sent to Peru for succor, but it was two years before any aid arrived. In the meantime, the people in Santiago lived, as a Chilean historian has described it, "without clothing, which they had lost in the attack of the Indians, and covered with the skins of animals, suffering the horrors of hunger; and they had to defend themselves from continuous attacks of the enemy."

This experience proved the necessity of building a town nearer Peru to aid communication with that colony. Soon, therefore, Chile's second city, La Serena, was founded on the coast some hundreds of miles north of Santiago. Other establishments were also made, among them Concepción, 1550, and Imperial, 1552, south of Santiago. From time to time other additions to the colony were made. Valdivia even went so far as to establish settlements on the eastern side of the Andes in the region of what is now the important Argentine city of Mendoza. For two hundred years an extensive trans-Andean district was administered from Santiago de Chile.

Wars with the natives continued. When Valdivia arrived, the central and southern region of Chile was occupied by the Araucanian Indians. They might be compared to the Navajos or Apaches of the Southwest or the savages of the Northwest, whom our government was not able to pacify completely until long after the Civil War. Tecumseh and Sitting Bull had their counterparts in Lautaro and Caupolicán, heroic and ferocious leaders of the Araucanians. While we were driving and crowding the Indians westward and eventually settling them on reservations, the Chilean descendants of Valdivia and his party were struggling with the Araucanians. In that case the Indians were crowded southward into the forests or eastward into the broken foothills of the Andes. The Bio-Bío River was for many years the boundary between Chilean whites and Indians, as was the Mississippi with us. The history of relations with the Indians in the two cases is a parallel.

In Chile in the early 1550's, the most skillful leader of the Araucanians was one Lautaro. He had served for a time in the armed forces of Valdivia where he had learned Spanish arms and methods of fighting. But, offended at his treatment by the Spaniards, he had deserted the whites and rejoined his people, becoming a valiant and brave leader in their struggle against the invader.

The year 1553 was fateful in the history of the Chilean colony and in the life of Valdivia. Some gold deposits had been discovered not far from Concepción, and great expectations were held. In the region to the south were some frontier posts. Late in the year, when movements of the Indians and rumors of revolt caused uneasiness, Valdivia led a force southward to this frontier to pacify the natives. Such movements as these became the themes of Spanish and Chilean writers. One of the great epics of Spanish literature is concerned with the wars of the Spaniards with the Araucanians in the period immediately following that of Valdivia. At that time the great Indian hero was Caupolicán, successor of Lautaro. The epic, *La Araucana,* was written by the Spanish poet, Ercilla, who participated in the war against Caupolicán. The poem might in some ways be compared to our *Hiawatha.* That Caupolicán was a respected opponent of the Spaniards in the Chilean colony is proved by the fact that today a fine bronze statue of the chief stands tensely on a ledge of rock on the side of Santa Lucía, staring alertly and fiercely down one of the main business streets of the Chilean capital. And just below the bronze Caupolicán is the fine National Library of Chile.

Valdivia no doubt anticipated a ready victory over the

Indians. He had beaten them before; he could do it again. But the situation was different now. The Araucanians had a great leader, who had inspired them with deep hatred of their foes and with an ardent determination to drive them from their country. As a Chilean historian puts it, the entire southern district was a "human furnace." A Spanish fort, Tucapel, fell before the Indian attack. Valdivia, then in Concepción, decided to retake it. He set out for the campaign with fifty Spaniards and a considerable number of Indians, most of them probably Peruvian. He sent orders to a lieutenant in a nearby fort to join him at Tucapel on December 25. The lieutenant was delayed in starting. When he arrived at Tucapel he was too late, for Valdivia and his entire force had been destroyed by the Araucanians. Horrible tales are told of the tortures which Valdivia was forced to suffer before he died, but as they are not historically provable, it is vain to recount them. It is quite possible that he was submitted to torture.

However, before his death, Valdivia had seen his colony— so poor, so struggling in its first years—firmly established. It was destined to have other leaders able to guide its development. Its founder deserves to be ranked with Cortés and Pizarro in the list of the *conquistadores*. Perhaps in some respects he deserves to be placed above Pizarro. And today, the white-marble Valdivia and the green-painted bronze Caupolicán are justified in gazing down proudly from the heights of Santa Lucía on the great Chilean city which has passed its four hundredth birthday. It represents the work of their people—a people in whom is united the strength and vigor and courage of the Spaniard and the Araucanian.

CHAPTER IV

DOÑA CLARA AND THE SILVER MOUNTAIN OF POTOSÍ

Like lava from a mighty volcano silver flowed down the mountain of Potosí. With this silver Potosí for more than a century brought the world to its feet. It practically paid for the "Invincible Armada" and helped to make Spain the mightiest nation in the world. Queen Elizabeth sent Drake and her plundering "sea dogs" to seize Spanish ships laden with Potosí's fabulous riches. The gleaming ore, like the rich veins of California or the Klondike, brought boom times. The *conquistadores*, the colonial officials, all the nobility and dregs of humanity, rushed in to stake their claims. The boom town of Potosí flashed into being, shone brilliantly as the metropolis of the New World fifty years before Jamestown was settled, then faded into a ghost city. Like any mining town of Colorado, Alaska, or South Africa, Potosí had its fleeting day of greatness. But Potosí was the greatest of them all.

Potosí was founded in 1545 in one of the cold, forbidding valleys of Upper Peru (present-day Bolivia). The valley lies almost fourteen thousand feet above the sea, as high as Pike's Peak, where frigid winds and violent storms make life difficult during much of the year. The horizon around the valley is broken by towering mountain peaks, majestically piercing the thin air. Like a mammoth cone, the hill of Potosí rises

This statue of Pedro de Valdivia stands on Santa Lucía Hill in Santiago, Chile. The *conquistador*, who for safety first made his camp on this elevated rock, now looks down on the great Chilean capital which he founded.

Chief Caupolicán, leader of Araucanian Indians, was a respected opponent of the Spaniards. The Chief's statue in bronze stands on a ledge of rock on the side of Santa Lucía, commanding a view of the main business streets of Santiago.

San Francisco Church in Potosí was one of the few buildings which escaped the damage caused by the bursting of the dams around Potosí in 1626. The superstitious saw the flood as a sign

Potosí Mountain, seen from Cobija Arch in Potosí, Bolivia. This mountain, barren today, was the scene of a tremendous boom when silver ore was found in it. Fortunes were made before the mines

two thousand feet above the floor of the valley, defying the puny efforts of man and nature to turn it inside out. The soft pinks, lavenders, browns, and yellows of its barren slopes lend dashes of color to the cold, somber setting. There is little about the mountain of Potosí today to suggest that hundreds of Spaniards struggled and thousands of Indians died to obtain its mines of wealth.

Among the Indians of Bolivia there are many legends about the discovery of the mountain of silver. According to one, an Inca chief encamped during one of his military campaigns near the site of Potosí. Suspecting that the hill might contain silver, he ordered Indian miners to dig for the ore. No sooner had the digging commenced than a mysterious voice commanded, "Take no silver from this hill which is destined for other owners."[1] Following this command, the Indians say, no ore was taken from the hill until its rediscovery in 1545. In that year an Indian herdsman accidentally came upon the rich veins. There are several versions of the manner of his discovery. Perhaps, in tending his llamas, he tied some of them to shrubs which the animals pulled out, revealing the shining metal. Perhaps the fire which he built of dry grass and twigs to warm himself from the chilly night air melted the ore near the surface, causing it to run in little trickles of pure silver. Perhaps the Indian, in chasing a stray animal, clutched at a bush to avoid slipping over a precipice and thus laid bare the silver ore.[2] In any case, the Indian kept his secret for a few weeks. Soon, however, his Spanish master learned of it and immediately began operations. The news quickly

[1] Quoted in Bernard Moses, "Flush Times at Potosí," in University of California Chronicle, XI (July, 1909), 217.

[2] These versions are recounted from Vicente G. Quesada, Crónicas Potosinas, I, 25-27, in Moses, op. cit., pp. 218-19.

spread, and within a few weeks the "silver rush" to Potosí was on. As in the California gold rush days of 1849, miners, adventurers, and camp followers appeared as if by magic to get in on the ground floor.

The earliest arrivals, eager to begin digging, did not even bother to build shelters for themselves. They lived in the open air, exposed to the rough mountain winds, and forced the Indians of the nearby valleys to bring them what foods they needed. As the population increased, however, and the storms of winter became violent, more Indians were brought in to construct houses, stores, and other buildings necessary for a growing community. By September, 1546, some fourteen thousand persons had flocked to Potosí, more than overflowing the twenty-five hundred houses built to shelter them. A swamp was drained to provide space for the spreading town, and a church was erected to care for the spiritual needs of the people. Even revolts by the conscripted Indian laborers failed to slacken the amazing growth. All sea routes from Spain and all roads in America led to Potosí, for Potosí was booming.

These thousands of early settlers, together with other thousands who followed, took millions of dollars of silver from their mines. Scratch the surface a little, burrow ever so slightly into the mountainside—there lay the rich ore, almost pure silver! Before 1600, the kings of Spain, who were supposed to receive one-fifth of all silver mined, had collected $396,000,000. In less than fifty years, therefore, the miners of Potosí made for themselves more than a billion and a half dollars. Many collected small fortunes, but the more fortunate —or the more ruthless—became millionaires. These newly-rich, even in far-off Potosí, demanded all the comforts and luxuries that money could buy and bring to them. No extravagance was too expensive for their inflated pocketbooks. They made Potosí the metropolis and the showplace of the New World.

No person better illustrates the fabulous growth and richness of Potosí than Doña Clara, truly a glamorous, mysterious "woman of silver." As in any mining town that enjoys boom days, the men of Potosí loved to gamble, loved to pay attention to beautiful women, and loved to bestow rich gifts on their favorites. Of all those who won the favor of wealthy miners Doña Clara was "the gayest, the most beautiful, the most accomplished, and the most elegant."[3] Her richly adorned home became the gathering place of the wealthiest men of the city, and she sought to cater to their every desire. They came to her palace to gamble, to give her lavish presents, and to enjoy the friendliness of her social circle. Doña Clara was typical of the best and the worst of her city. The worst that can be said of her is that she was a woman of the world; the best, that she was a product of the wild life of a mining town, and that she died sorrowful for the evil of her ways.

Soon after the discovery of silver Doña Clara came to Potosí from—no one knows where. Setting up her gambling room at first in modest quarters, by her charm and gaiety she soon attracted men who came to gamble and enjoy her attention. As the silver flowed out of the mountain in ever-increasing quantities, the stakes on her gambling tables grew ever larger, and her profits steadily mounted. Within a few months she was rich enough to build one of the most splendid of all the new palatial homes that were going up around Potosí. Her wealth, or the wealth of her patrons, brought to her door comforts and luxuries from all parts of the world. In the words of a Bolivian writer,

[3] Moses, *op. cit.*, p. 224.

Her table service was all of silver and gold; filigree with emeralds and rubies was abundant among her ornaments. . . . Her reception room was magnificent. The Venetian mirrors had frames of burnished silver; her furniture was adorned with gold and mother of pearl, upholstered with cloth of gold and silver from Milan; figures of gold taken from Quichuan antiquities adorned her tables.[4]

She received rugs from Persia and Turkey, tapestries and embroideries from Flanders, ivory and precious stones from India and Ceylon, and crystal glass from Venice.

In her more personal possessions, too, Doña Clara revealed the same sumptuous tastes. As Martínez y Vela wrote,

She had as many chemises of fine cambric and Dutch linen as there are days in the year, and a change was made every night; four rich bedsteads of wood and bronze, with featherbeds and draperies of beautiful cloths; and she changed from one to another every three months.[5]

For her wardrobe she imported silks and knitted goods from Granada, stockings from Toledo, linen from Portugal, felt hats from France, satins from Florence, gold and silver braid from Milan, and laces from Flanders. She used perfume from Arabia. For her table, China sent white porcelain, the Malay Peninsula furnished all kinds of spices, and South America gave vanilla and cocoa. Indian slaves and white servants were at her command. The world was Doña Clara's supply house, and her wealthy friends enabled her to draw on it freely.

But the glamorous Doña Clara was not the only glittering woman in Potosí. There were many Doña Claras, women of the type to be found in any society that grows up about a

[4] Quoted from Don Bartolomé Martínez y Vela, *Anales de la Villa Imperial de Potosí,* in Moses, *op. cit.,* pp. 224-25.

[5] *Ibid.,* p. 224.

mining camp. Few of the Spaniards who came to get rich quickly brought European wives with them. There were few homes, therefore, in which family life of the usual sort could be practiced, and in which children could be raised according to decent, Christian standards. Potosí was filled with adventurers, with men attracted by the tales of quick riches. Drinking, gambling, and fighting, rather than normal home living—this was the Potosí of Doña Clara.

Nevertheless, there is much about the early growth of Potosí to excite wonder and admiration. As the city grew by thousands each year, new homes, churches, and public buildings were erected to meet the needs of the population. Modest homes, as well as palatial ones, stretched out over the valley at the foot of the mountain. High balconies, huge double doors, and wrought-iron grilles were used in the construction of the homes of the wealthy. Master architects came from Spain to direct the building of beautiful churches, and religious paintings and carved figures were brought from Rome to decorate them. Local craftsmen designed silver chalices and sacred vessels of pure metal to adorn the altars. In the course of time, all the principal religious orders built convents and monasteries.

The immense quantities of silver which flowed from the mountain had to be collected, stored, and coined. The king's fifth had to be counted and shipped. For these purposes special public buildings were erected, such as the Royal Mint, the Exchange Bank, and the Royal Coffers. The first of these was built in 1572. Partially rebuilt since that time, it is still standing, one of the most beautiful buildings of modern Bolivia.

This growing city at the foot of the silver mountain came to be known as the "Imperial City." The first coat of arms, granted by the Emperor Charles V of Spain, bore the words: "I am the rich Potosí, the treasure of the world, the king of mountains and the envy of kings." Philip II, emperor of Spain after 1556, sent a shield, bearing the motto, still used by Potosí: "For the powerful Emperor, for the wise King this lofty mountain of silver could conquer the whole world."[6] When Philip was crowned emperor in Spain, only eleven years after the founding of Potosí, the city honored him with an enormous celebration costing eight million dollars. Upon the death in 1559 of the former emperor, Charles V, the city spent one hundred and forty thousand dollars on funeral ceremonies. Thus did the people of Potosí prove the truth of the oft-quoted statement, "Easy come, easy go!"

The population of Potosí continued to grow until by 1570 there were probably one hundred and twenty thousand inhabitants. As the numbers increased, life became gayer and more lavish. At least fourteen dancing schools were founded, and at one time thirty-six gambling houses were operating. There was a theater, which Doña Clara often attended in the company of her wealthy friends, and to which the admission was as high as fifty dollars. But most exciting to Doña Clara and to all the people of the city were the days of fiesta— feastdays of saints or national holidays in honor of the king's birthday. Upon such occasions Doña Clara put on her most expensive gowns, some of them costing as much as fourteen thousand dollars. She wore sandals of silk and gold, decorated with pearls and rubies, and embroidered overshoes, ornate with pearls worth hundreds of dollars. Gold bracelets and necklaces, set with other precious stones, hung about her

[6] These mottoes are quoted in William E. Rudolph, "The Lakes of Potosí," in *The Geographic Review*, XXVI (October, 1926), 536.

wrists and neck. With all this display of luxury, Doña Clara and many others like her would drive down the stony streets in beautiful carriages drawn by sumptuously decorated horses. Wealthy miners clad in rich apparel and mounted on prancing horses bowed as she passed; others came to share her carriage.

Sometimes the feature attractions of these fiestas were tournaments, staged with all the color and pageantry of feudal times. One of the most famous of these took place in January, 1552. Montejo, a celebrated horseman from Cuzco, Peru, had come armed with lances to fight a duel on horseback against Godines, the champion of Potosí. The two men first met in the house of Doña Clara, where Montejo, her favorite, challenged Godines. The duel attracted half the population of the community—men and women, Indians, Spaniards, and Negroes. On foot and on horseback they came to view the tournament, with its fine horses, its colorful costumes, and its bloody duel. For these people it was a gala event, much more like Europe than America. But for Doña Clara it was a sad occasion, for Montejo, the man who had won her favor, was killed. This tragedy brought to Doña Clara a long illness, from which she never fully recovered. When she did finally improve, it was only to discover that she was a poor woman; her Indian servants had disappeared, taking with them most of her wealth. In sorrow and mourning she turned now to the church she had so often shunned. The gaiety and proud revelry she had once known now changed to humble prayer and meditation.

But, with or without Doña Clara, life in Potosí went on. There were other women to take her place in the gay festivities; Doña Clara was not missed. There was still silver in the mountain of Potosí, and for many years more it continued to flow. For twenty years after the discovery of the silver mountain the ores were so high in silver content that only a little smelting was necessary to extract the pure metal. By 1566, however, the rich veins were exhausted, and new methods had to be devised. When Viceroy Toledo visited Potosí in 1573, he introduced the use of quicksilver or mercury in the process of refining the silver-ore. This was simple enough, for the mercury could be brought from the royal mines recently opened in Peru.

At about the same time a dam was built in the mountains above Potosí so that the summer rains might be caught and water furnished to the ore mills during the whole year. The viceroy ordered twenty thousand Indians to be brought to construct the huge dam. Within fifty years, thirty-two such lakes were built to furnish enough water to wash the ore and to supply the needs of the entire population of the city. A channel, with tunnels and twenty-two bridges, was constructed to carry the water three miles from the lakes to the mills in the city. One hundred and thirty-two mills thus received the water they needed. Much of the work on this construction, like that in the mines, was carried on by the Indians working under the Spanish system called the *mita*. Under this system adult males might be forced to work for the king, usually for pay. Sometimes, however, the Indians were not protected by the law, and many fled to escape the service.

By these methods did the Spaniards and their Indian laborers turn the mountain of Potosí inside out to get its silver. But get the silver they did—hundreds of millions of dollars' worth! Nevertheless, there was more to be done than simply to mine the ore; the royal fifth must be transported to faraway Spain. At fairly regular intervals shipments of silver were made on the backs of llamas and mules over the mountains and down to the Pacific, a journey of at least two weeks. Another month was required to ship by boat to the Isthmus of Panama. There the bars of silver were again loaded on the backs of mules to be carried forty miles over mountains and through the jungles to the Atlantic shores. Sailing into the harbors came the famed Spanish galleons, armed ships which bore the riches of Potosí to the kings of Spain. By such a hard and dangerous route was the wealth of the New World transported to fill the treasuries of the Old World.

The boom days of Potosí, however, could not last forever. The city, which, even before the landing of the *Mayflower*, had grown to be the largest in the Western Hemisphere, could not always remain unsurpassed. The mighty mountain of silver must one day begin to run out. That day was March 16, 1626. It was Sunday afternoon. Without the least warning one of the huge dams burst, hurling its waters over the city and valley below. Within two hours the work of half a century was wiped out. All but six of the one hundred and thirty-two mills were demolished, and a thousand homes were destroyed. Hundreds of people lost their lives. The dam was repaired, mills were rebuilt, and more Spaniards came in search of silver, but the great days of Potosí were at an end. Many of the miners saw the destruction of the city of evil and riches as a sign of divine disapproval. This interpretation was emphasized by the remarkable escape from the raging waters of the old and hallowed San Francisco church. Many miners became superstitious and lost their zeal for gain. Moreover, the bulk of Potosí's silver had already been taken. Potosí slowly declined until by 1825 the once largest city in the New World numbered only eight thousand persons.

Symbolic both of the rise and of the decline of Potosí was the career of Doña Clara. Even before the destruction of the city that had given her wealth and pleasure, she had disappeared from its streets. A Bolivian historian wrote that

on a day that was comparatively warm for the frigid climate of Potosí, an old woman of ninety-two years entered the church of Merced. She was poorly clothed, for she was accustomed to beg and lived from charity. She knelt and heard mass with great devotion, and prayed for a long time. This beggar was the splendid Doña Clara.[7]

[7] Quoted from Quesada, *Crónicas Potosinas,* I, 231, in Moses, *op. cit.,* p. 227.

CHAPTER V

FRANCISCO DE TOLEDO: VICEROY OF PERU

The dusty, narrow streets of Lima, Peru, on November 30, 1569, presented a scene of excited movement and bright color. On that hot and humid mid-summer day, the new viceroy, Francisco de Toledo, just arrived from Spain, made his official entry into his capital city. Wishing to save the people needless expense, the viceroy had asked that no special ceremony be held to celebrate his coming. The request was ignored. Men have always liked a pageant, the Peruvians perhaps more than most. They arranged for the new official a reception so magnificent that it served as a model for more than two centuries.

When Toledo came to Lima, he found the viceregal palace not prepared to receive him and his household, so he had taken temporary quarters in a village not far from the city. Here he had received callers and exchanged social courtesies with them. In the meantime, preparations for the official reception were being made in the city. Finally, all was in readiness. Decorations hung everywhere; imposing arches spanned the streets. Every soldier's equipment and uniform were shining and spotless, and every official of whatever rank was starched and dignified in the garb that his office required. Many ladies and gentlemen had spent more than they could well afford to secure the richest clothing that was obtainable.

The viceroy set out for Lima in a litter carried by footmen. Soon he mounted a horse, richly bedecked as befitted the horse that bore a man of the viceroy's rank. He was preceded by a body of men equipped with firearms and followed by a corps of pikemen. At the city limits an official presented the viceroy with another horse, much more brilliantly adorned than the first. A party of footmen in black, scarlet, and yellow livery joined his train. Proceeding, the viceroy met a company of infantrymen whose commander delivered an address of welcome. Presently the cavalcade came to an arch. Here it paused while Toledo took the oath of office. This ceremony completed, the regular judges of Lima took the reins of the viceroy's horse. Other high-ranking city officials took up the poles that supported a canopy over the viceroy, and the procession advanced. By this time it had become a thing magnificent to behold. It contained, besides the viceroy and his household, various bodies of soldiers in colorful uniform, the members of the faculty of the University of St. Mark, the officials of the city, the supreme court of the viceroyalty, and the officials of the church. Like a brilliantly colored serpent, the procession wound its way through the streets to the cathedral. The viceroy and the archbishop greeted each other, and a brief ceremony was held. The march then continued to the palace, now ready for occupancy. Here Toledo spoke a word of appreciation to the various elements of the procession, and they disbanded, going about their separate affairs. In this manner Peru's first great viceroy began his official activities.

Before going ahead, we must go back a bit; some explanations are in order. Every American, whether of North or South America, knows that Francisco Pizarro conquered Peru in 1532. An earlier section of this book has described the manner in which he captured and killed the Inca emperor, Atahualpa. The Spanish conquerors were a group of very courageous, but very hard, men. They may have feared God, but certainly they feared neither the Indians nor each other. One of Pizarro's lieutenants was Diego de Almagro. Almagro had reason, in fact, to consider himself a partner in the conquest of Peru rather than a subordinate of Pizarro. He became dissatisfied and, after Peru was more or less conquered, secured from Pizarro authority to lead an expedition to the southward. Setting out with a small number of Spanish soldiers and some hundreds of Indians, he crossed the Andes through Bolivia and went southward to Chile, touching Northwestern Argentina. In Chile Almagro found no natives with rooms full of gold. Instead, he found only deadly deserts and the fierce and inhospitable Araucanian Indians. He quickly decided that Chile had nothing for him and returned to Peru. There he got into a quarrel with Pizarro and his brothers. Hernando Pizarro's hatred could be washed away only by Almagro's blood, so Almagro was slain at Cuzco.

This quarrel was very serious for the Spaniards in Peru. Before long in Lima the son of the dead Almagro stabbed Francisco Pizarro, the conqueror. Dying, Pizarro dipped his finger in his own blood and traced a cross on the pavement. However, the spirit of the cross lacked much of determining the relations among the *conquistadores*. They became divided into two groups, "Men of Pizarro" and "Men of Almagro," and for a quarter of a century the history of Peru was mostly a matter of bloody feuds between the men of these groups and between them and the Indians back in the high Andean Sierras.

The government in Spain, headed in the latter half of the

sixteenth century by Philip II, found it impossible to control the Peruvian Spaniards. Communication between Spain and Peru was exceedingly slow. It sometimes required as much as two months for a ship to cross the Atlantic to the Isthmus of Panama. And the voyage from the other side of the Isthmus to Callao, seaport of Lima, often cost another month. The distance from Spain was more than five thousand miles. To the Peruvians, the king and his authority seemed very far away and the necessity for obedience correspondingly slight. In the absence of effective control, Peru had never actually been organized, although it had been made a viceroyalty in 1544.

A viceroyalty in the Spanish colonial system was something like one of our own English colonies—Virginia, for instance—before the Revolution. But there were some very important differences between our colonies and the Spanish viceroyalties. The viceroyalties were much greater in area than any of the English colonies; there were but four of them in all Spanish America at the end of the colonial period. Territorial extent alone would have made it hard to control from the viceregal capital all parts of one of these divisions. Moreover, the Spaniards in America did not enjoy any rights of self-government as did our English colonial forefathers. The powers of government in the viceroyalty were concentrated in the viceroy—the governor we would call him. The word viceroy might be translated "vice-king." And as a king is usually more powerful than a governor, so were the viceroys stronger than our colonial governors. Another important element of the governmental machinery of the Spanish colony was the *audiencia*. The English word that comes nearest expressing the idea is "court." However, the Spanish *audiencia* was something more than a court. If there was no viceroy or other executive officer at the capital, the *audiencia* acted as the executive. Sometimes, too, it exercised the law-making power.

The viceroy who was sent to Peru when it was made a viceroyalty had not been strong enough to control the situation. Nor were his successors. They fought with the *audiencia*. They were ignored by the church. The *conquistadores* refused to obey them. As late as 1568, Peru was still in a bad way. The church officials felt themselves above the civil authority and acted accordingly. They were not as conscientious as they should have been about caring for the souls of the Indians—and the Spaniards. The *conquistadores* —now owners of mines and plantations—were quarreling and fighting among themselves about land claims, mining claims, about the right to use the labor of the Indians. The civil power was unable to enforce obedience to itself. Taxes could not be collected properly, and the government in Spain was being cheated of a great part of its revenue.

Perhaps worst of all these evils was the plight of the Indians. Under the empire of the Incas, before the Spaniards came, the Indians had been dominated. There was order, and everyone had the necessities of life—though he had no freedom. With the destruction of the native government, the life of the Indians was completely disorganized. As the Spaniards had not yet been able to regulate themselves properly, they could not of course organize the Indians. The natives were idle, many of them in want, many of them vagrants. They were subject to mistreatment, even to enslavement, by the Spaniards. Churchmen, mine owners, plantation owners, even royal officials abused them.

This was the condition of affairs when Francisco de Toledo was appointed viceroy. A strong man was needed. No other type would have the authority necessary to dominate the scene in Peru. The man who went to Peru to rule was in the situation of the broncho-buster who prepared to mount the wildest, most undisciplined pony of the entire herd. He must be strong and skillful if he were to "ride 'em."

The viceroyalty of Peru at that time was a vast unit. It included the Isthmus of Panama and all of South America that was not claimed by Portugal—an area of more than six million square miles. However, Viceroy Toledo's attention was chiefly devoted to that part now included in Peru and Bolivia.

En route to Panama, the new appointee made brief stops at Cartagena, in Colombia, and Panama. One of the "good deeds" he performed in both places was to round up and send back to Spain all of the married men who had left their wives in Spain years before—and apparently forgotten about them. He also drove out of Panama—for immorality—all bachelors and unmarried women. It must have seemed to those wrong-doers that "the sword of the Lord and of Gideon" was swishing about their ears. At Panama the viceroy took ship for Callao. However, he stopped in Northern Peru and, being tired of the sea, decided to make the remainder of the journey to Lima by land. From Paita, where he landed, to Lima is a distance of about six hundred miles—the distance from Washington to Chicago. And there were in those days no broad concrete roads. As the viceroy progressed slowly, he gathered information about the country and the people. The journey required several weeks.

After his entry into Lima, the viceroy consulted the leading men in order to inform himself of the needs of the vice-royalty. The king had instructed Toledo to make a tour of inspection. This was one of the matters on which he needed

(Left) A Cuzco Indian of today. It was for the social and economic good of Indians like this that Francisco de Toledo worked. (Right) A street scene in modern Cuzco, where llamas are used as beasts of burden.

Arequipa, now the second city of Peru, was one of the stopping places of Viceroy Francisco de Toledo in his five-year tour of his viceroyalty. Here we see, towering over the modern city, El Misti, one of the most beautiful volcanic cones in the world.

This statue of the Virgin crowns the Hill of San Cristóbal in Santiago, Chile.

advice. Considering the size of the viceroyalty, it was not a question to be decided lightly. Aside from the huge size of this unit, there were the Andes everywhere—one of the highest and most rugged mountain systems in the world. And the roads of the country were only those of the Incas, good in some places but inadequate, generally speaking. Particularly was this true for horsemen. The inns which the Incas had built along these roads had not been kept up. That tour would be a difficult undertaking even for a strong, perfectly healthy man—and the viceroy was not that. However, his sense of duty was such that he decided, against some advice to the contrary, to make it. Of course he could not penetrate the jungles of the Amazon or go to far Chile and Argentina. But he could, and did, visit all of the important population centers of Peru and Bolivia. At each place he stopped to study local problems and to draw and proclaim reform laws. He also directed a number of campaigns against rebellious Indians. The tour required five years and covered a distance of some five thousand miles.

The viceroy traveled with a large retinue of officials and soldiers. The route led up to the high *puna*, or tableland, northeast of Lima, then along it southeasterly to Cuzco, the old Incan capital. Several months were passed there, in the course of which Toledo directed a campaign against some rebellious Indians. The viceroy then journeyed around Lake Titicaca into Bolivia. One of the places he visited in that section was the great silver mining city of Potosí, with a population at that time of a hundred and twenty thousand. Returning to Cuzco for another stay of some months—and correcting some abuses which had developed in his absence—he went down the western slope toward Arequipa. Here, in what is now the second city of Peru, some additional weeks

were spent. Then the party continued down to the sea, crossing a great mesa of sand and descending narrow, precipitous
canyons. A ship was awaiting them, and in it they sailed
back to Callao and returned thence to Lima.

Many of the wise laws of Toledo's almost thirteen years in
office were made while he was on this tour. Some had been
decreed before he left Lima, others were drawn after his
return. The most important of these laws are summarized
briefly as a means of indicating the general nature of the
colonial problems which the Spaniards had to face and showing the way in which Toledo tried to solve them.

One of the most serious of these problems concerned the
church. There were many churches and convents in Lima
and in other parts of Peru. But there were not enough ordinary priests, and there were more friars (or monks) than were
needed. Toledo caused the establishment of schools for training priests and saw that the curricula included courses in the
Indian languages. He ordered that friars be assigned to native
villages to instruct the Indians in the Christian religion. On
Toledo's arrival in Lima he found there many hundreds of
natives who were living very miserably and were receiving
no religious instruction despite the great number of churchmen in the city. He ordered a special section to be built for
the Indians and required that two Jesuit fathers reside in the
section and instruct its inhabitants. His reforms increased the
general efficiency of the church, especially as it related to
caring for the natives. He also brought the church under subjection to the civil authority, which is to say to his authority.

Toledo (and all of his predecessors and most of his successors) had much trouble in regulating the possession of
land. Pizarro had begun the practice of distributing land—
along with the Indians who lived on it—to his lieutenants.

A grant of land of this sort was called an *encomienda*. The Indians living on it were "commended" to the holder of the land, the *encomendero*. The *encomendero* could collect tribute from the Indians or require them to work for him. He was supposed to pay for this labor, and he was obliged to care for the Indians and make them Christians. From the beginning, there had been much trouble in Peru about these *encomiendas*. When one faction defeated another in a feud, lands were confiscated and redistributed. When Toledo arrived, he found many of these holdings in the possession of unauthorized persons or groups. He regranted many of them, usually to the great dissatisfaction of someone. There was difference of opinion concerning the period over which these grants should extend. Some wanted them to be perpetual; others believed they ought to expire in the course of one or two generations. The *encomienda* gave much trouble to Toledo and later viceroys.

Mining was in need of attention. Quicksilver and silver mines were at the time the most profitable. Toledo took possession of the former for the king, thus securing an important source of revenue. The silver mines were carefully inspected and placed under new regulations. These regulations made possible the honest collection of the percentage of metal which was due the king, usually a fifth. One of the king's most insistent instructions to Toledo was that he should increase the royal revenue. As another means of attaining that end, Toledo placed a head tax on the Indians. Thus the revenue was increased, but the viceroy was charged with being unjust to miners and Indians.

The regulation of the life of the Indians was one of Toledo's greatest cares. It has been shown that he cared for their spiritual interests in his reforms of church practices. For the social and economic good of the Indian, the viceroy decreed laws that regulated the terms on which he might be required to labor. These laws included rigid scales of pay for different types of service. The Indian was not to be enslaved. But, as the mines needed labor, the viceroy ordered that shifts of laborers be furnished by Indian villages, and he organized a system to govern them. He also drew up laws that forbade the use of the Indian as a beast of burden to carry heavy loads. The Indians were badly scattered throughout the mountains in small villages. In such a situation it was hard to Christianize them or to manage them for labor. Toledo ordered that they be brought together into larger towns. This would afford opportunity for the priests to reach them—and the labor agent as well. In the region of Cuzco, twenty-one thousand Indians who had previously lived in three hundred and nine villages were relocated in but forty.

One of the happiest features of Toledo's Indian reforms was that of using native Indians as village chiefs, elected by the Indians themselves. Such chiefs, appointed by the Inca, had been the rule in earlier times and in using them Toledo was continuing a tradition. The Indians were thus much more easily controlled. Tribute was to be collected by these chiefs. It was they who should provide the labor squads for the mines. Through them, most of the contacts between Indian and white were to be made. To this day in Peru the village chief may be seen proudly carrying his heavy, silver-decorated staff of office. Its survival for more than three hundred years suggests that the device was successful.

Toledo had trouble with the *audiencia*. Because of the succession of inefficient executives who had preceded Toledo, the *audiencia* had grown accustomed to acting quite independently. Its members wished to continue to do so. As a consequence, they frequently quarreled with the viceroy. They wrote letters to the king criticizing Toledo; *he* wrote the king criticising *them.* It was one of the viceroy's duties to preside at the meetings of the *audiencia,* though he had no vote in deciding points of law. On the other hand, the *audiencia* was the viceroy's council, and he had to consult it on certain matters. Perhaps, under these circumstances, it is not strange that there should have been differences. Before he left Peru, however, Toledo had succeeded in limiting the *audiencia* pretty much to its judicial functions.

The Inquisition was established in Peru at the beginning of Toledo's term. This was a special church court whose duty it was to try offenses against religion. There was no such thing as religious freedom in Spain or in Spanish America at that time—nor in most of the rest of the world. Any departure from strict obedience to the teachings of the church might bring the offender arrest and trial. If the accused were found guilty, his property was often confiscated. If the offense were a very serious one, death by burning might be the punishment. In Peru and Mexico (the viceroyalty of New Spain) during the entire colonial period, one hundred persons were burned after conviction by the Inquisition. One of the duties of the Inquisition was to see that no books which the church considered a bad influence were sold or read. Toledo had some trouble with the judges of the Inquisition because of their independent attitude but, as he held the purse strings and paid their salaries, he was able to control them and prevent their interfering with any of his civil functions.

The activities of the viceroy included, of course, a great many that have not been mentioned. One of them was his effort to preserve the history of the Indians. As these people had no written language, we owe much of our knowledge of them to this interest of the viceroy. He appointed Pedro Sarmiento, a learned Spaniard who had spent many years in Peru and had traveled over most of it, to write a history of the ancient inhabitants. The book was written, and it is still considered one of the best sources of information on the subject.

An American historian has written, "Toledo himself described the condition in Peru as being one in which the difficulty was not in making laws, but rather in getting obedience to the laws that were made."[1] Though Francisco de Toledo did not succeed in developing among the Peruvians a spirit that caused perfect obedience to the laws, he did much to lessen lawlessness. When he returned to Spain—after many pleas to the king to be permitted to do so—he left Peru with a well-organized government. The system of laws for which he is chiefly responsible was so well adapted to the conditions of the country that not only were many of them used in Peru for the remainder of the colonial period, but they became the basis of Spanish law in other parts of Spain's American possessions. He was one of Peru's best viceroys, perhaps the very best. He did not long survive his return to Spain, for he died in April, 1582. It would seem that his work had not been greatly appreciated by his sovereign. At any rate, Philip gave him no special gift or honor when he returned and, for many years after his death, Toledo's heirs were trying to secure from the government what they considered just rewards for their father's service in Peru. Throughout history, kings have not been noted for their gratitude.

[1] Arthur Franklin Zimmerman, *Francisco de Toledo, Fifth Viceroy of Peru, 1569-1581* (Caldwell, Idaho, Caxton Printers, 1938), p. 285.

CHAPTER VI

PADRE KINO: MAN OF GOD

"God, gold, and glory" were the great forces that moved the Spaniards in their work of exploration, conquest, and colonization in North and South America. These forces caused them to dare the perils of the Atlantic crossing and, once they had reached the American shores in safety, led them inland. These forces—sometimes "will-o'-the-wisps" they proved to be—drew them across almost limitless deserts, through well-nigh impassable jungles, or over the frigid, sky-piercing crests of some of the highest ranges of mountains on the globe.

Which of these forces was strongest it would be difficult to say with certainty. But it cannot be denied that religion was an exceedingly important feature of the lives of the conquerors and those who accompanied them. No Spaniard was permitted to come to America unless he was known to be a faithful Catholic and to have several generations of ancestors who also had been good Catholics. When some of the things that the Spaniards did are judged by the standards of our day (which would, however, be unfair to the Spaniards), it is found that they were not very Christ-like, to put it mildly. While this can be said of the soldier element of the early colonials, it cannot fairly be said of some who accompanied them. Many of the members of the Franciscan, Dominican, Augustinian, Jesuit, and other religious orders

73

were in the highest degree Christian—wholly interested in saving the souls and bettering the physical conditions of the American natives, self-sacrificing to the point of martyrdom. One of the very best examples of this type of pioneer was the Jesuit, Eusebio Francisco Kino. Padre Kino was admirable for his character and his work. He is interesting, too, because he was active among the Indians in a region which is now a part of the United States. He broke the trail into Mexico's Lower California and our Arizona.

Father Kino was born of Italian parents in Trent in 1645. In due time he gained an excellent education in universities of Austria. He made so fine a record in his studies that he was offered a place as professor of mathematics in the royal university of Bavaria. But already this man, who was to become an heroic American figure, had determined to offer himself for missionary service as a follower of Saint Francis Xavier. He made this decision because he credited his recovery from a serious illness to the intercession of that saint. As Saint Francis had spent many years in the Far East, in the Dutch East Indies in particular, Kino hoped to go there. However, when a call came for missionaries in New Spain (the name by which Mexico was then known), he came instead to America, arriving in the year 1681.

In the period between Cortés' conquest of Mexico and Kino's arrival in New Spain, the movement of colonization of the newly-discovered lands had been extending slowly southward and northward from Mexico City. In 1681 there were great areas in Northern and Northwestern Mexico which had not yet been settled and where the Indians were of course, living as they had lived before Columbus made his great discovery. Texas had not been occupied, nor had Lower California, Upper California, Arizona, and New Mexico.

Much of Northwestern Mexico was also unoccupied by white men. It was in the northern part of the Mexican province of Sonora and in Arizona that Father Kino was to do his great work. That region was known as Pimería Alta, its Indian inhabitants, Pimans. It was practically virgin territory, for missions had previously been established only on its extreme southern border.

Padre Kino arrived in 1687 on the scene of his life's future labors. (In the same year the French explorer La Salle met his death in Central Texas.) The new missionary went first to the northernmost mission in the Sonora region. It was located at Cucurpe on a little river called the San Miguel. The village is still there, nestling among the mountains and inhabited in large measure no doubt by the sons and daughters, many generations removed, of the Indians of Padre Kino's time.

Father Kino's first new mission foundation was that of Nuestra Señora de los Dolores (Our Lady of Sorrows), also on the San Miguel River. Nearby are fertile and easily irrigated bottom lands, necessary to settled life in that semi-arid region where rainfall alone is seldom sufficient to produce a crop. All about towered the mountains. The mission was placed on a high point, protected on three sides by steep cliffs. This was a very important consideration in a frontier region where, on occasion and perhaps not infrequently, the occupants would have to defend themselves against attackers. Of this mission, Professor Herbert E. Bolton, one of our great American historians, writes:

Here still stand its ruins, in full view of the valley above and below, of the mountain walls on the east and west, the north and south, and within the sound of the rushing cataract of the San Miguel as it courses through the gorge. This meager ruin on the

cliff, consisting now of a mere fragment of an adobe wall and sad-
dening piles of débris, is the most venerable of all the many
mission remains in Arizona and northern Sonora, for Our Lady
of Sorrows was mother of them all, and for nearly a quarter of a
century was the home of the remarkable missionary who built
them.[1]

Operating from this Mission of Dolores, Father Kino
extended his work across Arizona as far as the Gila and
Colorado Rivers. Often he was aided by small details of
soldiers. Particularly was he assisted by a fellow Jesuit, Father
Salvatierra. It was while he was on a journey of exploration
with this companion that Father Kino first saw the San Pedro
River near the present location of Douglas, Arizona. In this
region, not far from Tucson, he later built the mission of
San Xavier del Bac, which is still in use.

Father Kino had a great interest in the Indians of Lower
California. In 1695, as the result of much effort, he and Padre
Salvatierra were commissioned by the king of Spain to found
missions there. However, it was Padre Salvatierra who was
to found those missions, as Padre Kino was not able to leave
his red charges in Pimería Alta. It may be remarked in passing that it was Father Kino who first proved to the Spaniards
in Mexico that Lower California was a peninsula rather than
an island as was long thought. After Padre Salvatierra had
planted a number of missions in Lower California (crossing
the gulf by boat), food became scarce in the peninsula.
Assistance was needed. Father Kino was the nearest source
of possible aid, and he was appealed to. It was while he was
seeking a way to drive cattle to the starving missions of Salvatierra that the good Padre Kino found that Lower California

[1] From "The Spanish Borderlands," Vol. 23, *The Chronicles of
America,* 194. Copyright Yale University Press.

was connected to the mainland. After this discovery was made, cattle were driven to the assistance of the suffering missions—an aid that later was repeatedly given. Father Kino made a map of the region which was not improved upon for many, many years.

Padre Kino had a positive thirst for knowing the wild, but in many respects impressive and beautiful, country of the Southwest (i.e., *our* Southwest). He made scores of journeys, some of them covering distances as great as a thousand miles. As he traveled about over these sandy wastes or threaded his way through the passes of towering mountains, he made friends with the Indians. He taught them the simpler elements of the Christian religion and baptized them. He had them build many small huts, usually of stone or adobe, which served as chapels when he made his later visits. Father Kino was a most earnest Christian, and he had a great love for the humble Indians among whom he lived and worked. Merely to visit them at extended intervals was not enough to make and keep them good Christians. In the long periods between his visits they would slip back into their pagan tribal practices. He wished to teach them a settled way of life, to civilize them, as that was the only way to keep them Christians. So he built missions in many places in the extensive region under his spiritual control.

It is not to be thought that the institution which we call a mission was originated by Padre Kino. Already the Spaniards had built many missions on the frontiers throughout the two Americas, and they continued to build them during the entire colonial period. In fact, the twenty-three Franciscan missions which were built in Upper California (now the state of California) were founded as late as the years between 1776 and 1823, the last one after Mexico had become independent of the mother country, Spain. Texas eventually possessed a considerable number. A half dozen can be visited now in the neighborhood of San Antonio, some of them in ruins. The Spaniards endeavored with ill success to establish missions in what is now Southeastern United States—in the Carolinas, Georgia, and Florida.

The immense valley of the Amazon River was the scene of much missionary activity, as were other parts of Brazil. (Brazil, it must be remembered, was a colony of Portugal rather than of Spain.) In Chile, missions were established by the religious orders among the fierce, intractable Araucanians, an Indian people comparable in courage and fighting ability, as well as love of liberty, to the Navajos and others of our Plains Indians. One of the most famous groups of missions in colonial Spanish America were those of the Paraguayan region. There (in Southern Paraguay, Southwestern Brazil, and Northeastern Argentina) the native Guaraní Indians were gathered into more than a score of missions—"reductions" the Spaniards called them, because it was thought that the Indians were being "led back" to the Christian religion, from which many centuries before they had strayed away.

The mission, in addition to its religious work of Christianizing the Indians, was a great aid in the task of extending Spain's frontier. It frequently was the first step in the establishment of Spanish control in a new section. At times, particularly in the case of more barbarous tribes, the soldiers entered first. But with Indians such as those of Pimería Alta the missionaries went first, though the padres were sometimes accompanied by a half dozen or so soldiers, token of Spanish power and authority. The rule was that after the mission had been established and the Indians had lived under its civilizing influence for ten years, the padres passed along to farther and fresher fields. Then came the secular priests and the civil officials, and the Indians of the old mission became elements of civil group life, that is, they were absorbed into the normal life of the colony. The task of religious instruction, of spiritual assistance, was assumed by the secular clergy. And so, step by step, league by league, the dominance of Spanish civil government was pushed outward from settled centers.

One of the largest and most influential of Padre Kino's missions was that of San Xavier del Bac, previously mentioned. As a preliminary step to building this mission, Father Kino as early as 1696 had established stock ranches in the fertile valleys of the Santa Cruz and San Pedro Rivers. It was not until early in 1700 that the work of building the mission was actually commenced. Father Kino himself, in his diary, describes in these words this important beginning:

. . . we began the foundations of a very large and capacious church and house of San Xavier del Bac, all the many people working with much pleasure and zeal, some in digging for the foundations, others in hauling many and very good stones of *tezontle* [a porous stone much used by the Mexicans for building] from a little hill which was about a quarter of a league away. For the mortar for these foundations it was not necessary to haul water, because by means of the irrigation we very easily conducted the water where we wished. And that house, with its great court and garden nearby, will be able to have throughout the year all the water it may need, running to any place or workroom one may please, and one of the greatest and best fields in all Nueva Biscaya.[2]

[2] Quoted in *ibid.*, pp. 198, 199. Nueva Biscaya (or Nueva Vizcaya) was the Spanish name for the region of Northwestern New Spain in which lay Pimería Alta. It was named after Vizcaya, in Spain, after the manner of the English in naming New England.

Father Kino states that there were three thousand Pimans assisting with the construction of the buildings of San Xavier del Bac. When completed, this mission no doubt was similar to others that were built in this region and elsewhere in the Americas. The mission of San Luís Rey, in California, is another excellent example—still occupied but much reduced in size and in population.

The typical mission—and remember that they were to be found scattered widely over the tremendous sweep of territory from California to Southern Chile—was a self-sufficient community, or very nearly so. Its buildings, usually arranged around a square plaza, consisted of a church, a residence for the missionaries, storehouses for grains and other materials, less substantial huts which served as living quarters for the Indians, many of whom lived at the mission, and barns or corrals for stock. Often there was a guest house, particularly if the mission were a large one and so located as to have frequent visitors. Sometimes there were stationed at the mission a squad of soldiers, and, if so, there were quarters for them. Soldiers were, as a rule, not present when the Indians of the mission and the locality were peaceable. The Jesuit fathers preferred, if it were possible, to dispense with soldiers. It has been said that they saw in troops and governors only "diseases, epidemics, and political corruption." Usually there were but two padres at a mission. One of them was the superintendent of the farming and stock-raising operations. The other was responsible for the religious instruction of the Indians and for proper conduct of the mission. The larger missions sowed thousands of acres to crops and pastured many thousands of head of stock—sheep, cattle, horses, hogs—on adjoining slopes and valleys.

The many activities of the mission were performed by the

Indians. Among them were gardeners, carpenters, weavers, iron-workers, wood-workers, diggers of ditches. The name "mission" perpetuates the memory of a very substantial type of furniture, which was made by the humble mission Indian.

The Indians were regarded as children, spiritually and mentally. If they misbehaved, they were punished, sometimes by flogging, sometimes by being shut up, or by other means. They were taught the catechism, simple hymns, church responses, the rudiments of Spanish. It was very difficult for the ignorant, barbarous natives to understand many items of church doctrine. A story that well illustrates this point is told of Padre Tamarel who, like Padre Salvatierra, worked in Lower California. The natives of that country were accustomed to living in very rude huts—hutches rather, for they consisted of no more than rough walls three or four feet high with no roofs. Earthquakes brought roofs tumbling on the head, so the Indians just left them off. At a time when the natives were shivering in these highly ineffective shelters, Father Tamarel preached to them and threatened them with the fires of hell if they refused to listen to him. Whereupon, the simple people demanded that the padre lead them to that eternally warm place. When he refused to give them the warmth which they imagined he controlled, they killed him. It appears usually to have been the case that, while the native took on a veneer of Christianity, he retained a great deal of the pagan religion of his fathers. With so ignorant a people it could scarcely have been otherwise.

However, it is usually agreed that the church, of which the missions were a very important part, was the friend of the Indians, much more so than the Spanish civil government. In a great many regions, where the missionaries operated, the Indians assumed at least the appearance of civilization and Christianity. Warfare between tribes was lessened. A better food supply was provided through the grains and vegetables of the missions. The animals which were introduced made possible a somewhat more comfortable life for the native. Particularly was this true of the sheep which furnished wool for weaving. Many of the skills which were taught the native by the missionary are still practiced widely in the Indian pueblos of our Southwest. What person who has ever been in New Mexico or Arizona has not been intrigued and delighted by the bold colors and skillful weaving of Navajo rugs and blankets and by the beautiful silver work of Navajo and Pueblo Indians? The materials were introduced and the skills were taught originally by the padres of Spain.

Father Kino ranged widely over his domain in Pimería Alta. Often his companions were but a few Indians. Sometimes he traveled with considerable numbers of horses and mules from his ranches. His endurance and his hardihood were great in the discharge of what he considered to be his duty. Sometimes he found it necessary even to muster his Piman braves and send them against the marauding, merciless Apaches who were their neighbors to the north. The government paid a bonus for each Apache scalp taken, and it sometimes happened that, after one of these expeditions, there was disagreement concerning the sum due a claimant. One does not like to think of it, but at such times Padre Kino, with the interests of his charges at heart, would count the scalps himself and insist on a just payment.

In the later years of Father Kino's mission to the Pimans, the Spanish government was concentrating its resources on other sections of its vast American empire. For this reason it failed to provide the support that Padre Kino felt he should have for his work. His last days, therefore, were filled with disappointment. The heroic padre, worn down with his long and arduous period of self-sacrificing service, died at Magdalena, one of the missions he had founded. The year was 1711 and his age was not yet seventy. A companion who was with him at the end wrote of his passing:

He died as he had lived, with extreme humility and poverty. . . . His deathbed, as his bed had always been, consisted of two calfskins for a mattress, two blankets such as the Indians use for covers, and a pack-saddle for a pillow. . . . No one ever saw him in any vice whatsoever, for the discovery of lands and the conversion of souls had purified him. . . . He was merciful to others but cruel to himself.[3]

Father Kino had done little, if any, evil to live after him and, fortunately, the much good that he had done was not buried with his bones. Its effects live, and the memory of his fine life is still recorded in many pages of history.

[3] Quoted in *ibid.*, p. 201.

PART TWO

REVOLUTION

INTRODUCTION

The people of Latin America, like those of the Thirteen Colonies, won independence through revolution. At bottom, the cause of the Spanish-American revolutions was the same as that of the American Revolution—disregard by the mother country of the interests of the colonials. The British government forbade its American subjects to make felt hats or nails for export and regulated in other annoying ways the foreign trade in which they engaged. In the same fashion, and for the same reason, Spain forbade the Mexican colonials to grow olive trees and manufacture olive oil and the Peruvian to cultivate grapes and make wine. Nor could the colonials in Mexico trade with those in Peru. These activities would compete with the interests of the growers and merchants in Spain. The American market must be retained for the Spanish producer no matter how much the interests of the colonials suffered.

The truth of the matter is that, as time passed, the Spaniards and the Portuguese who lived in the Americas became Americans rather than Spaniards or Portuguese. To them, of course, their own welfare was of much greater importance than the welfare of a group of merchants back in the home country. Gradually the number of Americans grew greater, and with this increase in number grew the spirit of resentment against the mother country for its unfair restrictions. The time came, finally, when they would tolerate no more government from abroad.

Even before this time came, the weaknesses of Spain had been clearly demonstrated. It had failed to maintain the trade monopoly against British, French, and Dutch smugglers. Politically, Spain steadily, though slowly, declined after the famous defeat of the Armada in 1588. In the late years of the eighteenth century an effort was made to reform and strengthen the decaying political organization. The effort failed, however, for corruption and misgovernment were too deeply rooted to be eliminated. Hence, the American children lost respect for their Spanish mother.

There were other causes for revolution. In the eighteenth century, many intelligent young Spanish-Americans of wealthy families were sent to Europe for education. There they came into contact with the teachings of Rousseau and other French liberals. Many of them became members of the Masonic Lodge, at the time a highly liberal organization. These young men were to become the leaders of thought and action in the Spanish-American revolutionary movement. They had seen the success of the American Revolution and were inspired with a desire to emulate it and to gain for themselves the benefits of independence which we had achieved. These Spanish-American liberals were equally excited by the French Revolution of 1789. They read the Declaration of the Rights and Duties of Man and felt that they should have the freedoms expressed there. As to the *mestizos* and Indians in Latin America, they had never felt any love for Spain and could be readily persuaded to take up arms against her. In the early years of the nineteenth century, criticism of Spain was widespread in Spanish America. The invasion of Spain by Napoleon, therefore, was all that was needed to start the Spanish-Americans on the way to revolution.

Napoleon, in the course of his conquests, entered Spain

in 1807. He deposed the Spanish king, Charles IV, and caused the heir to the throne, Ferdinand, to surrender his right to rule. Then Napoleon placed his brother, Joseph, on the Spanish throne. The people of Spain did not tamely accept these changes. They organized a counter-movement against the government of Napoleon, and shortly, with the aid of England, undertook the Peninsular War against him. Although Spanish patriots claimed the right to rule the American colonies, the colonials denied the right and set up their own governments, presumably to rule until Ferdinand should come to the Spanish throne. In most cases this was merely a pretense, the actual end in view being independence. When Ferdinand later became king of Spain, he made no concessions to the Americans, but endeavored to restore the old restrictions, from which, of course, the colonials had for some years been free. Then, indeed, the movement became an open struggle for complete independence.

The Spanish-American and the Brazilian revolutions present some highly interesting contrasts with our own revolution. Ours was a unified movement. General Washington commanded all the armies, the entire venture was directed and sustained by one congress, and the area affected by military campaigns was comparatively limited. Among the Spanish-Americans there were many movements, though they were concentrated mainly in three large areas—the revolution in Mexico, the revolutions in northern South America, and the revolutions in southern South America. There were many armies operating independently of one another, and several congresses legislated in various regions. Moreover, the area of the Spanish-American revolutions was immensely greater than ours, and the difficulties of terrain much more formidable. They were obliged to cope with cloud-piercing mountain ranges, great jungles, and wide deserts. All these obstacles produced another important difference in the two independence movements: that of the Spanish-Americans endured more than twice as long as ours. Beginning in 1810 in several regions, the wars were not actually finished until 1825, though in some places military activities ceased at an earlier date.

Furthermore, the Spanish-Americans fought their wars of liberation without allies, while we were aided by France, a powerful European nation without whose help we should probably have lost the war. As with us, the Spanish-Americans had great difficulty in properly equipping the soldiers, for they, too, were forced to import much of their war materials. Though no foreign government aided them, they received valuable assistance from many foreign individuals, who enlisted in their armies. One of these was Lord Cochrane, the English naval genius, who was associated with military activities in Chile, Peru, and Brazil. Several North Americans, such as William Rawson in Argentina, also helped. But it cannot be said that this aid was decisive, as was the aid of France for us.

In those days, it should be remembered, there were very few newspapers—even fewer in Latin America than in the Thirteen Colonies. This makes it all the more remarkable that the spirit of rebellion could be kept alive through so long a period as fifteen years. Finally, this extended period of warfare and chaos had the sad effect of producing in many regions the feeling that warfare was a normal condition. This was one of the reasons for the failure to create stable governments and organized society until long after the wars ceased.

Brazil, in her independence movement, presents some sharp contrasts with Spanish America. After Napoleon had entered the Iberian Peninsula, he shortly invaded Portugal, Brazil's mother country. With the aid of an English fleet, the Portuguese royal family and many nobles removed themselves to Brazil and set up court at Rio de Janeiro. Immediately the former colony of Brazil was raised to the status of a kingdom and as such enjoyed many liberal reforms. Later, with the overthrow of Napoleon, the Portuguese court returned to Lisbon. The Portuguese had not been popular with the Brazilians. Just as the Spanish-Americans had become Americans, that is, Mexicans, Peruvians, or Chileans, so the Portuguese-Americans became Americans, that is, Brazilians. Therefore, when John VI left Rio, he gave precise instructions to his son, Pedro, whom he appointed regent. If an independence movement should begin in Brazil, he instructed, Pedro should put himself at its head and declare for an independent kingdom. Thus, Brazil would be kept in the family. That is precisely what happened. In 1822, Pedro became Emperor Pedro I of the independent Brazilian Empire. As a result, the Brazilian Revolution was practically bloodless.

As with us, so with the Latin-Americans, this period of revolution against the mother country was a "great moment." It brought forth their national heroes—Bolívar in Venezuela and Colombia, San Martín in Argentina and Chile, O'Higgins in Chile, Hidalgo and Morelos in Mexico, and many, many more. As new nations came into being, national flags were adopted and days of independence were commemorated. The history of these revolutions was on the heroic scale. It deserves to be known.

CHAPTER VII

FRANCISCO DE MIRANDA: FORERUNNER
OF REVOLUTION

The half century from 1775 to 1825 was a remarkable period in the history of human liberty. It witnessed three great revolutionary movements which remade the political map of Western Europe and the Americas. These movements were the American Revolution, the French Revolution, and the Latin-American revolutions. The first divorced the Thirteen Colonies from the British Empire and established the world's first great republic. The second destroyed the old French absolute monarchy and commenced a movement which in time established the freedom of peoples in Western Europe. The third broke the hold of Spain and Portugal on immense possessions in North and South America, and made the Americas preëminently the continents of republican government.

Only one man who could be called a personage had the glorious experience of being associated with every one of these famous revolutions. He was the Venezuelan, Francisco de Miranda. Today Miranda's countrymen and Latin-Americans in general call him *El Precursor*, or "The Forerunner." More than thirty years of his life were devoted to the cause of Spanish-American independence. Awake, he worked persistently for the cause; asleep, he doubtless dreamed of it.

Professor William Spence Robertson, an American historian, has called him "the knight-errant of Spanish-American liberty."

The place of Miranda's birth was Caracas, now the capital of Venezuela; the time was March 28, 1750. In Caracas he spent the first twenty-one years of his life and there he received his formal education. There, too, he began to see the bad features of Spain's colonial government.

Venezuela, at the time of Miranda's birth and for sixty years afterward, was ruled from Madrid, Spain, as the captaincy-general of Venezuela. Its relation to Spain could be compared in some respects to the relation of the British colony of New York to the home government at London. But there were some important differences. Venezuela's governor was called a captain-general. His power was not limited by an elective assembly as was the case with the governor of New York. The people of Venezuela had absolutely no voice in their government. The captain-general and other important officials were sent from Spain, and they took their orders from the Spanish court. In Venezuela there were many educated, intelligent native-born whites (called creoles) who felt that they were quite capable of filling those offices—and drawing the good salaries attached to them. Because of what they felt was an unjust discrimination, they bitterly disliked the Spaniards who ruled them. As time passed, the creoles became more numerous and more influential. In Venezuela, as in the whole of Spanish America, taxes and the laws which governed trade were much more oppressive than those against which New York and the other British colonies rebelled. As Miranda was an intelligent youth, he saw all of these injustices and formed adverse opinions about them.

In Spain and in Spanish America most young men of good

family found their opportunities in either the church or the army. Miranda early centered his interests on the army, and when he reached manhood his father, a man of some means, provided him with the funds necessary for a voyage to Spain and the purchase of a commission in the Spanish army. As an army captain, Miranda pleased some of his superiors and displeased others. Part of the displeasure was perhaps, owing to the jealousy of less able men, part to the impatience and extreme frankness of Miranda himself. Nevertheless, in the course of time he was promoted to a colonelcy.

After Spain, in 1779, joined France in the war against England (at the time when the United States was fighting for independence), Miranda's regiment was sent to the West Indies. Miranda spent two years there and participated in the actions which resulted in wresting from England Pensacola and the Bahamas. Of course Spain was not an ally of the United States in these years. Nevertheless, since these activities embarrassed and hindered Great Britain's war effort, Miranda may be said to have aided the cause of the United States.

During this West Indian period, Miranda again got into difficulties with high-placed Spanish officers. Charges were brought against him, he was convicted by a court, fined heavily, and sentenced to spend ten years at a lonely Spanish military post in Africa. In these circumstances, Miranda decided that the time had come for him to make the educational tour which for some years he had been considering. He evaded arrest (the conviction was made in his absence) and found passage to the United States. His difficulty was not cleared up by his interested friends, and never again did he serve the Spanish government in any capacity. Letters from discontented Venezuelan friends had strengthened his conviction of

Spanish abuses there, and now that he was personally injured, he resolved to devote his life to freeing his native land from Spanish domination.

Now began for Miranda a period that would have been highly enjoyable to any young man, and must have been in the fullest degree educative for Miranda. Already, while serving in Spain, he had met some attractive English people and had come to admire the English political system, which was much more liberal than that of Spain. In the year and a half which he spent in the United States, he had an opportunity to observe the operations of a liberal republican government and so had his liberal convictions strengthened. He was particularly impressed by our practice of religious toleration—something which was unknown in any part of the Spanish Empire. Most of the liberal practices which he observed here he credited to the influence of England, and his admiration for the English system was further strengthened.

From the United States Miranda crossed to Europe late in 1784. His travels there embraced England, Holland, Prussia and other German states, Austria, Italy, Russia, and Switzerland. Already the alert and industrious Venezuelan had mastered most of the languages spoken in Europe and had read widely. These accomplishments now stood him in good stead. He was an interesting person, and, wherever he went, he was received in the best society. He passed several months at the Russian court of Catherine II. His dislike for Spain seems to have been growing during these years, when he had so many opportunities to make comparisons—many of them to the disadvantage of Spain. While he was at Catherine's court, a diplomat wrote of him:

He is a man with a haughty disposition and vast knowledge who speaks very freely about everything but particularly denounces the Inquisition, the government of Spain, the King, and the Prince of Asturias. He makes many offensive allusions to Spanish ignorance.[1]

In mid-year of 1789 Miranda returned to London, drawn perhaps by the French Revolution which had just begun. His travels had wonderfully increased his knowledge and broadened his views. They had also afforded him many opportunities for arousing in persons of influence an interest in the cause of his people. Whatever respect he had had for Spain was gone, and after his return to England he entered seriously upon what became his life work—the freeing of his country and all of Spanish America from the dominance of Spain. Wherever he saw an opportunity to encourage an enemy of Spain, there Miranda was to be found. As England, from 1790 to 1810, most often presented such possibilities, he was usually in London in those years. He was subsidized by the British government and was constantly busy advancing the cause—writing for the press, making plans for military expeditions to liberate Venezuela, drawing drafts of constitutions for independent governments in Spanish America. As the Spanish government considered him a traitor and made many efforts to seize him, his steadiness in support of the cause proves that he possessed no small degree of personal courage.

In these years Miranda gradually built up a fine library. He loved books and lost no opportunity to buy works of value—on history, on military science, on literature, on many subjects. His love for books quite outran his resources. An Englishman estimated in 1807 that his library was worth

[1] Quoted in William Spence Robertson, *The Life of Miranda* (Chapel Hill, University of North Carolina Press, 1929), I, 79. The Prince of Asturias was the heir to the Spanish throne.

about forty-five thousand dollars, and that he owed London booksellers twenty-five thousand dollars. After he left the Spanish army Miranda never had a regular income. His father gave him nothing after 1790. He was supported by loans from friends interested in him or in his cause and by grants from the British treasury. This accounts in a measure for his constant financial troubles. It is a tribute to his abilities and the worth that he was thought to have that he should have been able to live rather well and to build up so fine a library with no regular or dependable resources.

Quite naturally, Miranda's interest was tremendously excited by the French Revolution. He crossed to Paris, and such was his fame as a military expert that he was commissioned a general in the revolutionary army. He participated in some important campaigns but, it must be admitted, not very successfully. In fact, he was accused of having been responsible for a military defeat in Belgium. He was tried on the charge and found guilty. Many persons declared that he was not actually guilty of the charges of cowardice and mismanagement that had been brought against him. Forced to remain in hiding for some months, he finally escaped from France— with a collection of books—and returned to London. This sorry experience did not dampen his ardor for liberal government or discourage him in his efforts to liberate Venezuela.

General Miranda established in London a home in which to keep his fine library, to entertain his friends, and to work on his projects for emancipation. It was here that his two sons, Leander and Francisco, were born. Their mother was Miranda's housekeeper, Sarah Andrews, a woman of common origin and no education.

It was from London that he planned an expedition to liberate Venezuela. He got together some funds and crossed to New York. There he purchased a small boat, which he named the *Leander* (after his son, presumably), and enlisted some hundreds of adventuresome men. With these he sailed for the coast of Venezuela. James Briggs, one of the group, wrote an account of this expedition. In it appears this description of Miranda:

He is about five feet ten inches high. His limbs are well proportioned; his whole frame is stout and active. His complexion is dark, florid and healthy. His eyes are hazel-coloured, but not of the darkest hue. They are piercing, quick, and intelligent, expressing more of the severe than the mild feelings. He has good teeth, which he takes much care to keep clean. His nose is large and handsome, rather of the English than Roman cast. His chest is broad and flat. His hair is grey, and he wears it tied long behind, with powder. He has strong grey whiskers, growing on the outer edges of his ears, as large as most Spaniards have on their cheeks. In the contour of his visage, you plainly perceive an expression of pertinaciousness and suspicion. Upon the whole, without saying he is an elegant, we may pronounce him a handsome man. He has a constant habit of picking his teeth. When sitting he is never perfectly still; his foot or hand must be moving to keep time with his mind, which is always in exercise. He always sleeps a few moments after dinner, and then walks till bedtime, which with him is about midnight. He is an eminent example of temperance. A scanty or bad meal is never regarded by him as a subject of complaint. He uses no ardent spirits; seldom any wine. Sweetened water is his common beverage. Sweetness and warmth, says he, are the two greatest physical goods; and acid and cold are the greatest physical evils in the universe. . . .

. . . He appeared the master of languages, of science and literature. In his conversations, he carried his hearers to the scenes of great actions, and introduced them to the distinguished characters of every age. He took excursions to Troy, Babylon, Jerusalem,

This statue of San Martín in Plaza San Martín, Buenos Aires, is backed by the tallest building in South America.

An Ecuadorean Indian of today, carrying her baby safely on her back. Ecuador, or the territory of Quito, was added to the Republic of Colombia by Bolívar, on his march toward Peru.

Caracas, where Francisco de Miranda was born in 1750, is now the capital of Venezuela. It was here that he was welcomed as Precursor by Venezuelans in 1810. Here they built a shrine for his body, but it has remained empty because no one knows what was done with his bones when La Caracca cemetery, his original burial place, was closed.

Rome, Athens, and Syracuse. Men famed as statesmen, heroes, patriots, conquerors, and tyrants, priests and scholars, he produced, and weighed their merits and defects. Modern history and biography afforded him abundant topics. He impressed an opinion of his comprehensive views, his inexhaustible fund of learning; his probity, his generosity, and patriotism. After all, this man of blazoned fame, must, I fear, be considered as having more learning than wisdom; more theoretical knowledge than practical talent; too sanguine and too opinionated to distinguish between the vigor of enterprise and the hardiness of infatuation.[2]

The *Leander* expedition was not a success. It merely added another item to the list of Miranda's military failures. The disappointed leader returned to London to resume his plotting and planning with the British government. (It is worth mentioning that the first printing press of Venezuela was taken in by the *Leander* expedition.)

At this period Miranda had great hope that England could be induced to assist him in freeing the Americas. The British merchants had long wanted admission to the trade of Spanish America, but had constantly been denied it in conformity with Spain's idea of maintaining a commercial monopoly. An English army did operate in the Río de la Plata region in 1806 and 1807, capturing and holding for a short time the city of Buenos Aires. Miranda's hopes ran high. But just then, in expanding his dominance of the European continent, Napoleon occupied Spain and placed his brother, Joseph, on the Spanish throne. Though the Spanish king submitted, his people did not. For several years England had been fighting Napoleon, but had found no place on the continent where they could strike at him. The turn of affairs in Spain offered

[2] Quoted in N. Andrew N. Cleven, *Readings in Hispanic American History* (New York, Ginn and Company, 1927), pp. 407, 412-14.

an opportunity. England immediately made an alliance with the patriot opponents of Napoleon and sent an army to the Iberian peninsula. This alliance meant that, for the time at any rate, no further thought could be given to aiding revolutionary movements in Spanish America. Miranda's terrible temper is revealed in the uneasiness that the English officials felt in breaking the bad news to him. No less a person than the Duke of Wellington, the "Iron Duke," was appointed to perform the fearsome task. How he did it the Duke many years later described in these lines:

I think I never had a more difficult business than when the Government bade me tell Miranda that we would have nothing to do with his plan. I thought it best to walk out in the streets with him and tell him there, to prevent his bursting out. But even there he was so loud and angry, that I told him I would walk on a little that we might not attract the notice of everybody passing. When I joined him again he was cooler. He said: "You are going over into Spain (this was before Vimiera)—you will be lost—nothing can save you; that, however, is your affair; but what grieves me is that there never was such an opportunity thrown away!"[3]

These developments caused important movements in Spanish America, one of the first of them in Venezuela. When Napoleon forced the Spanish king to quit the throne, his American subjects felt that they owed no allegiance either to Napoleon's brother or to the opposing government which the Spanish patriots organized. The Americans took the attitude that they were free to rule themselves until such time as their legitimate king should regain his throne. With many of the Spanish-Americans this was only an excuse, adopted to make easier the first step toward independence. In several colonial

[3] Quoted in Robertson, op. cit., II, 23.

centers European officials were replaced by local governments formed by the people themselves under the leadership of prominent creoles. This was the case in Venezuela. The captain-general was displaced on April 19, 1810.

When Miranda learned what was going on in Venezuela he was deeply interested. It was not long before agents from his native country and from other revolutionary governments in Spanish America began to appear in England. Miranda received them and aided them in every way possible. However, England was far too busy with Napoleon in Spain to give any assistance to the independence-hungry revolutionist from across the sea. Finally, Miranda, unable to do anything effective in England, decided he must return to Venezuela. Wishing to have him at hand in case an opportunity should arise for using him, the English government refused its consent. Nevertheless, Miranda could not be restrained, and he left without the government's permission—and thereby forfeited any further allowance from the London treasury.

The Precursor, after his long exile, returned to his native land in mid-December of 1810. He was given an enthusiastic welcome by the Venezuelans, and he himself aided the display by entering Caracas "mounted on a beautiful white charger." Though some doubted his value to the cause, most felt that he could give valuable assistance. Had he not been for decades working for the end toward which they were now swiftly moving? Was he not a general and an authority on military matters? It is therefore not strange that he was almost at once chosen as a delegate to the national congress then being formed. Of that body he shortly became the most influential leader.

The congress met early in March, 1811. The great question of the hour was whether or not independence should be declared. In the discussion of this matter it was asserted that the people of Venezuela had desired independence ever since the movement of April 19 of the previous year. The establishment of a republican form of government was early agreed upon. Miranda argued that it would be illogical to establish a republic without declaring independence. Independent, Venezuela would be in a position to seek foreign alliances; without a declaration, no alliance could be sought. This and other strong arguments convinced the members of congress. The all-important declaration was voted on July 5, and the document signed on July 7, 1811.

It must not be thought that every Venezuelan favored independence. Venezuela had its Royalists, or Tories, just as the United States had them in the American Revolution. There had been many Spanish soldiers in Venezuela when the revolution was begun, and it was expected that others would be sent, if that were possible. It was necessary to organize a revolutionary army. This was quickly done, and Miranda was placed at its head, with orders to suppress the Royalist opposition. Again the great expert in military matters was in command of an armed force and had a chance to put his theories into practice.

It must be borne in mind that Venezuela was beset with all the customary troubles of a new revolutionary state. In addition to difficulties arising from the opposition of the Royalists, the serious inexperience of the leaders in political matters, and important differences about the form which the new government should take, there was a decided lack of financial resources. This meant a lack of equipment for the army, of adequate support in its campaigns. Despite these disadvantages, Miranda had some successes. One of these was the recovery of the city of Valencia. However, he was accused of causing unnecessary bloodshed and of securing supplies in an illegal fashion. Again, as in Spain, in the West Indies, and in France, Miranda had to defend himself against charges of misconduct. In this case his defense was successful.

The entire political picture in Venezuela was changed by a terrible earthquake which shook the country on March 26, 1812. Many thousands of people were killed. The churchmen, most of whom were Royalists, declared that the tragedy was an act of Divine Providence to punish the people for their infidelity to their rightful king. This argument had great influence with the mass of the ignorant and the credulous, and many former supporters deserted the cause of the Patriots. In these grave circumstances, congress made Miranda dictator and charged him with the task of putting down the growing Royalist opposition. Miranda was now both the chief civil and the chief military executive of the country.

Meanwhile, the Royalists, under command of the acting captain-general, Domingo de Monteverde, were approaching the capital from the west, gathering strength as they came. Miranda exhibited indecision in meeting the threat. He had placed Simón Bolívar, then a young captain, in command of the important town of Puerto Cabello, on the seacoast not far from the capital city. Lacking the force to meet his attackers, and the means of enduring a siege, Bolívar had to surrender to Monteverde. After this reverse Miranda seemed to lose his spirit and his confidence. At any rate, not long afterward he signed with the Royalist commander the capitulation of San Mateo, which contained fairly liberal terms for the revolutionists. Miranda apparently felt that for the time being the cause was lost. He probably believed that the future would present opportunities for renewing the struggle under more favorable conditions.

Now a strange thing happened. Miranda was arranging to quit the country and had gone to the port of La Guayra to take ship. It is thought that he intended to flee to Colombia or to the West Indies and there encourage revolution. However, before he could board ship he was seized by a number of his former officers, who were angered by his capitulation. They locked him in the Castle of San Carlos, a prison in La Guayra, and notified Monteverde of their act. The Royalist commander arrived shortly and took Miranda into custody. One of the officers who thus made possible the capture of Miranda was Simón Bolívar, who was later to become one of the greatest heroes of the Latin-American revolutions. This action is one of the incidents in that remarkable man's life which his admirers have great difficulty in explaining away or justifying.

For the time being, the revolution in Venezuela was at an end. Bolívar fled to the West Indies, whence he later was to return and assume leadership in the movement. Miranda was taken to Spain where he spent the remaining four years of his life in prison. He died on July 14, 1816, at La Caracca, where he was buried. As the cemetery many years later was closed without Miranda's bones having been moved, it is not known today where they are. Venezuela later built a splendid shrine to contain them, but the shrine remains empty.

Historians still disagree over many passages in Miranda's life. He appears to have been much better at theory than at practice; as leader of the military forces of revolution he was not a success. But it would be distinctly an error to think of the great "Forerunner" as an "also-ran." His achievement lay in the all-important phase of preparation. As a great Spanish-American historian once wrote, "the revolution had first to be made in the man before it could be made in the country." Miranda ploughed the field of revolution with unwavering determination and planted the potent seed with steadfast resolution. It was his misfortune that he did not contribute materially to bringing in the harvest. But the soil and the seed ultimately produced richly—and that not long after Miranda's death. As the great Precursor, Francisco de Miranda deserves a high place in the history of Venezuela and in the wider history of Spanish America.

CHAPTER VIII

MARIANO MORENO: A FOUNDER OF THE ARGENTINE REPUBLIC

Wars for independence, such as the American Revolution, do not burst into full flame in a single day. The farmers, artisans, and merchants of the Thirteen Colonies had to be made to see the advantages of independence before they would fight for it. Months, even years, of mental preparation—thinking, debating, writing, speaking—were necessary before these peace-loving colonists would shoulder their muskets against the soldiers of the king. Patriots like Samuel Adams, Patrick Henry, and Thomas Paine had great difficulty in convincing the people that separation from England was desirable.

In quite the same way, the average man of Latin America had to be taught to believe in separation from *his* mother country, Spain. Of course, if he happened to be living in Brazil or Haiti, his mother country was Portugal or France, instead of Spain. In any of these cases his attitude toward Europe was very much like that of the English colonist. Just as the latter was persuaded by Adams, Henry, and Paine, so the colonist in Latin America was influenced by *his* leaders. In Venezuela, in Mexico, in Haiti, in Brazil, in Chile, in Argentina—in fact, in all the new nations that were to spring up in Latin America—such leaders came to the front. Although the names of most of them are new and strange to us, they are quite as much national heroes in their countries as are Samuel Adams and Patrick Henry in ours.

One of the most brilliant of these heroes was Mariano Moreno, who, like Alexander Hamilton, was a very young man at the time of the struggle for independence. He lived and worked in the city of Buenos Aires (Good Airs), soon to become the capital of a new nation, Argentina. Moreno was not exactly a Samuel Adams, a Patrick Henry, or a Thomas Paine, but he had some of the abilities of each of those men. Like Adams, he was a planner and an organizer. Like Henry, he was a lawyer and a speaker. Like Paine, he was a writer and a journalist. Like all three, he was a genuine believer in freedom of speech and press and the democratic form of government. Like all three, too, he dared to speak out his convictions and to show his fellowmen exactly where he stood.

Mariano was born in Buenos Aires in 1778, not many years after that city had become the center of a new viceroyalty, the fourth in Spanish America. (The other viceroyalties were those of New Spain, New Granada, and Peru.) Although he came from a large family—he was the eldest—his parents saw to it that he received the best education to be obtained. They sent him to El Colegio de San Carlos (The College of Saint Charles), a primary and high school. He loved to study, and he eagerly took every course offered and borrowed every book he could. He quickly mastered Latin. Early in life, therefore, Mariano developed a vivid memory and an ability to express his ideas clearly and forcefully.

Such talent did not pass unnoticed. When he had finished the *colegio*, his teachers and parents determined to send him to a university. Because no university had yet been established in Buenos Aires, he had to go away to college. There were three places to which he might have gone: Córdoba, over in the north central part of Argentina; Santiago, across the high Andes Mountains, in Chile; and Chuquisaca (the present-day city of Sucre), far away to the northwest in Upper Peru (present-day Bolivia). Even today, with modern trains and automobiles, it is a long, tiresome, though exciting, journey from Buenos Aires to any one of these places. In 1800, of course, such a trip was a daring adventure. Nevertheless, Mariano determined to go to Chuquisaca, most distant of the three, two thousand miles away. Across the perfectly flat *pampas* (treeless plains) of Central Argentina he went, on to the hot, dry lands of Northern Argentina, up the steep Andes to the plateau where Chuquisaca was located. The whole journey had to be made on foot or by horse or burro. On that arduous trip to his college Mariano must have learned a lot of geography and collected a great deal of information about people—farmers, *gauchos* (Argentine cowboys), Indians.

Chuquisaca, when the twenty-one-year old student arrived, was not a really large city—there were fourteen thousand inhabitants—but it was an important one. An archbishop, with all his officials, lived there, as well as the officers of the royal *audiencia* and the families of the wealthy mine owners of Potosí, rich mining town a hundred miles away. There were ten convents and a number of other religious institutions. But, to Mariano, the most interesting institution of all was the university which he had come so far to enter, one of the finest universities in the New World at that time. The University of San Francisco Javier, as it was called, was nearly two hundred years old (founded in 1624, thirteen years before Harvard), and was especially famous for its studies in law and theology.

Mariano's parents had sent him to the university to study

for the priesthood, and he himself had wished to enter the clergy. By the time he was ready for ordination, however, he had become interested in the study of law and determined to stay on for three more years so that he might become a lawyer. He soon became a member of the Caroline Academy, a kind of debating society for advanced law students. Here with fellow-students he could practice public speaking and debate the great economic and political questions of the day. He dared to discuss (in secret, of course) the evils of Spanish colonial government—high taxes, cruel treatment of the Indians in the mines, tight control of colonial trade, harsh policies of the colonial governors. In the Caroline Academy, too, he read books, especially French books which had to be smuggled into South America because the Spanish rulers did not wish the colonists to read them. These were books by Rousseau, Raynal, and the same French thinkers who were writing about the ideas of free speech, free press, and popular government that had influenced our own leaders of independence. He even read of the American Revolution and learned how the Thirteen Colonies had become the United States of America and were developing into a strong nation. The young law student, perhaps without realizing it, was really preparing himself for the day when he should become a leader in the struggle to free his own people in Buenos Aires.

Therefore, when he returned to his home after five years, Mariano Moreno was a mature young man. He had seen new lands, met new people, and gained new ideas. He had learned of the democratic movements in the United States and France. He had become a critic of the unjust and unfair policies of Spain toward his city and toward other parts of Spanish America. With these ideas he returned to Buenos

Aires just in time to become a leader in Argentina's stirring struggle for independence.

Moreno at once passed the examinations entitling him to practice law, and very soon he was made legal counselor of the *audiencia*. While he was serving in this position in 1806-1807, there occurred some of the most important events leading to Argentina's fight for independence. The young legal adviser—now twenty-eight—was an eager participant. On two separate occasions—one in 1806, the other in 1807—English forces sailed into the Río de la Plata (River of Silver) and seized the city of Buenos Aires. Spain, once a great power, had grown too weak to give aid to the faraway colony. The colonists, therefore, raised their own army and twice expelled the raiding English redcoats. The people of the city had proved, to their own satisfaction at least, that they were not wholly dependent upon Spain and could protect themselves if necessary. They became aware of their own strength. They received a taste—a very delicious taste, they thought—of making their own decisions. They began to feel that they were Argentines rather than Spaniards. By helping to plan measures for the expulsion of the British soldiers, Mariano Moreno and his brother, Manuel, nurtured this feeling.

But the people of Buenos Aires were still not ready to attempt independence. They had not yet reached the point where separation from Spain seemed desirable; nor had they leaders who could guide them along the way to independence. In fact, quite the opposite seemed to be true in 1808. Not long after the British were driven away, news came to Buenos Aires that Napoleon had invaded the mother country and taken captive Ferdinand VII, heir to the throne. Immediately, the *porteños* (citizens of Buenos Aires) expressed their loyalty to Ferdinand and said they wanted no other ruler, certainly not Napoleon or one of his puppets.

At this critical moment a new viceroy arrived from Spain; he was sent out by the *junta* (council) which was defying Napoleon and attempting to rule in the place of Ferdinand. This viceroy, a lieutenant-general in the Spanish Navy, soon discovered that business conditions in the colony were very bad, that there was really an economic depression. There was little legal commerce going in and out of the port. There was much smuggling. The farmers could not sell their products. All this was happening because, after the English had been driven out, the Spanish had restored their old colonial policies. These were much like the familiar Navigation Acts which the British had used against the Thirteen Colonies. Just as the British had tried to keep all the trade of their colonies in their own hands, so the Spanish tried to develop a commercial monopoly in Spanish America. The Spanish government had used these strict policies for three hundred years, but once the business men of Buenos Aires had tried the freer trade which prevailed during the British occupation, they discovered they liked it. They could no longer put up with the Spanish monopoly. They became more and more discontented and, in the spirit of the English colonists at the Boston Tea Party, they grumbled openly.

Among those who encouraged the grumbling was the young lawyer, Mariano Moreno. A little like Thomas Paine with his *Common Sense*, Moreno composed the *Memorial of the Landowners*, a long attack on the commercial practices of the mother country. He argued that the Spanish commercial policies had brought ruin to the people on both sides of the Río de la Plata. The public treasury was empty because foreign goods were smuggled in. Farmers and stock raisers had no markets for their goods. Prices of necessities were too high for the poor. Misery was everywhere. Much of this could be prevented, said Moreno, if English goods were admitted by law. Then the common people would be healthier, wealthier, and happier.

But Moreno was not yet pleading for revolution or independence from Spain. He was simply describing the condition of his people and the remedies he thought would relieve their misery. Nevertheless, his *Memorial* was important, because it linked his name, for the first time, with great national and international events. It was effective, too, because it gave the people something to think about. It showed them how unfair and unjust were the policies of Mother Spain. They began to wish for better schools, for greater opportunity to govern themselves, for freedom of speech and freedom of the press. Their wishes led to discussion. Their discussion led to discontent and restlessness, and restlessness eventually led to rebellion.

Just as we celebrate July 4, 1776, as the beginning of the United States of America, so the Argentines commemorate May 25, 1810, as the birthday of the United Provinces of the Río de la Plata. (The name Argentine Republic was adopted later.) On that day was created a new government known as a *junta*. Mariano Moreno became one of its first secretaries, as the nine members of the *junta* solemnly swore to defend their land in the name of the king, Ferdinand VII. But this was actually only a disguise to conceal their real desire for independence. This desire was realized, too, for Spain was never able to reconquer these courageous people. Since that day the United Provinces have been independent—the first independent nation in South America.

If independence were to be assured, however, more than

wishes and declarations was necessary. There was still much for Moreno and his colleagues to do. At once they invited the people of other parts of the viceroyalty of Buenos Aires to send delegates to represent them in the new government. They passed rules for the guidance of the leaders. As one of the secretaries, Moreno assumed charge of military and political affairs, a duty which he carried out efficiently and energetically. One of his first tasks was to found a newspaper, *Gaceta de Buenos Aires* (Gazette), so that the people might know what was going on in their country and in the rest of the world. As its editor, Moreno could tell the people of the need for information and truth. He argued for free speech and free press. He said that people should have books to read, many books; and he, more than any other man, was responsible for the founding of the national library which still exists in Buenos Aires. He organized an academy of mathematics and set up a discussion club. Moreno was a true champion of the methods of democratic government in his country.

In every way possible he worked to make his new government a republican one. In July, 1810, he drew up a Plan of Operations to guide the officials. In this plan he praised the spirit and success of George Washington and the United States, when he wrote:

Let me say that at times accident is the mother of events; for, if a revolution is not directed aright, if intrigue and ambition destroy public spirit, then the state will relapse into the most horrible anarchy. My fatherland, what changes you may suffer! Where, Oh noble and grand Washington, are the lessons of your politics? Where are the rules which guided you in the construction of your great work? Your principles and your system would be sufficient to guide us:—lend us your genius so that we may accomplish the results which we have contemplated![1]

With Washington as his inspiration, therefore, Moreno gave every effort—without thought of his own health—to make his new nation strong. He attacked the problems of public instruction and public health. He conducted a census. He tried to improve business and foreign commerce. Moreno was a dynamo seeking to drive his people to strength, unity, and democracy. He worked with the energy and the vitality of a Thomas Jefferson or a Benjamin Franklin.

But any man who works so forcefully is sure to make enemies as well as friends. So it was with Moreno. To Cornelio Saavedra, president of the *junta*, Moreno seemed too hasty, too liberal, too democratic. Saavedra feared that the people were not yet ready for real democracy. He believed that changes in government must be made slowly and gradually. Therefore, he wished to be the balance wheel to slow down and govern the speed of the dynamic young lawyer. The difficulties between the two leaders came to a head in December. Moreno, like Jefferson and other founders of the United States, wished to get rid of all relics of the pomp and ceremonies of the days of kingly control. The new nation must be democratic. There must be no titles, no crowns, no expensive pageants. In this first serious break with Saavedra, Moreno came off the victor, for these practices of royalty were abolished forever.

It was not so in the second dispute. Late in December delegates came to Buenos Aires from the provinces, from the

[1] Quoted in W. S. Robertson, *Rise of the Spanish-American Republics, as Told in the Lives of Their Liberators* (New York, D. Appleton-Century Company, 1918), p. 157.

The Christ of the Andes stands at Uspallata Pass, marking the end of a boundary dispute between Argentina and Chile. On the base is the inscription: "Sooner shall these mountains crumble into dust than Argentinians and Chileans break the peace sworn at the feet of the Redeemer."

(Left) This memorial to Mariano Moreno, a founder of Argentina, is on the Congress Plaza, Buenos Aires. (Right) The Cabildo in Buenos Aires is on the Plaza de Mayo (The Plaza of May), so named in honor of the birthday of the United Provinces of the Río de la Plata, later the Argentine Republic. This building, recently restored, was the scene of the meeting of Moreno and his fellow revolutionaries on May 25, 1810.

The Andes. Around these dangerous chasms, up these peaks, with snow and freezing temperatures making it even more difficut, San Martín led his Army the Andes into Chile, to help win independence for that country.

Plaza San Martín in Lima, Peru, is a monument to this great general, who was appointed "Protector of Peru" when he forced Spanish troops to evacuate the city and paved the way for Peru's declaration of independence.

rural regions of Argentina, asking to be admitted to the new government. Moreno was opposed, for he feared that the government was not yet strong enough to rule over so large a territory unless it resorted to undemocratic means. But he was outvoted in the *junta*, and the provincial delegates were admitted. This was the unfortunate beginning of a long conflict between the people of Buenos Aires and the citizens of the provinces, a conflict which has not yet been satisfactorily settled in Argentina.

This defeat was too much for anyone as sensitive as Moreno. He felt that his honor compelled him to resign. Almost at once he dropped out of active participation in the government. Nevertheless—even without Moreno—the struggle to make Argentina free and strong went on. Several unsuccessful attempts were made to unite the outlying parts of the old viceroyalty of Buenos Aires with Argentina. These provinces, however, preferred to set up their own governments, and, soon, there were three other new nations in the southern part of South America—Paraguay, Bolivia, and Uruguay.

Meanwhile, fiery leaders like Mariano Moreno were busy in other parts of North and South America, working, as Moreno had worked, for the freeing of the people from Spanish bonds. Flames of revolt flashed up and down the hemisphere, from Mexico to Chile. Writers and orators were preaching that the time was ripe to strike for independence. Yet, as every American knows, it takes more than writing and preaching to win wars for independence. It takes armies, generals, money, and courage. To create these forces, months and years are sometimes required. Many parts of Latin America, therefore, did not win independence until ten, even fifteen years after Argentina, and Cuba, so close to our own shores, did not succeed until 1898.

There remains a little to be said about Mariano Moreno, one of the daring youths who had led the way toward the independence of a whole continent. In January, 1811, shortly after his resignation from the government, he was sent on an important diplomatic mission to Brazil and England. However, through these last trying and exciting months, Moreno had worked beyond his strength. The stormy voyage in a little ship was too much for him to endure, and he died before he reached the equator. His body was buried at sea, wrapped, it is said, in an English flag. When President Saavedra, Moreno's political enemy, heard of his death, he said, "It took so much water to extinguish so much fire!" Mariano Moreno had no part in the drafting of Argentina's declaration of independence in 1816, but his fellow countrymen today will tell you that he made the declaration possible.

CHAPTER IX

BOLÍVAR AND SAN MARTÍN: LIBERATORS OF
A CONTINENT

Three great figures, by their leadership and inspiration, won for the New World independence from Europe. These leaders were George Washington, Simón Bolívar, and José de San Martín, who, with scores of other equally devoted patriots, fought and bled to liberate the people of the Americas. Washington, with a steadfastness that would not die, won freedom for the Thirteen Colonies and launched a wave of independence that washed to the southernmost shores of South America. Bolívar and San Martín, working separately but simultaneously, freed from Spain's control every inch of her once proud empire in the continent of South America. In 1775 the whole of the Western Hemisphere, from the Arctic Ocean to Cape Horn, was owned by European nations. Fifty years later only Canada, Alaska, Guiana, and a few Caribbean islands remained colonies of Europe. Such was the astonishing achievement of three great Americans and the millions who followed their leadership.

Simón Bolívar and José de San Martín are the greatest of all the great liberators of Latin America. Memories of their achievements live today in the hearts and minds of many Americans, North and South. Though the one was born in Venezuela and the other in Argentina, they are the heroes of the hemisphere, and their monuments are to be seen from New York and Washington to Buenos Aires and Santiago. Each devoted ten years or more to the cause to which he had pledged his faith. Each solicited funds, organized armies, fed and clothed his men, and personally led them across the tremendous mountain wall of the Andes from the Atlantic side to the Pacific. Each accomplished feats greater than those of Hannibal or Napoleon when they crossed the Alps into Italy.

Bolívar, by leading armies through swollen rivers and over ice-covered mountains, freed an area ten times as large as Spain; San Martín, by scaling the Andes twelve thousand feet above the sea, assured independence to countries half as large as the United States. Bolívar, moving across the northern part of South America, gave freedom to the people of Venezuela, Colombia, and Ecuador; San Martín, marching from the south, guaranteed independence to the inhabitants of Argentina, Chile, Paraguay, and Uruguay. In Peru and Bolivia both men contributed to the defeat of the last Spanish soldiers. Their campaigns, considered together, operated like a giant pincers to squeeze out the slipping Spanish grasp on South America. Together, Bolívar and San Martín aided the founding of nine new nations, and helped to create in the New World a stronghold of republican governments. They are the real "George Washingtons" of South America.

In order to understand the mighty encircling movement of these generals, let us follow their exploits, first those of Bolívar, then those of San Martín. Simón Bolívar was born in Caracas, the capital-to-be of Venezuela, on July 24, 1783, the year of the treaty of peace between Great Britain and the United States of America. His wealthy parents, descended from noble families, died before he was ten years of age. His education, therefore, was entrusted to relatives and teachers, one of whom was Andrés Bello, one of the greatest learned men of Latin America. When Simón was only fifteen, he made his first trip to Europe, visiting Mexico on the way. After some time in Paris, he went on to Spain, where, still only eighteen, he was married to the niece of the Marquis of Toro. His wife, however, died in 1803, soon after their voyage to Venezuela. Again Simón went to Europe, living a dissipated life in England, France, Italy, Austria, and Spain.

In those countries he lived extravagantly on the four million *pesos* (more than four million dollars today) he had inherited. In one period of three months in London he spent one hundred and fifty thousand francs (thirty or forty thousand dollars). But his life was not entirely worldly, for during these years he read widely of the writings of the French philosophers, and watched closely the rise of Napoleon Bonaparte, whose exploits he admired. His readings and his observations were filling his mind with ideas of his own. These ideas reached a climax on the day in 1805 when, on one of the hills of Rome, he swore to dedicate his life to freeing the people of America from Spanish domination. Two years later, after a visit to the United States, he was back in the land of his birth, ready to join those of his countrymen who were plotting against Spain.

By April, 1810, the plotters were prepared to act. Even before Mariano Moreno and his fellow Argentines had set up the first independent government in Buenos Aires, Venezuelan patriots in Caracas took the first timid step toward independence. They soon learned, however, that revolution could not succeed without arms and other aid from abroad. Bolívar and two of his countrymen were sent to London to secure what help the British government would secretly give. Back in Venezuela in the late months of 1810, Bolívar went to work to carry out his stated resolve: "We must fearlessly lay the foundation of South American liberty; to hesitate is destruction." Under Miranda, whose activities we have already noted, Bolívar began his military career, only to share unhappily in the surrender of that elder general. However, the defeat of Miranda, whatever it may have meant to the cause of Venezuelan independence, gave Bolívar his great chance. From that time on, he was the leader, the first leader, in the revolutionary campaign against Spain in northern South America.

Meanwhile, Bolívar must make his plans on the Dutch island of Curaçao, where he had sought refuge from the Spanish leaders. There he reavowed his determination to free the people of his native land and its neighboring colonies. There, as during his whole career, he never lost hope. There he worked with an energy that would have weakened most men. Early in 1813, he appeared in the northern part of Venezuela's neighbor, New Granada (present-day Colombia), where he was given the rank of colonel. The cause of Venezuela became the cause of New Granada, and Bolívar worked for the liberation of both colonies. Soon the entire coastal area of New Granada was freed of Spanish soldiers, and Bolívar led his army over the mountains for more campaigns in Venezuela. Fighting without mercy, he declared a "war to the death" on all Spaniards, even on neutrals who would not aid the cause of revolution. In August, he entered Caracas in triumph, his carriage drawn by beautiful young ladies. Always a lover of display and glory, he was proclaimed "Liberator of Venezuela" by his adoring countrymen.

This early success of the "Liberator," however, was not to endure. The Spanish leaders reorganized their armies, secured reinforcements, and a second time forced Bolívar to flee. A second time, too, he went to New Granada, received command of an army, and proceeded to subdue Bogotá, the principal city. Again he was acclaimed wildly and given a title, this time "Illustrious Pacificator." But, as before, complete victory eluded him, and in May, 1815, he escaped to the British island of Jamaica.

Now, indeed, the cause of the patriots seemed lost. Everywhere over Venezuela and New Granada waved the Spanish flag of crimson and yellow. Ten thousand Spanish troops, veterans of the Napoleonic wars, arrived in dozens of warships and transports, with enormous supplies of arms to stamp out the last sign of revolt in every corner of South America. The cause of Latin-American freedom had never seemed so hopeless. But, to Simón Bolívar, in his hideaway in Jamaica, these were only other obstacles to be overcome. He continued to dream of the independence of all Spanish America and to make plans for winning it. To him there was never doubt of the final victory; he remained firm and unconquered. To him, as to Washington at Valley Forge, bright spring must follow black winter.

By 1816 Bolívar was back in Venezuela to continue his ceaseless campaign. The new army which he organized was reinforced by thousands of English, Irish, and German adventurers, who volunteered to aid the patriot cause. Months were necessary to train the men, mold them into a fighting force, and gather the supplies for the long marches he planned. By 1819 everything was ready. On to Bogotá! Ford the raging rivers! Wade through flooded plains! Once the men marched for a week with water to their waists, their rifles and supplies carried over their heads or on their shoulders. Their clothing became ragged, their rifles rusty, as they fought against the swirling waters. Then, fresh food, a few hours of rest, and

"Forward!" again. Climb the mountains! Climb the towering Andes at thirteen thousand feet, higher than the passes through which Hannibal or Napoleon invaded Italy. Slow climbing, hard breathing, nose-bleeding, frigid winds blowing against ill-clad bodies—these were only a few of the torments which attacked the courageous soldiers. But Bolívar drove them on, tired, hungry, dirty, tattered.

On August 7, 1819, the weary little army fought the battle of Boyacá, and three days later entered the city of Bogotá. The Spanish hold on the colony of New Granada was broken forever. Now Bolívar must hasten back to Venezuela, where the patriot congress, jealous of his success, was plotting to undermine him. Appearing unexpectedly before the plotters, he quickly cowed them by his commanding manner, his piercing eyes, and his sharp language. They voted to unite Venezuela and New Granada in the "Republic of Colombia" and made Bolívar the first president and military dictator. Spanish troops, however, still held much of Venezuela, and the "Liberator" must form a new army to free his native land. Six thousand men were mustered—Venezuelans, New Granadans, Englishmen, Scotchmen, Irishmen, Indians. On June 24, 1821, inspired by hopes of quick success, this tough patriot army routed the Spanish foe at the battle of Carabobo. What Yorktown had been to the United States and Boyacá had been to New Granada, the battle of Carabobo was to Venezuela.

Venezuela was now free. New Granada was free. Together they formed the new nation of Colombia. Bolívar had liberated Spanish colonies four times as large as Spain itself. He had driven a deep wedge between the Spanish possessions in North America and those to the south. Still, with all this success, Bolívar had only begun. Vaster dreams now drove him on. To the south of Colombia along the Pacific, lay Quito (present-day Ecuador) and Peru, home of the old Inca Empire. These were the new prizes that beckoned the "Liberator."

Once more Bolívar took to the battle trail. Up and over the mountains again to Bogotá, south from Bogotá to Quito, the new army gained recruits as it marched. Antonio José de Sucre, one of his most trusted aides and the ablest general, was sent by sea for the attack on Quito. Gradually the two armies converged on the city, entering in triumph on May 25, 1822. The territory of Quito, or Ecuador, was now added to the growing Republic of Colombia. But, Quito, the city on the equator, was only a stopping place. There was still Peru, where Spanish forces were very strong. Bolívar must have Peru. There was Lima, "City of the Kings," and the real capital of all Spanish possessions in the New World. Bolívar must have Lima.

Far to the southward, however, the other great South American liberator was also dreaming of Peru and Lima. Already San Martín had secured the freedom of his native Argentina and had crossed the Andes to liberate Chile. Now he was eyeing Peru and preparing to march northward. The story of the achievements which had brought him this far is as remarkable as that of his contemporary, Bolívar, whom he was soon to meet.

Although his blood was pure Spanish, José de San Martín was a true son of America, a real child of the frontier. He was born on February 25, 1778, in the Indian village of Yapeyú, in the district of Misiones. Misiones, which means "Missions," had been an area of dozens of Jesuit missions; it is today the northeasternmost territory of the Argentine Republic. José spent his early years there among the Indians in a land of butterflies and brilliant flowers, of deep forests and groves of wild oranges and lemons. When José was seven, his father, a Spanish military officer and governor of Misiones, was transferred to Spain. After four years, still only *eleven*, the youth joined the Spanish army. For the next twenty-two years he served in campaigns in Spain, France, Portugal, North Africa, and even on the Mediterranean. Between campaigns there was time to participate in the gay life of Madrid and to study mathematics, geography, and history. He learned a little of French and English.

All these years of valiant service to Spain, however, did not dim San Martín's devotion to the land of his birth. In 1811 he prepared to return to Buenos Aires for reasons which he himself, years later, described as follows:

In 1811, I was serving in the Spanish army. Twenty years of honorable service had gained for me some consideration in spite of the fact that I was an American; I heard of the revolution in South America; and—forsaking my fortunes and my hopes—I desired only to sacrifice everything to promote the liberty of my native land. I arrived at Buenos Aires in the beginning of 1812:—thenceforward I consecrated myself to the cause of Spanish America.[1]

San Martín reached Buenos Aires in March, 1812, a young man of thirty-four, and at once offered his services to his native country.

For two years the United Provinces (present-day Argentina) had been struggling to maintain the independent government they had set up on May 25, 1810. San Martín was at once given a commission as lieutenant-colonel. Brilliantly successful in his first action against the Spaniards, he was soon made general-in-chief of an expedition to be sent to Peru.

[1] Quoted in Robertson, *Rise of the Spanish-American Republics, as Told in the Lives of Their Liberators* (New York, 1918), p. 182.

However, three months later, in April, 1814, he resigned his command, then accepted the governorship of the provinces of Cuyo in Western Argentina.

San Martín had given up his command of the army, but he had by no means given up his resolve to make secure the independence of his country and the neighboring Spanish colonies. He had chosen to go to Cuyo because Mendoza, its chief city, lay at the foot of the best passes through the Andes to the Pacific. He was convinced that the Spaniards in Peru could best be defeated by attack from the Pacific coast. With this conviction, he devoted three years of unceasing effort in Mendoza to the preparation of an army which would be strong enough to defeat the enemy wherever it might be met.

The immense task which San Martín undertook in the years from 1814 to 1817 is almost without parallel in history. The success with which he overcame every obstacle is almost unbelievable. In a little inland town, far removed from Buenos Aires, he undertook to raise an army. Almost without money and without factories at his command, he had to manufacture cannon, ammunition, and uniforms. He had to work secretly, lest the Spaniards learn of his plans before he was ready. Mendoza became "The Nest of the Argentine Eagle," as its men, women, and children helped with their labor, their money, even with their jewels. San Martín himself lived cheaply and ate little, so that every available *centavo* might go to the preparation of the army.

Perhaps the most important of San Martín's aides was a Franciscan friar, Luís Beltrán. After fighting against the Spaniards in Chile, he had returned to Mendoza with a bag of instruments and tools, which he had invented and manufactured with his own hands. He was skilled in mathematics, chemistry, and physics. He knew how to make cannons, watches, and powder. He was a carpenter, an architect, a blacksmith, a draughtsman, and a physician. To Friar Beltrán, San Martín entrusted the task of outfitting the army. Three hundred men were soon at work under the padre's skillful direction, casting cannons and shells, forging horseshoes and bayonets, making knapsacks and uniforms. On the walls of the little factory he drew charcoal designs of the special wagons to be made for transporting supplies over the steep mountain passes. Beltrán was the "Archimedes of the Army of the Andes," and when at last preparations were complete he donned the uniform of an artillery lieutenant.[2]

After two years of this slow, tedious preparation, events promised a brighter future for San Martín. On July 9, 1816, the government of Argentina formally declared the independence of the country. About the same time it approved the general's plans for the invasion of Chile, and appointed him captain-general of the Army of the Andes. Moreover, during the late months of the year, the army grew to more than four thousand by the addition of seven hundred Negro slaves, induced to fight by the promise of liberty. Bernardo O'Higgins, son of an Irish father and a Chilean mother, brought a large detachment of Chileans who had already been fighting for the independence of their country. With these reinforcements, therefore, San Martín by January, 1817, was ready to scale the Andes.

To the cheers of the loyal people of Mendoza, the Army of the Andes set out on its great adventure. More than nine thousand mules and sixteen hundred horses were laden with the tents, provisions, cannons, a portable bridge, bandages,

[2] This account is based on Bartolomé Mitre, *Historia de San Martín y de la Emancipación Sudamericana* (Buenos Aires, 1907), II, 118-19.

medicines, and all the other supplies needed for an army on the march. Three detachments were to work their way separately through the difficult mountain passes, then converge on the Chilean side with the accuracy of clockwork. Exact timing was necessary if the army, in full force, was to meet the Spaniards.

Day after day for nearly a month the soldiers clambered up and down the steep trails, making their roads as they went. Skirting dangerous chasms, scaling craggy peaks, wading through snow, they tugged at their heavy equipment. At night there were frightful hail storms and freezing temperatures. The dreaded mountain sickness, which causes violent nose-bleeding and heart failure, attacked many. Scores of the soldiers perished, and over half of the livestock. Through these terrible weeks, only the inspiration of San Martín, O'Higgins, and Beltrán, and the loyalty and comradeship of the men kept the armies moving forward. Early in February the three divisions joined forces at the exact time and place arranged.

The Army of the Andes barely had time to descend into Chile when, on February 12, it met and routed a Spanish force at the battle of Chacabuco. A year later to the day the patriot government felt strong enough to declare the independence of Chile. San Martín fought another battle, that of Maipú, to clinch the independence. The Chileans offered to make San Martín "supreme dictator," but, unlike Bolívar, he had no political ambitions, and he declined in favor of Bernardo O'Higgins. This Irish-Chilean leader for years had been working for Chilean independence, and the honor of being the first head of the new nation was rightfully his. He had sometimes had the assistance of foreigners, one of whom was the American, Joel Roberts Poinsett. (Later Poinsett represented the United States in Mexico, where the flower, the poinsettia, was named in his honor.)

Just as Quito was only a stopping place for Bolívar, marching from Colombia to Peru, so for San Martín Chile was only a way station on the road to Lima. Peru alone, of all the Spanish possessions in South America, still remained in the hands of the Royalist armies, numbering twenty-five thousand men. Moreover, Peru lay far to the north and was difficult for an army to reach. San Martín must have a fleet. He and O'Higgins, therefore, called upon Lord Thomas Alexander Cochrane, once a celebrated officer in the British Navy, to assemble the ships. *El Diablo* (The Devil), the South Americans called him. Again it was a case of slow, arduous preparation.

Not until August 20, 1820, was the fleet ready. Then Lord Cochrane's great expedition of eight war vessels and sixteen transports sailed for Peru. The ships carried nearly forty-five hundred men, over half of whom were veterans of the Army of the Andes. There were uniforms and equipment for fifteen thousand more, for San Martín hoped to enlist that many recruits in Peru. Progress along the coast was slow, however, and not until thirteen months later did the fleet capture Callao, the port of Lima. In the meantime, Spanish troops had evacuated the capital, San Martín had entered the city, and Peru had declared its independence (July 28, 1821). The great general was appointed "Protector of Peru." His plans had worked out exactly as he had wished. "I want not military renown," said he, "I have no ambition to be the conqueror of Peru. I want solely to liberate the country from oppression. . . ."

As "Protector of Peru," San Martín's task was tremendous. Yet he undertook it with the same energy and enthusiasm with which he had organized armies. Now, however, for the first time, influences began to work against him. Some persons suspected him of seeking to create a dictatorship. His own long-devoted soldiers criticized him for not proceeding at once against the remaining Spanish troops in Peru. He himself seemed unsure of his next action. He lacked troops to move alone against the Spaniards, and the Peruvians had not flocked to his standards as he had expected. He must secure assistance. News had come that Bolívar was in Quito, moving victoriously down from the north. Perhaps he and Bolívar could work together for the final liberation of Peru. He must see Bolívar at once. He decided to go to Guayaquil, Ecuador, to meet him.

The Guayaquil meeting between the two great liberators was one of the most dramatic meetings in history. Both men were of distinguished appearance, striking and dignified. San Martín, forty-three years old, was dark-skinned, with black eyes and long chin. Bolívar, thirty-nine, was slender of figure, with thin face and piercing eyes. The Argentine was patient, earnest, and capable of great self-sacrifice; the Venezuelan was proud, sensitive, and ambitious for power. Both were sincere patriots, profoundly devoted to the cause for which they struggled.

The two men held three interviews, all behind closed doors and without witnesses. No one knows, therefore, exactly what took place. Some believe that Bolívar refused to give any real aid for the final campaign in Peru, even though San Martín offered to serve as a subordinate officer. Perhaps they disagreed, too, over the form of government to be set up in Peru. San Martín believed that Spain's former colonies should be independent monarchies ruled by European princes. Bolívar wished to create one great republic in South America with a president chosen for life. Perhaps he hoped to be that president. But whatever the two generals may have talked about in their historic meeting, it is clear there was no agreement.

San Martín returned at once to Lima, a sad and disappointed man. He found Lima in revolt, a strong wave of opposition threatening to engulf his government. He explained his position in a long letter to Bolívar:

> The results of our interview have not been what I hoped for the prompt termination of the war. Unfortunately, I am fully convinced, either that you did not believe in the sincerity of my offer to serve under your orders with the forces at my command, or that my presence is embarrassing to you. . . .
>
> Finally, general, my decision is irrevocably made. I have convened the first congress of Peru for the 20th of next month. The day after it is installed I shall embark for Chile, convinced that my presence is the only obstacle which hinders your coming to Peru with the army under your command. It would have been the crowning happiness for me to end the war of independence under the orders of a general to whom America owes her liberty. Destiny deposes otherwise, and it is necessary for me to conform to it. . . .[3]

True to his promise, the great Argentine resigned his position as "Protector of Peru," in September, 1822. He returned to Chile, then crossed the Andes once more to Mendoza. There, in the city where he had forged the Army of the Andes, he spent a few months almost without recognition. His sadness was magnified a thousandfold by the news of the death of his wife in Buenos Aires. Returning to the Argentine capital in 1824, he received none of the honor and praise he rightfully deserved. Poor now and without resources, San Martín found a loyal friend who paid his ship passage to

[3] Translated from Mitre in Chapman, *Colonial Hispanic America* (New York, 1933), p. 284.

The Casa Bolívar in Vieja Magdalena, near Lima, Peru, is the house where first San Martín and then Bolívar established headquarters. It is now the Bolivarian Museum.

Modern native farmers at Port au Prince, Haiti. L'Ouverture gave these natives the status of free wage earners rather than slaves.

A native Haitian with basket on head and live chickens suspended by a string around her neck. She is typical of natives in modern Haiti.

A street in modern Cap Haitien, Haiti.

Europe. In Belgium and France he spent the remaining days . of his saddened life. He died in 1850.

The honor of ridding Peru of its last Spanish soldier went to Bolívar rather than to San Martín. But it was a long, grueling struggle. Not until December 9, 1824—two and a half years after the meeting at Guayaquil—was Bolívar able to deliver the decisive blow. It was the battle of Ayacucho. In the following year General Sucre invaded Upper Peru to defeat the last Spanish army in South America. There, high on the plateau of the Central Andes, he created the Republic of Bolívar, which later changed its name to Bolivia. Its capital was called Sucre in honor of the general who became its first president.

With the final liberation of all the Spanish colonies in South America, Bolívar returned to Bogotá. For fifteen years he had marched up and down the Andes, braving hardships, fighting battles, freeing peoples. He had rejoiced at the other revolutionary movements which had freed Mexico, Central America, and Brazil. He was pleased with the recognition of the new countries by the governments of the United States and Europe. Now he must turn his attention to establishing order in the nation he had created—*El Gran Colombia,* comprising Venezuela, Colombia, and Ecuador. Many of his enemies feared he might try to crown himself king, though again and again he denied that he had such ambitions. "I am not Napoleon," he said, "nor do I wish to be; neither do I want to imitate Caesar, . . ." Until 1830 he labored to put down the political dissensions which were tearing his country apart. Then, sadly disappointed and failing in health, he resigned the presidency and prepared to leave the country. "He who dedicates his services to revolution plows the sea," he declared. On December 17, 1830, he died, before he could bring peace to his people. Even before his death his Great Colombia was falling to pieces. Venezuela, Colombia, and Ecuador had become the independent nations they are today.

Thus, in death ended the fantastic careers of the two great generals—Simón Bolívar and José de San Martín. They had freed a continent. Today, Bolívar lies buried in Caracas, his birthplace, where Venezuelans revere his memory. The body of San Martín lies in the Cathedral of Buenos Aires, where Argentines pay deep respect to the man whom they once neglected. But both liberators, like their predecessor, George Washington, are heroes of all the Americas.

CHAPTER X

TOUSSAINT L'OUVERTURE: HAITIAN SPARTACUS

He has been called "the Black Napoleon." This is an injustice, for Toussaint L'Ouverture was in many respects a "whiter" man than Napoleon Bonaparte. Napoleon's whiteness was largely a matter of the surface; L'Ouverture's was inside. History has few stories more heroic than that of the Negro slave who fought as if inspired to free his colored brothers from their shameful bonds and sacrificed his life for his cause. Though he acted on a much smaller stage, Toussaint's generalship and his administrative ability would bear comparison with Napoleon's. If the comparison be a matter of unselfish virtues and morals, Napoleon fares very poorly indeed. The Republic of Haiti, sometimes called "The Black Republic," the only Latin-American nation that speaks French and whose people are chiefly Negro, is a striking memorial to Toussaint, its founder. There today no unsympathetic master cracks the whip over the cringing back of an enslaved Negro.

The history of Haiti[1] in the years before Toussaint includes some unusual passages. It was originally settled, after the

[1] Today the island as a whole is called Haiti. The French end is occupied by the Republic of Haiti, the eastern end by the Dominican Republic. While it was controlled by France, the region called Haiti was denominated Saint-Domingue. In this account the word Haiti will be used instead of the longer Saint-Domingue.

destruction of the native Indians, by pirates of the type of Captain Kidd and his crew. Most of these early settlers (or perhaps they were "unsettlers") were of French blood. For that reason, the French king, Louis XIV, by a treaty made with Spain in 1697, was able to make good a claim to the western section of the island of Haiti. Shortly afterward the French organized a government for the colony.

Haiti is not a large country. The French colony occupied that part of the island which is now the Republic of Haiti, that is, the western third. In area it is comparable to the state of Vermont, slightly less than ten thousand square miles. But before the end of the eighteenth century that small region had become famous as the richest tropical colony in the world. Its wealth was derived chiefly from the cultivation of sugar cane and indigo, though there were other tropical products.

The Haitian plantations were organized and operated much as were the cotton plantations of the southern states before the Civil War. The land was owned by a small number of whites. Plantations were very large and were worked by thousands of Negro slaves. Most of the plantation owners dreamed of the day when they would be able to dispose of their possessions and retire to Paris to spend the rest of their lives in idleness and gaiety. This dream caused them to feel little concern about social conditions in Haiti.

The Frenchmen in the island had no rights of self-government. Their laws were the decrees of the French king, enforced by a governor sent out from France. The whites were not troubled by this condition, however, for there was no self-government in France until after the French Revolution commenced. But with the first movements of that revolution, the politics of the French colony became a matter of extreme importance.

In the century which preceded the year 1789, a complicated society had developed in Haiti. The whites there were of two classes, "Big Whites" and "Little Whites." The former class included the owners of the great plantations and the few professional people; they were the lords of the island. The second class were people of much less means, small farmers, small merchants. The "Big Whites" looked down upon the "Little Whites," and the "Little Whites" were jealous of the "Big Whites" whose wealth gave them so much more power and position. Very early in the colony's history the blood of white and black began to be mixed. To discourage this development, Louis XIV decreed that when a Negro woman bore a child whose father was white, both mother and child should be free. As the mixing nevertheless continued, there eventually came into being a large class of free mulattoes. Some of them were able to gain considerable wealth, and their children, when they showed more than ordinary intelligence (and this was not infrequent), were sent to France for an education. The whites had no liking for these people. Mulattoes could own property, but they were denied social rights, were burdened with special duties and restrictions, and were made to feel in many ways their inferior position. Though they were personally free, they felt that their condition was not much better than that of the slaves. They hated the whites bitterly.

Of the slaves there was a great number. They were ill-used by both masters and mistresses. They were forced to work long hours and were flogged unmercifully. Each year tens of thousands of new slaves were imported from Africa, most of them under conditions of extreme barbarity—packed between low decks, poorly fed, many of them smothering to death.

Mulattoes who had plantations saw nothing wrong in owning large numbers of slaves to work them. Thus, while the mulattoes hated the whites, at the same time they looked down upon their Negro slaves and were in turn hated by them.

In 1789 the population of Haiti numbered about forty thousand whites, fifty thousand mulattoes, and probably five hundred thousand slaves. As long as the French government supported the whites and strongly controlled the colony with an army of French soldiers, the whites were able to hold their dominant position. But the French Revolution brought island-shaking changes.

The basis of these changes in Haiti was the French Declaration of the Rights and Duties of Man of 1789, with its ideas of "Liberty, Equality, and Fraternity." All men were declared to be born free and equal. When the French government was reorganized to give Frenchmen representation in it, the "Big Whites" sent delegates to Paris to become members of the National Assembly. They expected that Haiti would secure some form of self-government—and that was satisfactory to them as long as *they* controlled the government. But there were many educated Haitian mulattoes in Paris, and they demanded for their class a right to participate in the colony's government. A society, The Friends of the Blacks, was formed among the Frenchmen to support the demands of the mulattoes. Under the persuasions of the mulattoes and their friends, the French National Assembly decreed that a colonial assembly should be formed in Haiti, and that mulattoes should have the right to vote for its members and even to be elected to membership. The Haitian whites bitterly objected; the mulattoes just as bitterly demanded their rights. In Haiti riots broke out. Brutal murders became common; mulattoes were tortured. In the face of this critical situation, the Parisian government wavered in its policy—now the colonial mulattoes could vote and hold office, now they could not. This wishy-washy course added to the confusion in Haiti.

As to the Negroes, neither white nor mulatto gave them any consideration. Both would retain the Negro in slavery. This was the situation that gave Toussaint L'Ouverture his great opportunity.

Toussaint was born in 1743 on the plantation of Bréda. Fortunately for him, Bayou de Libertas, manager of the plantation, was a better-than-ordinary master. The parents of Toussaint were full-blood Negroes of the same African tribe. The father was Gaou Guinou. Toussaint was one of eight children, eldest of the five boys. For the first fifty years of his life he was known as Toussaint Bréda. Then, for a reason that is not entirely clear, he took the surname of L'Ouverture. The name Toussaint L'Ouverture translates from the French into "All-Saints Opening."

As a child, Toussaint was scrawny and delicate, but by the time he was twelve years old he was powerful and athletic. He was never handsome. He passed his early years with the other slaves in crowded, uncomfortable, unsanitary quarters. No doubt he witnessed cruel floggings and became acquainted with the institution of slavery in all its hideous features. As was customary with young Negroes, his first work was to look after flocks of sheep and goats. He liked animals and had a way with them, particularly with horses. He showed great patience, intelligence, and good humor. These qualities attracted the attention of his master, and Toussaint was promoted to the post of coachman.

This promotion was a great event in the life of Toussaint. It took him out of the fields and gave him some leisure for study. Somehow he learned to read, write, and draw. As he was very religious, he also picked up bits of Latin from the church service. An old slave taught him the uses of medicinal plants. His mind was alert and keen, and his memory was unusually good. In short, Toussaint early proved himself a much more than ordinary person. The fact that he could read and write seemed to his fellow slaves something magical and gave him great standing with them.

A friendly priest is said to have given Toussaint some assistance with his studies. It was through this priest that he secured a book written by the brilliant Frenchman, the Abbé Raynal. The black boy was deeply affected one day when, reading this book, he came across a prophecy to the effect that one day the Negro slaves would find among their own number a chief to lead them to liberty. Henceforth, Toussaint felt himself to be that chief and awaited his opportunity. He knew his body to be the property of a master, but he knew also that his soul was his own. No one should possess it, and some day he would free his body and those of his fellow bondsmen. So, while the "Big White" masters were dreaming of the day when they should have sufficient riches to retire to Paris, the slave nursed his dream of being the liberator of his suffering people. While he waited, he prepared himself.

At twenty-five, Toussaint decided to marry. The woman of his choice has been described as "a good-natured Negress of enormous girth named Suzanne Simon." For more than thirty years, until they were separated by Napoleon, they lived together happily.

When the magic words of the French revolutionists, "Liberty, Equality, and Fraternity," set the whites and the mulattoes at each other's throats, Toussaint recognized his opportunity. For almost two years after the beginning of the

French Revolution, the slaves of Haiti seemed to pay no attention to it. But they were hearing something of it and were watching the examples which were being set them by the whites and the mulattoes, and some of the more intelligent and daring were planning for action. They were ready to act on August 23, 1791. They arose in a terrible insurrection. Having once broken the bonds of fear, it was hardly to be expected that the abused slaves should act with moderation. Plantations and crops were destroyed, houses were burned, masters and their families were tortured and killed. A hundred thousand slaves were pitting themselves against the whites and four thousand soldiers. The horrors committed by the Negroes were equaled by those of the whites. Every Negro taken was killed. Entire roads were lined by gallows from which swung the bodies of Negroes. Many a tree also bore this terrible crop.

Toussaint must have known what was being planned, but he took no part in the original insurrection. Unrestrained violence was not in his nature. He remained on his master's plantation, placed himself at the head of the other slaves, and defended the plantation and the family of the master. Presently he helped the family to escape to Baltimore. Later he gave them various kinds of assistance.

In three weeks the original insurrection had run its course. It had cost the lives of two thousand whites and ten thousand Negroes and had caused property damage of two million dollars. The mulattoes were thought to have inspired the insurrection, and one of the sequels of the terrible event was the hunting down and the assassination of scores of them.

The destruction in the northern part of the colony had in fact been the work of Negroes. But in the southern section mulattoes and Negroes operated together. However, at a critical point the mulattoes refused longer to coöperate with the Negroes and made an arrangement with the whites. They let the whites know that they had taken up arms to protect their own interests and not to free the slaves. Thereupon, whites and mulattoes made a truce, and the Negro was left either to win his freedom unaided or to submit to a continuance of his enslavement.

When the insurrection had been in progress for a month, Toussaint placed himself at the head of the slaves of the Bréda plantation and joined a band headed by the Negroes, Jean-François and Biassou. The leaders suspected him because he had protected his master's family, so he was not permitted to command. Instead, he was put in charge of the wounded where he was able to make use of his medical-plant lore. But soon his intelligence was needed in a more important post. He was declared a brigadier-general and made an aide of Biassou. Toussaint's abilities won him the confidence of the Negroes of the band and when, somewhat later, the two leaders quarreled, Toussaint was able himself to assume command.

Now followed six years of fighting, the details of which it would be profitless to follow. But let us look at its broad outlines. The French National Assembly at Paris in 1792 declared that mulattoes and all free Negroes of Haiti should have equal political rights with the whites. A commission was sent to the island to put the decree into effect. The mulattoes were delighted, but the Negroes saw in the move no reason for rejoicing. They were legally still slaves. However, the whites refused to accept mulatto equality, and again there was bloodshed. Then the French commissioners, to secure force to control the situation, decreed the freedom of all slaves who should enroll to assist them. By this time the news of the overthrow of the French King had reached Haiti, and Toussaint refused to fight for the republic that had been proclaimed at Paris. His horror was great when, some months later, he learned of the execution of the king, Louis XVI. Thereupon, Toussaint, along with Jean-François and Biassou, crossed over and joined the Spanish commander in the eastern end of the island.

To understand this move it must be recalled that, after France had deposed its king, Spain joined an alliance of other European nations to destroy the French Republic and replace the king on the throne. With the Spanish forces, Toussaint could feel that he was fighting for his king. But another complication arose for him when the "Big Whites" called in English soldiers, promising to assist them in conquering the French colony if England would restore to them their estates and their slaves. England was an ally of Spain. When Toussaint learned that England would restore slavery, he could no longer coöperate with the Spanish forces. So, with a well-equipped and well-trained force of four thousand Negroes, he crossed into Haiti and placed himself at the disposition of the French commander, General Laveaux.

Toussaint's services to Laveaux were so great that he was made lieutenant-governor of the colony and, not much later, commander-in-chief of the French army there. In the course of some months, after Toussaint had fought several bloody campaigns, some of them against Haitian mulattoes, the English commander made a peace with Toussaint and withdrew from the island. Spain, in the meantime, had withdrawn from the European alliance and made a peace with the French government. One of the terms of the peace was that Spain should turn over to France its part of the island of Haiti. The entire island thus became Toussaint's domain.

Various commissions and individuals were sent from Paris to displace Toussaint from the powerful position which he had gained. But he foiled all of their attempts. He did not, however, declare the island independent. Rather, he exercised control in the name of the French government.

Having cleared out the Spaniards and the English and put down the jealous opposition of the mulattoes, who could not endure the idea of being ruled by a Negro, Toussaint was able to undertake the reorganization and rebuilding of the life of the island. After all of the years of strife and destruction through which it had passed since 1790, reconstruction was badly needed.

One of his first acts was to invite the planters to return to their estates and resume activities. The Negroes were now free, but they were required to return to work as wage earners. Pardon for everyone, forgetfulness of the past, honest work to rebuild the colony—that was the program of Toussaint. He established his control in the Spanish end of the island and eliminated the slave trade which had been continued there. He got under way a program of roadbuilding and returned to Haiti, leaving his brother, Paul, as governor in Santo Domingo, the former Spanish colony.

Haiti was divided into districts and over each Toussaint placed a general. Over all he exercised a close personal supervision. He was continually dashing about the country to see that everyone was working, that every man was doing his duty.

Some of the things Toussaint did might tempt one to laugh. To impress the Negroes, he felt that it would be wise to do everything with much display. He wore gaudy uniforms in public, though he dressed very modestly in the privacy of his home. When he went out he was always attended by a brilliant retinue. He had a personal guard of fifteen hundred men, flashily uniformed. In public he was always preceded by two trumpeters in red uniforms and silver helmets. Before one laughs too loudly, he should remember that European kings did much the same. Even President Washington drove abroad in a fine coach drawn by splendid white horses, preceded and followed by outriders, and probably for much the same reasons. Toussaint's only extravagance was fine horses, of which he possessed many. He ate little and drank sparingly. His capacity for work was tremendous; often he slept no more than four hours. His tirelessness and his good sense brought order again to Haiti and gave it the best government it ever had.

Late in 1799 Napoleon Bonaparte became first consul of France. This was a fateful event for Haiti, particularly for Toussaint. Napoleon could endure no rivals, and he had a very strong prejudice against color. The first proclamation that Napoleon sent to Haiti did not recognize the principle of Negro freedom. This omission worried Toussaint; he feared that Napoleon would attempt to restore slavery. In these circumstances he decided that the wise course was to draw up a constitution for the colony, have it approved by the population, and send it to Napoleon. It is an interesting and significant fact that of the ten men whom Toussaint appointed to draft the constitution seven were whites and the others were mulattoes. There is no prejudice here; the best brains were needed for the task, and the wise Negro, disregarding color, chose men with intelligence. Notable clauses of the document which the commission produced were those which declared that slavery was forever abolished, that religious tolerance should exist, and that Toussaint should be governor for life. Duly ratified, the constitution was dispatched to Napoleon, along with a personal letter from Toussaint.

But Napoleon had no intention of leaving Toussaint and Haiti in peace. He sent his brother-in-law, General LeClerc, with an army of twenty thousand men, to bring him under subjection and to restore slavery in the island.

Forewarned, Toussaint prepared for the struggle, for re-enslavement was not to be thought of. He lacked equipment. Some of his subordinates were shortly bought off and deserted him. After some months he found himself in great difficulties. In these circumstances, LeClerc suggested a conference. Toussaint consented, though he was warned that treachery might be planned. However, he trusted to French honor and kept his engagement. When he reached the appointed place, he was seized. His family was also arrested. All were sent to France. There, at the explicit orders of Napoleon, Toussaint was handled with every precaution to prevent his escape. He made repeated efforts to see Napoleon and wrote him many letters. He neither saw the first consul, nor were his letters given the courtesy of a reply. Toussaint was imprisoned in the Chateau de Joux, in the Alps not far from the Swiss border. There he was held during the winter of 1802-1803. He was not given sufficient clothing or bedding to keep him warm—a particular hardship, for he had never actually known cold. Nor was he given enough food. He was annoyed by constant watching. The cold and the systematic neglect to which he was exposed produced his death on April 7, 1803. Eighteen years later, Napoleon, himself at that time near death on his tropical island of exile—as uncomfortably hot, let us hope, as Toussaint had been cold—remarked to one of his companions, "I have to reproach myself with the attempt made upon Santo Domingo during the

Consulship. I should have been satisfied to govern the colony through Toussaint L'Ouverture."[2]

Many years ago, when the style in oratory was much more florid than it is now, Wendell Phillips, in an oration on Toussaint, spoke these eloquent words:

I would call him Napoleon, but Napoleon made his way to empire over broken oaths and through a sea of blood. This man never broke his word. I would call him Cromwell, but Cromwell was only a soldier, and the state he founded went down with him into his grave. I would call him Washington, but the great Virginian held slaves. This man risked his empire rather than permit the slave-trade in the humblest village of his dominions.[3]

Though Toussaint had been removed from the scene, LeClerc and fifty thousand Frenchmen were unable to conquer Haiti. Toussaint's black people and their powerful ally, yellow fever, defeated this formidable host. And Haiti, which Toussaint L'Ouverture founded and for which he died, still lives—and will never forget its heroic founder.

[2] Quoted in Percy Waxman, *The Black Napoleon; the Story of Toussaint Louverture* (New York, Harcourt, Brace & Company, 1931), p. 10.

[3] Robt. McL. Cumnock, *Choice Readings* (New York, Grosset & Dunlap, 1938), p. 336.

CHAPTER XI

JOSÉ MARTÍ: APOSTLE OF CUBAN
INDEPENDENCE

When José Martí met his death in 1895, he was wearing on a finger of his left hand an iron ring. It had been fashioned from part of a chain which had bound and bruised his leg while he was held for long months in a Cuban prison. The ring was a constant, grim reminder of the corrupt, unjust Spanish government that ruled Cuba for many years after the mainland colonies of Spain had won their freedom. The metal of the ring was no harder than had been the iron determination of Martí as he strove for the liberation of his country from the Spanish yoke.

To the Spaniards for more than three centuries, Cuba was "the Pearl of the Antilles." With its wealth in sugar and tobacco, it was a colonial jewel that rightly deserved the title. Since it remained with Spain after the great revolutionary wave of 1810-25 had subsided, it was baptized with another complimentary name, the "Ever-Faithful Isle." This title was less fitting, for always, from 1825 until independence was won, there were many Cubans who worked and plotted for release from Spanish rule. They planned several revolutions, actually broke out into insurrection a number of times, and from 1868 to 1878 fought a civil war, quite properly called the Ten Years War. It cost two hundred

Morro Castle, Havana, is an old Spanish fortress which dominates the harbor of the capital of Cuba. It is a constant reminder of the corrupt Spanish government that ruled Cuba before Martí and other patriots struck for Cuban independence.

Old residences like this in Havana reflect the Spanish influence in modern Cuba.

The National Capitol at Havana. This splendid building, representing Cuban independence, rests on the foundations which Martí built when he prepared the way for revolution against the Spanish yoke.

Columbus Cathedral, one of the old churches in Havana. Here Christopher Columbus was first buried.

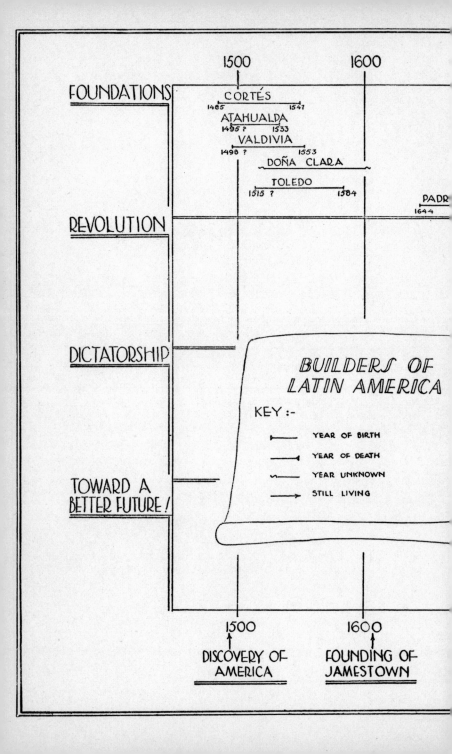

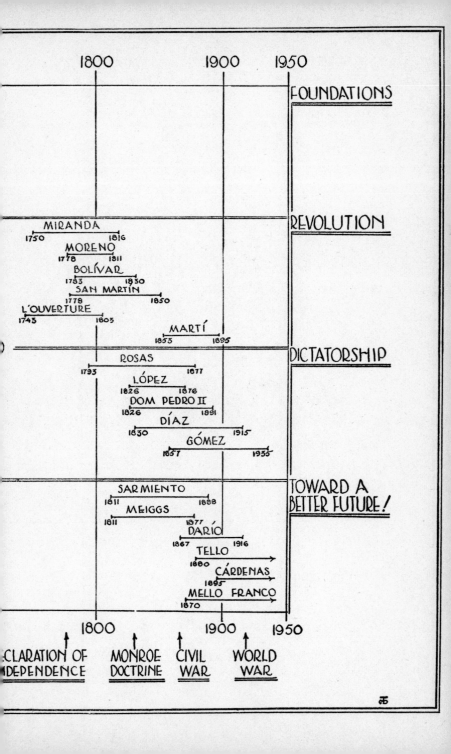

thousand lives and property worth seven hundred million dollars.

Seldom have Spain's rulers been noted for wise government. They were too blind, or too unintelligent, to learn a lesson from even the empire-shattering loss of their colonies in North, Central, and South America. With only slight changes, the mistakes which led to that great loss were continued in the only American colonies that remained to Spain, Cuba and Puerto Rico. The islanders had no share in their government; those who ruled them were sent across from Spain. The economic interests of the Cubans were not considered, as the case of flour clearly shows. Cuba did not produce wheat, but across a few miles of water in the United States much wheat was grown, and any amount of flour was obtainable. However, the tariff charge for its direct entry into Cuba was so high that it was cheaper to send a barrel of flour the long voyage to Spain and back to Cuba than to bring it directly from the United States. The Cuban consumer, of course, paid the cost of the unnecessary voyage. But any Cuban who was independent enough or indignant enough to criticize his government was in danger of imprisonment or death. It was natural that such conditions should produce a Ten Years War. In the treaty that ended that war, Spain promised some liberal reforms, but in actual fact there was little betterment of either Cuban politics or Cuban economy. Defeat of the revolutionists silenced some, but it did not end their activities. The period from the end of the Ten Years War to 1895 was scarcely more than an armed truce between the motherland and these dissatisfied islanders. It was in this period that José Martí did the great work of his too brief life.

José Martí, the man who was to become the flame of the Cuban revolution, was born in Havana early in 1853, just after the failure of a number of attempted revolutions. As his parents were exceedingly poor, he grew up in poverty. However, very early he gave evidence of great intelligence and, through the assistance of interested friends, he secured the elements of primary and secondary school education. He was but fifteen years old when the Ten Years War began. But, despite his youth and the fact that his father occupied a post (though a humble one) in the government, he sympathized warmly with the movement and gave it such support as he was able. While yet of junior high school age, he began writing in support of the revolutionists. In January, 1869, he published the first, in fact the *only*, number of a paper, *The Free Fatherland*. In it was printed "Abdala," a poetic drama which he had written "expressly for the fatherland." Though expressed in figurative language, it contained severe criticism of Spain's treatment of Cuba. It brought José unfavorably to the attention of the authorities. Later in the year, because of other seditious activities, José was arrested along with several other young men. After they had been held in jail for some months, they were tried and various punishments were decreed for them. That of José was six years' imprisonment.

At the age of seventeen, José spent six months at hard labor in a stone quarry with a ball and chain attached to his right leg. He suffered physical injuries from which he never fully recovered. The iron scarred his flesh indelibly, and the painful experience fixed firmly in him the determination to work ceaselessly for Cuba's freedom. After these first months, his imprisonment was softened somewhat. He was placed in the care of one Sarda, a friend of the captain-general, who had an estate on the Isle of Pines, just off the southwest coast of Cuba. Sarda had the chains removed and, at José's request, gave them to him. He carried some links of the chain in his pocket by day and slept with them under his pillow by night. Later he had the ring made from one of the links. It was more convenient than the chain and was as good a reminder of his mission.

Early in 1871, the Cuban authorities decided to deport Martí to Spain. This was not an unusual procedure. Perhaps it was hoped that life in the motherland—or the "step-motherland"—would soften his spirit of revolt. At any rate, it would spare the government the expense of caring for the prisoner. For, arrived in Spain, he was released from arrest and was free to move about as he wished. He could not, of course, return to Cuba without permission before the end of his six-year sentence.

Looking back, one may call Martí's exile a piece of good fortune. It gave him an opportunity for advanced study which he would probably never have had in Cuba. Though he was ill much of the time, his four years in Spain were a period of astonishing activity. Without delay he made contacts with a group of intellectual Spaniards who condemned the government's policy toward Cuba. Very shortly he became known as a flaming orator and a writer of remarkable ability. He was able to make a living, though a somewhat scanty one, by journalistic work.

During almost the whole of this Spanish period, Martí was a student, first in the Central University in Madrid and later at the University of Zaragoza. His studies, though directed chiefly toward securing a law education, were broad. They included Roman law, political economy, commercial and criminal law, oratory, general and Spanish literature, Roman and Greek literature as well as the Latin and Greek languages, Hebrew language and literature, universal history, psychology, logic and ethics, physics, chemistry, natural history, physiology and hygiene, and much else. He took a degree in civil and church law and another in philosophy and letters. In all of his school work he showed himself a brilliant student. Eventually he learned both French and English well enough to write in them. All the time he read with unwearied appetite. He had a thirst, it seems, to learn everything.

Toward the end of 1874, Martí decided to quit Spain. He spent some weeks visiting Paris and other European cities, then went to Mexico. There he rejoined his family, for his father had moved to the Mexican capital in search of better opportunities.

Martí's wanderings from this point are numerous. From Mexico he returned under an assumed name to Cuba for a brief visit. Back in Mexico, he fell in love with and became engaged to a young woman of good family and some means. Then he went to Guatemala where he had Cuban acquaintances and was for some months professor of French literature, English, Italian, and German, and the history of philosophy in the Central Normal School of that country. Few young men of twenty-three have the abilities necessary to carry such a difficult program. In Guatemala he fell in love again but, impelled by promptings of honor, he dashed back to Mexico and married the fiancée whom he had left there. This was an unhappy marriage, however, though the son born to the young couple had Martí's fervent devotion all his life. To this son, also called José, one of Martí's books of poems, *Ismaelillo,* is addressed. The couple went to Guatemala, but politics soon caused Martí to quit his position at the Normal School.

The six years of his sentence having expired, Martí returned to Cuba in mid-year of 1878 and took up the practice of law. However, his political views again got him into trouble and, in September, 1879, he was again deported to Spain. He remained in Spain only a short time; in January, 1880, he was in New York City. The remainder of his life, except for brief absences now and then, was spent in our great city, which Martí called "a city of iron." One of these absences took him to Venezuela, where he thought of establishing himself. As always, however, his liberal political views were irrepressible, and the Venezuelan dictator, Guzmán Blanco, ordered him from the country. He returned to New York City.

By 1880 Martí had a reputation that was international. He was known not only as a political writer and propagandist for Cuban freedom, but he was recognized as a poet of great merit. In the course of time some volumes of his poems were published. He wrote charming children's stories, one of the best being "The Black Doll." He founded and printed a few numbers of a monthly magazine for children, *The Golden Bough*. In New York he gained fame as a literary critic. As an orator he was probably unexcelled by anyone of his time. Besides his creative literary work, he made some excellent translations from the English to the Spanish, among them being Helen Hunt Jackson's *Ramona* and Thomas Moore's *Lallah Rookh*. Very early in life Martí proved himself a master of the Spanish language.

Martí's means of livelihood, except for the brief periods of law and teaching, was journalism. Even when he was a lawyer or a professor, he wrote continuously for newspapers and reviews. For years he was a contributor to the New York *Sun*. At the same time he was a correspondent for the great Argentine daily, *La Nación,* and for various other newspapers in Mexico, Central America, and South America. Martí founded several newspapers and reviews, but most of them, for lack of financial support, were short-lived.

Enough has been said to suggest that life in Cuba was not comfortable, to say the least, for critics of the government. It was impossible for those who were open advocates of independence. This meant that hundreds of the most intelligent and most independent Cubans lived abroad, as did Martí. There were colonies of Cubans in Mexico, in several of the Central American countries, in Haiti and Santo Domingo, and at several points in the United States. The most important were in New York City and Tampa, Florida. The latter colony was composed in great part of Cubans who were engaged in the cigar-making industry. Most of them were revolutionists.

The Cuban colony of New York City was less numerous and, generally speaking, was composed of persons of a more intellectual type. It provided the best thinkers of the revolution. One of these, Tomás Estrada Palma, a schoolmaster for several years in the vicinity of the city, was later (1902-1906) to be the first president of independent Cuba. But preëminent as the thinker of the Cuban Revolution was José Martí. When the Cubans wished to celebrate a day of importance in their revolutionary movement, such as that on which the Ten Years War had been commenced, it was almost always Martí who pronounced the oration which was the chief feature of the celebration. It was he who explained in the newspapers of the United States and Latin America the abuses to which the Cubans were subjected and the type of government which the revolutionists wished to establish in Cuba.

By 1884 Martí felt that talk had gone far enough and that it was time to make plans for action. He induced the two

most prominent surviving military men of the Ten Years
War to come to New York. These men were Generals Máximo Gómez and Antonio Maceo, the second a mulatto. They
were at the time living in Honduras. In the course of an extended talk with these two men it became clear to Martí
that there were important differences in their views. The
generals, in the usual manner of Latin-American military men, favored a military government for Cuba. Martí,
a civilian, had always been critical of militarism. He believed
that the leadership of the revolution, aside from essentially
military matters, should be civil. In Martí's mind this was an
exceedingly important difference. For two days after the conference he thought the matter over carefully and coolly, then
he wrote a letter to General Gómez in which he stated his
position. "A people," he declared, "is not to be founded like
a military encampment." Public liberties were the only jus-
tification for plunging a country into a war. Martí expressed
the fear that General Gómez regarded the coming Cuban
war as his own "exclusive property." If Cuba must be enslaved, Martí preferred that it be the slave of someone other
than its own sons. If he *must* be a foreigner, he would prefer
being one in some country other than his own. General Gómez
felt himself insulted, and he and General Maceo returned
to Honduras. This difference among leaders delayed for
some years the struggle for Cuban independence. Perhaps
the delay was not entirely to be regretted, as it afforded time
to bring the exiled patriots nearer to agreement. It also gave
time for political changes in the United States which very
probably were necessary to the success of the movement
when it was at length begun.

There were other grounds of difference among the exiles
as well as among their sympathizers in Cuba. There were

many who believed that the island's welfare could best be served by annexation to the United States. Martí was not one of these. For him the great end was the complete independence of Cuba—not only from Spain, but from every country.

In these years the Cubans in exile grouped themselves into societies. A New York group was the "Cuba Aid Society," of which Martí was president. Another society there called itself "The Independents." In Tampa a corresponding organization was named the "Patriotic Cuban League." All of them assisted exiled Cubans and agitated for Cuban independence. In November, 1891, Martí was invited to Tampa to make a commemorative address before the "League." He accepted, and while he was in Tampa he and other leaders drew up a set of resolutions. Back in New York, on January 5, he and the Cubans there, on the basis of these resolutions, produced a document which they called "Secret Bases and Statutes of the Cuban Revolutionary Party." Thus the Cuban Revolutionary party was organized. Thereafter it took the lead in preparing for the revolution and, finally, actually began it. Martí was at once chosen president of the party, a position which he held for the remainder of his life.

Martí had always been an active man, but beginning January 5, 1892, his activities could properly be described as feverish. From that day on, he lived and breathed the Cuban Revolution. Money had to be raised to buy war materials, to buy or lease boats. Groups of Cubans in widely separated localities had to be visited to stir up their enthusiasm and organize their support. The workmen in the cigar factories in Florida pledged one day's pay in thirty to the revolution. Wealthy Cubans gave large sums. Martí's eloquence was more valuable than ever.

General Gómez, who, Martí knew, must be the commander of the revolutionary army, had moved to Santo Domingo. Martí visited him there, and they became reconciled. Their cause was too big to be hindered by personal differences. Thenceforth they coöperated loyally in the patriotic project. Several times in the years after 1892 Martí revisited Gómez, and once Gómez voyaged to New York to confer with Martí. Martí went to Mexico City to raise money and to assure, if possible, Dictator Díaz' friendliness to the proposed movement. He went to Costa Rica, to Panama. He made innumerable trips between New York and Tampa. It seems almost impossible that one physically weak man (Martí was often ill in these years) could have done all that Martí did in the three years after 1892. But his enthusiasm never wavered. In the face of serious miscarriage of early plans for beginning the revolution, he maintained his courage and his determination, and inspired his helpers to new sacrifices and new efforts. It was at this time that his fellow revolutionists began calling him El Apóstol, "The Apostle."

Early in 1895 the final plan was made. General Maceo would lead a group from Costa Rica, to which country he had moved from Honduras. A second party was to move into Cuba from Southern Florida. The third, led by General Gómez and accompanied by Martí, was to enter the island from Santo Domingo. It was hoped that the Spanish officials in Cuba would be confused by a number of uprisings at different points.

In Cuba already were most of the men who would compose the revolutionary armies. They had been kept informed of the progress of the movement abroad, but they were growing impatient. Two or three premature insurrections were begun in Cuba, but they were smothered by the authorities who knew that action was being planned and were on the alert. Martí and the other leaders counseled patience and hastened their plans. At the end of 1894 everything was in readiness, both outside and inside Cuba.

On January 30, 1895, Martí sailed from New York for the last time, bound for Santo Domingo to join General Gómez. Instructions to move had already been given to the other groups. However, it was not until April 11 that Martí and General Gómez, with half a dozen other daring revolutionists, set foot on the island of Cuba. The landing took place in the dead of night at a little village called Playitas. On reaching land, the general, like Columbus before him, knelt and kissed the soil.[1] One of his followers imitated him. Martí did not thus salute his land, but it may be imagined with what deep emotion he again found himself standing on the soil, sacred to him, about which he had written so many poems and on which he had not had the happiness of setting foot for eighteen years. It had been a cruel absence from the beautiful country where, as he wrote, "the palms are highest."

Before long it was learned that General Maceo also had made a successful landing, and Martí and Gómez set out to meet him at a place agreed upon. En route, a handful of some sixty men were gathered, the nucleus of Gómez' army. General Gómez, to make everything official, recognized Martí as delegate of the Revolutionary party and named him major-general of the Liberating Army. It was decided that before the campaign was opened a Chamber of Deputies should be brought into being. This was in line with Martí's insistence

[1] Gonzalo de Quesada y Miranda, *Martí, Hombre* (Havana, 1941), p. 261. This work has been drawn on heavily for this chapter.

on providing for the supremacy of the civilian element in the revolutionary movement. Already the soldiers were saluting Martí as *Señor Presidente.*

On May 5, the Gómez party met General Maceo, who had got together some three hundred men. Again the old issue of civilian against military came up, Maceo this time representing the military. In the course of a discussion with Martí, Maceo said to him with a disdainful air, "Revolutions, Mr. Martí, are not made with speeches." But Martí remained firm in his position. The army must have its place, of course, in the contest, but he insisted that the free country be represented with all dignity and by a civil government. Maceo departed with injured feelings. Such incidents were not infrequent in the course of the revolution.

The Cuban Revolution, which merged into the Spanish-American War when we declared war on Spain in 1898, lasted more than three years. But for Martí it was very, very short. On May 19, 1895, Gómez' forces, by then about four hundred, encountered a superior force led by the Spaniard, Colonel Sandoval. In the action that followed Martí received three balls and fell, mortally wounded. Death came swiftly.

Considered as an event in literary history, Martí's early death was a tragedy. It is not certain that it was so tragic considered as an event of the Cuban Revolution. Martí's task had been one of preparation. In the preparatory stage of the revolution, his power as a thinker and a writer and his skill as an orator and propagandist had been of the highest possible value. These qualities were not of such great importance once action was under way. His work had been so well done that, although the Cubans had to wade through blood for three years before Spain was defeated, they never wavered before their terrible task. Martí's dream was realized at the end of the war when Spain abandoned all claim to the "Ever-Faithful Isle." The simultaneous loss of Puerto Rico left Spain with nothing of that colossal empire which it had once possessed in the Americas.

PART THREE

DICTATORSHIP

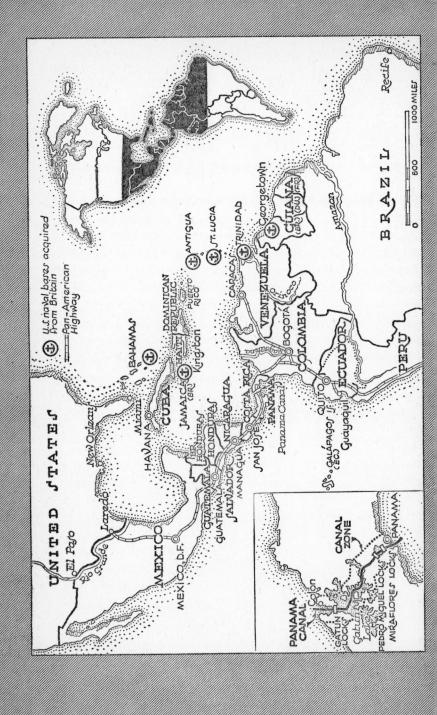

UNITED STATES

⊕ U.S. naval bases acquired from Britain
--- Pan-American Highway

El Paso
Laredo
Rio Grande
New Orleans
MEXICO
MEXICO,D.F.

BAHAMAS ⊕
Miami
HAVANA
CUBA
DOMINICAN REPUBLIC
HAITI
JAMAICA (BR.) ⊕
Kingston
PUERTO RICO ⊕
ANTIGUA ⊕
ST. LUCIA ⊕

GUATEMALA
HONDURAS
EL SALVADOR
NICARAGUA
MANAGUA
COSTA RICA
SAN JOSE
PANAMA
Panama Canal

GALÁPAGOS Is. (EC.)
QUITO
ECUADOR
Guayaquil

TRINIDAD
CARACAS
Orinoco
VENEZUELA
GEORGETOWN
GUIANA (BR.)(DU.)(FR.)
BOGOTA
COLOMBIA
Amazon

PERU

BRAZIL
Recife

0   500   1000 MILES

PANAMA CANAL

Colon
GATUN LOCKS
Gatun Lake
CANAL ZONE
PEDRO MIGUEL LOCKS
MIRAFLORES LOCKS
PANAMA

INTRODUCTION

Many North Americans wonder why there have been so many dictators in Latin America. And, not knowing the reasons, they have been inclined to look down upon our Latin-American neighbors as troublesome people, ignorant of the elements of good government. When the facts are known, however, it is seen that the dictatorships have been a natural consequence of Latin-American history. In fact, the well-informed person wonders that there has not been more bad government in Latin America than has actually existed.

The critic calls attention to the fact that the United States, after the Revolution, established rather shortly a well-organized, efficient government. Comparisons follow that are, to say the least, uncomplimentary to the Latin-Americans. This critic must not forget the long period of training in self-government which the Anglo-Saxon had had, a training that was entirely lacking in the history of the Spanish and Portuguese peoples. When Englishmen came to America in the first years of the seventeenth century, England had already been for some centuries developing representative government. Without exception, the colonies themselves had some degree of self-government, and some of them were almost independent of political ties with England. Thus, when independence had been won through the Revolution, they had merely to continue to govern much as they had been doing for many years. The one great problem that was new to them was that of forming a union, and they were able to do that, in large measure, because the practice of centuries had accustomed them to making political compromises to realize political ends.

With the Latin-Americans the situation was vastly different. Even the leaders of the armies and of the congresses had had no training in the democratic process of government. They had had, in fact, practically *no* training in *any* type of government. Everything had to be built up from the ground. It is true that they had before them the examples of the United States and France. But that was not altogether good, for governments were copied after one or the other of these examples without much regard to their fitness for Latin-American conditions. Often, indeed, the results were disastrous. It may be, as some have argued, that the Latin-Americans were not ready for democratic government. Even Bolívar, before his death, expressed this idea more than once. The reasons for this lack of preparation in good government need to be understood if one is to judge the Latin-Americans fairly.

Lack of experience in representative government was undoubtedly the chief reason for inefficiency in Latin America. Lack of education and of educational facilities was another. Illiteracy was widespread. Until the people of a nation are able to get thought from a printed page, teaching them to govern themselves is a very slow process. This has been the case with Latin-Americans. It can be said that political stability today exists to the greatest degree in precisely those Latin-American countries where literacy is highest. It is quite true that our own revolutionary forefathers were far from being perfectly literate, but at least we were better off in that respect than the Latin-Americans. In our country, moreover, condi-

Palermo Park, Buenos Aires. This was formerly the estate of Dictator Rosas. It is now the most beautiful park in the city.

Gauchos in modern Argentina, drinking mate on an *estancia* (cattle ranch). On such a ranch Rosas worked and lived the life of a *gaucho* before he became dictator.

"La Carreta" monument in Montevideo, Uruguay, a remarkably life-like covered wagon in memory of the pioneers of that country. For years little Uruguay was a buffer state between Spanish Argentina and Portuguese Brazil. In 1828, however, it won its independence, and in 1865 joined its old enemies, Argentina and Brazil, against López of Paraguay.

A Bolivian Indian chief. Ninety per cent of the population of Bolivia, with which Paraguay fought over the swamplands of the Chaco, is made up of such pure-blood Indians.

tions were such that we could carry forward an educational movement with greater speed than they.

Another disadvantage of many of the Latin-American nations was—and is—great racial diversity. In some regions there are many Negroes, and in most of the countries at the beginning of independence there were many more Indians than whites. This condition made it hard to form a united citizenry with common views on social and political matters, even with the best intentions on the part of the leaders. But the best intentions did not always exist, for, generally speaking, the small white element refused to believe the Indian could be educated or desired to keep him in ignorance so that he might be dominated the more easily. With the passage of time the *mestizo* element has increased in comparative numbers. In a few countries, notably Mexico, the *mestizos* have been able to take control of the government and secure reforms designed to better their condition, as well as that of the pure Indians.

A fourth obstacle to the attainment of unity was the great area of Latin America, most of it sparsely occupied, together with the natural barriers thrown up by mountains and jungles. The whole of Latin America is nearly three times as large as the United States, and, except in Argentina, there are few plains areas where roads and railroads could be built cheaply and quickly. Moreover, the countries had little capital to spend on these improvements, and for decades communication was very slow, much as it was with us before our railways were built. Of course, after a time, the Latin-Americans too began to build railways and to improve communications in general. Now they are doing some excellent work in creating automobile roads. Nevertheless, for many years distance and separation prevented the people within each nation from understanding one another. The same difficulty has operated, naturally, to prevent the development of good understanding among the various nations.

By the comparative brevity of our Revolution we escaped some of the ill effects that afflicted the Latin-Americans. The whole Latin-American generation that grew up between 1810 and 1825 came to feel that war was the normal state of being, and that it was the natural method of settling differences. Such a notion, once formed, is hard to eradicate. It is one of the reasons why some of our Latin-American neighbors still have recourse to violence at times, when it seems to us they ought to accept the result of the ballots.

We sometimes wonder why the people of a dictatorial country accept the government of a dictator. In the case of Latin America, there are several explanations. The Indians of America were under absolute rule when the Spaniards came. The Spanish people, themselves, for many centuries had been dominated by their kings and their priests. To neither class, therefore, did it seem unnatural to accept authority at the hands of a superior. And, when their government became too odious, it seemed to them only natural that force should be used to remove the ruler. In fact, it was difficult to remove him in any other manner, for the dictator did not allow the ballot-box to get out of his control.

Furthermore, the long wars of independence had been frightfully expensive, and the average man did not know how the debts should be met. It was easy, therefore, to entrust the problem to a leader who did know how, or who said he knew. These leaders were usually the generals, in whom the people had great faith. In addition, the young nations had to face many dangers, especially the dangers of conquest from abroad and of revolution from within. They were weak and insecure, and often a strong dictator seemed the best protection. Thus, in every country the dictator appeared, ruled by the use of force, and passed on his power to, or was forced out by, the next dictator.

Not all Latin-American dictators have been bad. Some of them tried in all honesty to improve the condition of their people. Dom Pedro II, emperor of Brazil, has often been called a benevolent dictator. But so admirable was the system which he backed that with time he had educated his people to the point where they preferred the freedom of republicanism to the imperial form of government, no matter how liberal. So, exit Dom Pedro! And he went in peace. Frequently, however, a dictator used his country and its resources to satisfy his own desires, financial or otherwise. Two of the worst of this type were Francisco Solano López, of Paraguay, and Juan Vicente Gómez, of Venezuela. The fact that Gómez passed from the picture as recently as 1935 indicates that the period of dictatorship in Latin America is not a thing of the distant past. Some nations relieved themselves of it rather early, Chile being the most prompt. Mexico has only lately emerged from the period, and today dictatorships are the rule in about half the twenty Latin-American nations.

Thus, the dictators have been of all types. A few were devout Catholics, though most completely ignored religious matters. A small number were well educated, but the majority had never been in a classroom. Some were generals, others, civilians. There were dictators good and bad, religious and irreligious, literate and illiterate. On the whole, they were courageous but violent, strong but intemperate, patriotic but selfish. They appeared in every one of the countries of Latin America.

As citizens of a democracy, we deplore dictatorship

wherever it exists. As intelligent people, however, we must recognize the fact that in some of the Latin-American countries, where illiteracy still is as high as 80 or 90 per cent, democracy as we know it cannot be practiced. The people are not ready for it. But what we must condemn without reserve is the tendency of dictators to neglect the education of their people; for with education there is the hope and expectation that one day the people will have reached the point where their intelligence, their general information, and their knowledge of what good government ought to be will make possible genuine democracies. Many dictators can be criticized on this ground.

The American dictatorship must not be confused with that of Europe. That of America is not totalitarian. And, no matter what the type of dictator who wields power in Latin America, he makes a pretense of governing through democratic processes. This proves the strength in America of the spirit of democracy, and gives ground for hope that in time democracy will prevail in actuality throughout the Americas.

CHAPTER XII

JUAN MANUEL DE ROSAS: COWBOY DICTATOR OF ARGENTINA

When the American Revolution came to an end, the people of the new nation eagerly prepared to settle down to times of peace and order. With difficulty, but without bloodshed, they adopted a constitution, chose the members of their first congress, and elected George Washington their first president. Then came Adams, Jefferson, and other presidents, all chosen by the people in peaceful election. As we have seen in the previous section, the American people had practiced self-government in the days of the Thirteen Colonies, and it was fairly easy for them to learn how to live together in a united democracy.

The people of Latin America were not so fortunate. For them, after independence, stormy days lay ahead. Instead of one united nation, there were, at first, eight, then thirteen, eventually twenty nations. Instead of regular elections, there were fighting and disorder. Instead of presidents who governed democratically, there were autocratic leaders, often dictators, who ruled without consulting the people. Even Argentina, one of the first to gain actual independence and today a great, progressive nation, had to endure this period of disorder and dictatorship. Like every other country in Latin America, Argentina had a succession of these "strong-arm" rulers. It is to her credit, however, that, as time passed, dictators came to power less frequently. Today, the Republic of Argentina is rapidly becoming a true democracy.

The best-known of the Argentine dictators is Juan Manuel de Rosas. The Argentine people often refer to the "Age of Rosas," for this dictator kept himself in power more than twenty-three years (1829-1852). During six years he controlled the province (or state) of Buenos Aires, and for seventeen more he extended his authority to the whole of Argentina. During these years, Rosas reigned without a constitution, without even a fair election. His methods were the methods of violence—spying upon, terrifying, murdering his political opponents. To establish himself in power, he hunted down lesser military chieftains and put them out of the way. To keep himself in power, he founded newspapers in his own and in foreign countries and closed the newspapers of his enemies. He made his name known in the churches, in the schools, and in the foreign countries. In his own country he was supreme, and in neighboring countries he interfered in local affairs. Even the interests of Great Britain and France were affected by his acts, and the United States had difficulty in maintaining cordial relations with him. Rosas brought some benefits to Argentina, as we shall see, but these can hardly justify the terror he caused or the lives he took. But we should not condemn Rosas—or any dictator—without attempting to understand and to explain him. We can try to explain, if not to excuse, him.

Rosas came into power, of course, because conditions produced him and gave him an opportunity. He stayed in power because conditions kept him there. What, then, were these conditions? The leaders of the Argentine people, as we have seen, set up a new nation in 1810. This they did without the least experience in self-government and, in fact, without knowing exactly what kind of government they wanted. They knew they wished to be free from Spain, but beyond that there was no agreement. For twenty years they experimented, trying first one type of administration, then another —government by one man, government by three men, government by an assembly. Most persons favored a republic, but some believed in monarchy. There were some who wished a federal republic like that of the United States, but others who thought all power should be concentrated in the capital at Buenos Aires. No government endured more than three years, some only a few months. In one year, 1820, there were at least twenty-four changes, three of which came on the same day.

After the terrible year 1820, some genuine attempts were made to improve the life of the people. Under one of Argentina's greatest heroes, Bernardino Rivadavia, many reforms were begun: the University of Buenos Aires was founded; schools were opened; a national bank was organized; harbors were improved; a charity organization was established. These reforms, however, were largely lost when Rivadavia attempted to set up a strong national government. Many of the people from the interior of the country did not wish to be governed by officials at Buenos Aires. Among these people were the wealthy and conservative landowners, who, in many of the provinces, invited local military chieftains— caudillos they were called—to resist the power of the government at Buenos Aires.

The soldiers of these armies were recruited mainly from one of the most colorful elements of all South American people, the gauchos. The gaucho was the Argentine cowboy, who roamed on his horse far and wide over the pampas, which, like our Texas plains, stretch hundreds of miles without a tree or hill. The *gaucho* was a hard-riding, hard-fighting, hard-drinking cowman. He learned to ride a horse almost as soon as he could walk and spent most of his life in the saddle. At the drop of a hat he would fight a wild steer or a man. As a soldier he was strong and courageous; as a man he was cruel and brutal. Yet, he might even carry a guitar and compose crude ditties as he rode over the countryside or visited country stores. He made his living by chasing wild cows, as this description shows:

The *gaucho* began life, then, as a *mestizo* [one of mixed Indian and Spanish blood] hunter for hides. But eventually hides became hard to find. In a very literal sense, the cow had been the foundation of Argentinian society. Steak, served with the Paraguayan tea called *maté*, was almost the exclusive food of Argentinian rural society. Bones and fat were used as fuel for fires. Ropes and cords and lassos were made from strips of leather. Boats were made of hides, as were such other items as Indian tents, the curtained doors of ranchos, buckets used for drawing water or for carrying ore in mines. . . . Gleaming cattle skulls served as chairs. Cart wheels were bound with hide which, drying, tightened to provide the extra strength needed in long cross-country hauls. Besides their manifold local uses, hides were the chief export. They were exchanged for all the other things for which the land had need. When the pampas Indian tried to still his almost unquenchable thirst for strong drink—and, by the way, he mixed it with mare's blood or gunpowder to make it more potent—he stole Spanish cattle and used the hides as the coin with which to make his purchase.[1]

Juan Manuel de Rosas was one of these *gauchos*, although

[1] Quoted from Madaline Nichols' unpublished paper on "The Gaucho" in C. E. Chapman, *Republican Hispanic America: A History* (New York, The Macmillan Company, 1937), pp. 323-24.

much wealthier and better educated than most. He was born in Buenos Aires in 1793, one of *twenty* children. His father owned extensive lands in the country to the south of the city. The Rosas family was related to some of the most important people in this section of Argentina. Like his mother who managed the family household, young Manuel was one to have his own way. Once, so his nephew declared, his teacher sent him home because he refused to do a task required of him. His mother tried to punish him. She

did not hesitate; she took him by the ear and led him to his room, where she locked him up, with this warning, "Here you shall stay and have only bread and water until you obey me."

Juan Manuel said nothing. A day passed with only bread and water. . . . Then, as the household slept, he broke open the blinds, wrote a few words on a piece of paper, undressed himself and, almost as Adam himself was, descended to the street and thence to the house of his cousins the Anchorenas. . . .

The following day . . . they found the note, which read as follows: "I leave all that which is not mine—Juan Manuel de Rosas."[2]

It was in this way that Rosas, still in his teens, became a *gaucho*. He went to work on a large cattle ranch, and learned to live as the *gauchos* lived, soon riding and fighting as well as the best of them. The cowboys knew many tricks, but there was none at which Rosas could not excel. He could throw a lasso with unfailing accuracy, either on foot or from a running horse, at a fleeing animal or man. He could shoot, straight and true, even from the saddle. To slaughter a cow

[2] Translated from Lucio V. Mansilla, *Rosas: ensayo histórico-psicológico* (Paris, 1899), pp. 10-11, in A. Curtis Wilgus, *South American Dictators During the First Century of Independence* (Washington, George Washington University Press, 1937), p. 106.

he could wield with ease the long butcher's knife he carried at his side. Sometimes, at the head of his men, he rode hundreds of miles. It was said he could vault over seven horses lined up side by side. By his cunning and superiority he soon became the leader of the *gauchos*.

When only twenty-two Rosas went into the meat-salting business. He invested his earnings in ranches and more ranches. Within a few years he accumulated more than seven hundred square miles of land and became one of the richest men in Argentina. Always, however, he retained the respect of the *gauchos*, and he became a kind of protector of the lower classes.

Because of his wealth and because of the military experience he had had in fighting the Indians, Rosas was also in favor with the wealthy merchants and landowners. Therefore, in 1829 they arranged that he be appointed governor of the province of Buenos Aires. They hoped he would be able to establish and maintain order. Rosas came into office, then, with the support of both the poor and the rich, an unbeatable combination.

During his three years as governor, Rosas did bring about a kind of peace, as his supporters had hoped, even in the whole of Argentina. He destroyed the power of local military chiefs. By abolishing tariff barriers, he tried to improve trade between the provinces. In order that the provinces might be united against foreign danger, he took charge of their foreign policies. When his term of office was finished in 1832, Argentina was more orderly than it had been for many years.

Then, however, eager to get back into the saddle, Rosas refused reappointment. He wished to lead his soldiers against the Indians of the South and push back the frontier for further settlement by the whites. This he attempted, but with only fair success. All the while he was absent in the field, he kept his finger in the politics of Buenos Aires. Not long after his return from the Indian wars, the provincial legislature again invited him to accept the governorship of Buenos Aires, this time for five years. From that time on he was regularly "reappointed." For the next seventeen years, or until his downfall in 1852, he was master in the province of Buenos Aires and in most of Argentina.

When he was not in the army, Rosas lived in his beautiful mansion in Palermo, then near the edge of Buenos Aires, but today the most beautiful park in the city. His estate, with its great and lovely gardens, was open to all to wander in as they wished. There, until her death in 1838, his wife was mistress of the household. There lived his three children, including the charming and gentle Manuelita, who, with her tenderness and tolerance, possessed greater influence over her father than did any other person. At times she was able even to persuade him to treat his enemies with some mercy. Steadfastly loyal to him, she refused to marry against his will until after his exile from Argentina in 1852. After the death of her mother, Manuelita helped her father entertain the many guests who came to Palermo—famous persons, like Charles Darwin, diplomats, wealthy friends, poor friends. Friendly and enthusiastic, though grave and easily moved to anger, Rosas liked to have his friends about him in his home. With them he found diversion from making war, reading documents, and from all the other duties of a harsh dictator.

But the task of being a dictator involves much more than entertaining friends. There are enemies—many of them—who command attention. These Rosas handled by the most cruel and violent of methods. To spy upon and terrorize them he worked through a secret society called the *Mazorca* (ear of corn). It was given this name because its members were said to fit together like the kernels on an ear of corn. The mysterious *Mazorca* was a kind of Ku Klux Klan whose members—some criminals, others patriotic citizens—did not hesitate to use murder and violence against Rosas' enemies. Thousands of his opponents fled to Montevideo, Santiago, or Asunción, where they conspired against the cruel dictator.

All persons in Argentina who believed, as Rosas did, in the federal form of government, were expected to wear something red, for blue was the color of his opponents and, therefore, unpatriotic. The Federalists flew red flags from their homes, and sometimes had a wide border of red painted around their buildings. They wore red ribbons upon which was printed the party slogan, "Federation or Death! Long live the Argentine Confederation! Death to the filthy, loathsome, savage Unitarians!" (The Unitarians were political opponents who believed that all power should rest with the national government and that the power of the Catholic Church should be reduced.) Men wore red waistcoats. Every school child had to wear a red sash and could use only those textbooks which were acceptable to the government. The dictator's image was carried in religious processions, and his picture hung in the churches and schools. In these ways did Rosas seek to make himself a national hero and to unify his country.

One of the tricks by which dictators take the minds of the people off their hunger, poverty, or lack of freedom is to direct their attention to foreign adventures. Rosas used this trick several times. On one occasion he engaged in a diplomatic dispute with the United States. Argentina had claimed the Falkland Islands, located off her southern coast in the Atlantic Ocean. When in 1831 two American sealing vessels put in at the islands, they were seized by agents of Rosas for violating the fishing laws. To secure revenge the United States sent the warship *Lexington*. Captain Duncan, by taking away all the settlers, broke up the Argentine settlement. In 1833, while the islands were unprotected, officers of the British Navy pulled down the Argentine flag and took possession. Although she has never been able to get them back from England, Argentina still claims the Falklands. Rosas blamed the United States for the loss, and several times tried to secure payment of an indemnity from us. We, however, have never admitted the responsibility.

In other disputes with foreign nations, Rosas fought a successful war against Argentina's neighbor, Bolivia (1837), and on several occasions intervened in the local affairs of another neighbor, little Uruguay. He risked quarrels with both France and England, and these nations retaliated (France in 1838 and France and England in 1845) by blockading the port of Buenos Aires. Repeatedly, during these quarrels, diplomatic agents of the United States tried to assist Rosas in settling them, but without success. The latter of these blockades was really the beginning of Rosas' downfall. During almost five years after 1845 Argentina had little trade with the outside world. Income from tariff duties fell to a trickle. The treasury was nearly empty. The government gradually grew weaker.

This was the moment for which Rosas' many enemies had been waiting. First they began to fall away from him, then to conspire with one another, finally to unite under their ablest leader, General Justo José de Urquiza. On the battlefield of Caseros, near Buenos Aires, in February, 1852, they defeated the army of Rosas and put an end to his power. To avoid capture, he fled to England on a British warship. There in a small hotel in Southampton, he lived for the next twelve years. Then he moved to a small farm, where for thirteen years, often dressed as a *gaucho*, he tried to relive a little of his youth in Argentina. He passed these twenty-five years in England without a visit from his lovely daughter, Manuelita. Married to her childhood sweetheart, she lived apart from him in London.

It is difficult to pass judgment on Rosas and his twenty-three years as dictator of Argentina. Shall we condemn him completely for the distress he caused? Or shall we justify his terrorism by the benefits he brought the country? Neither of these courses would be wholly correct. Certainly he must be held responsible for every life he took and every crime he committed. He must be blamed for all the oppression he inflicted upon his people. He gave them no constitution and few personal liberties. He did very little to improve economic or cultural conditions. He built no railroads or great public works, he gave no help to public education, and he permitted the University of Buenos Aires to decline. Although foreign commerce doubled and the number of cattle trebled during his rule, these were accidents rather than results of his policies.

Furthermore, Rosas must also be seen against the background of his times. He came to power after twenty years of anarchy. No government had succeeded in unifying the nation. The violent methods he used were also the methods of his opponents—inherited from years of anarchy and common on the untamed frontier. At the same time, two facts at least may be noted in his favor. He ruled the nation's finances with absolute honor. He had spent a fortune in the governing of his country. Once a millionaire, he died, not in poverty, but with scanty means. A military chieftain himself, he had rid Argentina of the dozens of smaller chiefs who were dividing the country. By this accomplishment, he prevented the breaking up of the nation. Rosas brought neither peace nor unity to Argentina, but he did introduce a feeling of nationalism upon which his successors could build peace and unity. Today, more and more, the historians of his country are coming to feel that the "cowboy dictator" made real contributions to the growth of Argentina.

CHAPTER XIII

FRANCISCO SOLANO LÓPEZ: DICTATOR ON HORSEBACK

Napoleon Bonaparte never ruled in Argentina. Yet there is exhibited today in one of the historical museums of Buenos Aires a model of Napoleon's imperial crown. Argentine schoolboys and schoolgirls love to see it there, shining with gold and brilliant with precious stones. It reminds them of one of the glorious moments in their country's history—the military defeat in 1870 of the hated dictator of Paraguay, Francisco Solano López. Their teachers tell them that López never wore the crown, never even saw it, although he had ordered it made in Paris. When it was sent from France to Paraguay, the Argentine authorities seized it and refused to send it on to López. Since that time it has remained a prized possession of the Argentine people, a reminder to them of an ambitious Paraguayan who was prevented from carrying out his dreams of imitating Napoleon.

Among the nations of Latin America, since independence, peace has been the rule. In a time when the many countries of Europe were fighting dozens of wars, the equally numerous nations of the New World were learning to live together in harmony. True, there were frequent border clashes, but seldom did these break out into actual armed conflict. In fact, only six of these can truly be called wars, and six wars be-

Bernardino Rivadavia, first president of Argentina, began many reforms in the country which were, unfortunately, lost later when Rosas became dictator.

Executive offices in Asunción, Paraguay. This building, once used by Francisco Solano López, is still the office of the executive of Paraguay.

Iguassú Falls, on the narrow boundary between Brazil and Argentina. Some o the falls belong to Brazil, some to Argentina. Here we see the Fall of Three Musketeers, property of Brazil.

Petropolis, high in the mountains of Brazil. Here Dom Pedro II spent summer with his family. And here in a little church he is buried.

tween twenty countries in a century and a quarter is a very good record.

Strangely enough, one of the smallest nations of Latin America involved itself in the two bloodiest of these wars. It was little Paraguay, landlocked in the heart of the South American tropics, which foolishly fought almost to the death against three of its neighbors (1865-1870). It was the same little Paraguay which only a few years ago needlessly struggled with another of its neighbors for possession of the great, green wastes of the Gran Chaco, a tropical lowland between Paraguay and Bolivia. In the first of these disastrous wars, Paraguay was controlled by one of the most ruthless of dictators, the cruel, vain López. It was he who drove his people almost to destruction to attain his crazy dreams of power. Before we can understand López, however, and the tragic story of the Paraguayan War, we must know a little of his country and its history.

Paraguay is a land of perpetual summer, a land of brilliant flowering trees, of lush tropical growth. Its soil is so rich that the people usually have been able to eat well without diligent cultivation of native food plants. Still, if Paraguayans have found it easy to feed themselves, they have found it much harder to maintain connections with the outside world. By river their country lies a thousand miles from the sea, and, hemmed in by powerful neighbors, is difficult to reach. For this reason, the native Indians, the Guaraní, and the early Spanish settlers soon developed a feeling of independence. Spain was a long way off, and officials seldom reached Asunción, chief Paraguayan city. Moreover, if the Paraguayans wished to defend their land against the hostile Portuguese in Brazil, they had to do it themselves; few Spanish soldiers ever came to help them. Thus, the Paraguayans learned to shift for themselves, minding their own business when possible, but protecting themselves when necessary.

Paraguay was one of the first Spanish colonies to set up its own government. Its people were unwilling to be ruled by Spain or even to become a part of an independent Argentina. Once independence was won, however, Paraguay found itself surrounded by larger and stronger neighbors. To the east and north, sprawling like a well-fed boa constrictor, lay huge Brazil, second largest empire in the world. To the south was Argentina—six times as large as Paraguay—hungering to feast on adjoining provinces. Even little Uruguay—down the river—was not always friendly. To the west was Bolivia, not yet strong, but large and very rich. To protect its land and its life, therefore, Paraguay entrusted itself to three successive dictators. Until 1870, they made the country a kind of island in the middle of a continent.

The first of these three autocrats was the mysterious José Gaspar Rodríguez de Francia, a shrewd but terrible man. He preferred to be known as Dr. Francia, though many of his people, who both feared and worshiped him, called him *El Supremo* (The Highest One). Dr. Francia was supreme in his country from 1811 to 1840, protecting it from all enemies. When his opponents were suspected of plotting against him, he tortured or executed them. In one period of nine days, he put to death seventy-two of the plotters, eight each day. He was a man controlled by fear. So much did he fear Paraguay's neighbors that he built, under his own command, the strongest possible army. By forbidding people to enter or leave without his consent, he cut Paraguay off from the world. In order that the people might learn to live on their own resources, he permitted few products (except munitions) to enter the country. He improved agriculture and stock-raising and encouraged the building of public works. Although his policies were harsh and brutal, *El Supremo* did give the country enduring peace. During his rule the population more than doubled, and, when he died in 1840, he left his "children" much more united and loyal than they had been twenty-nine years before.

Francia was followed in office by the two López, father and son. The father, Carlos Antonio, was the best of Paraguay's three well-known dictators. So important did he consider himself that he received distinguished guests without removing his hat and without rising from his chair. He was unattractive, very ugly and fat, so fat late in life that he could not ride a horse. Yet he was a man of some ability and brought distinct benefits to his country. Under him, the people of Paraguay received their first constitution, although not a very democratic one. He established the first newspaper, built the first railroad and first telegraph, and began the abolition of slavery. He also improved educational opportunities and gave assistance to agriculture.

The elder López, unlike Francia, believed that Paraguay could best be made strong by intercourse with the outside world. Accordingly, he encouraged foreigners to enter for settlement, promoted foreign trade, and secured from the United States and other countries the recognition of Paraguay's independence. He settled boundary disputes with Brazil and Argentina, and encouraged foreign scientists, including some from the United States, to explore the rivers of his country. Nevertheless, López had his troubles with foreign governments. On one occasion, his soldiers fired on an American exploring vessel, killing a seaman. On another he quarreled with an American consul. Because President Buchanan resented these insults to our government, he sent to Paraguay a fleet of nineteen warships and twenty-five hundred men. This show of strength forced from the Paraguayan ruler an apology and an indemnity for the family of the slain seaman. Yet, in the main, Carlos Antonio López kept the peace and brought unity to his nation. He died in 1862, knowing that his people, now nearly a million, were happier and more prosperous than they had ever been.

Francisco Solano López was the reckless, swaggering son of Carlos Antonio. Although he ruled only eight years (1862-1870), he brought misery and bloodshed to his people. Many persons think he was the most vicious of all the dictators of Latin America. There is nothing about him, except his courage, to admire or praise, and his country would have been far stronger and happier had he never lived.

Francisco was born on July 24, 1826, and from the very beginning was trained to be his father's successor. He was spoiled and pampered and grew into a proud, ambitious young man. As commander of a Paraguayan army at nineteen, he strutted about like a young Napoleon. In 1853 his father sent him to Europe as representative of Paraguay. In Russia he visited the battlefields of the Crimean War where he saw in action the greatest armies of the world. In Paris, because he greatly admired the French Army, he employed several military experts to visit Asunción to train his army. In Paris, he became a great admirer, too, of Madame Eliza Lynch, an attractive Irish lady, who returned with him to his country. Though never his wife, she became the mother of his four sons, and remained loyal to him to his death. Like other Latin-American dictators, López employed artists to make portraits and busts of him, all in the pattern of the Napoleon he hoped to be. These, like the model of the Napoleonic crown, were shipped to Paraguay; most of them, unlike the crown, reached Asunción in safety. When López returned from Europe, he felt he was ready to become an emperor.

Once López came to office, he worked to make Paraguay the great power of which he and Madame Lynch had dreamed. In Europe he had made plans for a huge building program. He would build a great cathedral, a vast theatre, and a splendid palace. The palace would become the home of the daughter of a great emperor whom he would invite to become his own empress. If López were to become the ruler of a great empire in South America, he must have the recognition of the emperor of Brazil, Dom Pedro II. If López were to be an emperor, he must have as his wife a princess of royal blood. Thus he offered to marry Isabel, the daughter of Dom Pedro. The vanity of the half-blood, López, was great enough for such an offer. But, Dom Pedro was not interested, and refused even to answer.

This humiliation at the hands of the Brazilian emperor was too much for López' pride. He turned now to the strengthening of Paraguay's military defenses. He improved railroads, steamship lines, and telegraphs. He imported munitions, built forts in strategic places, and increased the army to fifty or sixty thousand men. He would create his empire without the approval of Dom Pedro. He would create his empire even by war against Brazil. In less than three years he felt prepared to lead his armies into war against, not one, but three of his neighbors. The great tragedy of Francisco Solano López and of Paraguay was under way.

The causes of the Paraguayan War are somewhat complex. For forty years, powerful Brazil had been interfering, sometimes with justice, in the affairs of its little southern neighbor, Uruguay. In 1864, a Brazilian army invaded Uruguay to restore to power the political "outs," the *Colorados* (the Reds). López immediately came to Uruguay's aid by sending an army into Central Brazil and by capturing a Brazilian river steamer. He gave no direct aid, however, to the Uruguayan "ins," the *Blancos* (the Whites). Later, López decided to attack the part of Brazil which lies just to the north of Uruguay. To do this he had to send troops across the northeastern part of Argentina. Although Argentina refused permission, he sent his armies on their way. Now López was at war with the two most powerful countries of South America. Meanwhile, the *Colorados* had become the "ins" in Uruguay, and they too declared war on Paraguay. On May 1, 1865, these three nations—Argentina, Brazil, and Uruguay—formed a triple alliance, and resolved to fight together until López was exterminated. They agreed to force Paraguay to bear the total cost of the war and to give up whatever portions of its territory they wished. The poor people of Paraguay were now to pay the price of the follies of their ruler, but not without a bloody, five-year struggle.

Not all of the advantages in this war were on the side of the allies. The ability of the Paraguayans to hold out for five long years of fighting is proof of their courage and their thorough preparedness. López' army was composed of well-trained men, ready to follow his every command. This force, at the beginning of the war at least, greatly outnumbered the sixteen thousand soldiers of Brazil and the smaller armies of Argentina and Uruguay. To aid this army the Paraguayans had constructed a mighty fortress at Humaitá on the Argentine frontier at the junction of the Rivers Paraná and Paraguay. Moreover, because he knew that both Argentina and Brazil were torn by internal quarrels, López planned on a quick victory.

In counting on a short war, however, López had erred.

But he erred no more than the allied leaders who were confident that Paraguayan resistance could quickly be beaten down. Asunción, they thought, could be captured within three months. During the first year of the war Paraguay suffered defeats, but all on foreign soil. When the allies tried to storm the fortress of Humaitá in 1866, they lost four thousand men, the Paraguayans, only two hundred and fifty. The war then settled down into a long, exhausting conflict. Foreign governments, including that of the United States, tried several times to halt the fighting, but always without success. Not until 1868 did Paraguay surrender its "Gibraltar" at Humaitá. Even after the loss of that stronghold, the Paraguayans were not ready to quit. The allies required another six months to work their way up the Paraguay River to enter the capital of Asunción. "Conquest or death!" was the battle cry of the men of López, and often the latter alternative was grimly real as the general tortured or executed officers for losing a battle, or shot men who were willing to surrender.

The fall of Asunción might well have concluded the war. With its capture Paraguay was doomed. Its armies had been cut to pieces. Most of the able-bodied men in the country had been killed, and now the armies were made up largely of boys, old men, and even women. Because hospital facilities were inadequate, many died needlessly. The non-fighting population suffered almost as bitterly as the soldiers, for there were insufficient workers to raise the crops and carry on other necessary work. Hunger and disease gripped the entire country. Still López was true to his slogan, "Conquest or death!" Retreating slowly to the north, fighting as he went, he led his army over bad roads and through swamps and jungles. Men and women, young and old, strong and weak, staggered loyally after him, stealing food, fighting battles, dying as they went.

Not until March, 1870, were the last pitiful shreds of his armies cut down, and the general himself slain on the battle-field. The five years of carnage were at an end. The survivors of the war, starved and shattered, could begin to breathe again and to hope for better times.

In the following June, the allies signed a treaty of peace with a temporary government which had been set up after the fall of Asunción. By this treaty the prostrate people of Paraguay were required to support enemy soldiers in their midst for several years and to pay the entire cost of the war. (The payment of this indemnity, however, was never pressed.) Brazil took a large section of territory in Northern Paraguay, and Argentina exacted two generous portions in the southern part. Argentina also claimed more land farther to the north, but agreed to submit this to the arbitration of the president of the United States. In 1878, President Ruther-ford Hayes awarded this portion to Paraguay. To express their appreciation to President Hayes, the government of Paraguay changed the name of a village to Villa Hayes, a name it still bears.

In the misery and prostration of his people, then, terminated the grand dreams of Francisco Solano López. In the five years of tragedy, the population of his country had been re-duced from over a million to perhaps a quarter of that num-ber. Of these, no more than 10 per cent were males. López had been responsible for the shooting of his brothers, the torturing of his mother, and the execution of many of his of-ficers and men. He had brought starvation, disease, and poverty upon his people. He had all but wiped out an entire nation.

But the distressed people of Paraguay were heroic in peace as in war. They turned to work in field and shop to rebuild their shattered nation. Bravely and loyally, they struggled to find a new morale, enduring depression, revolts, and bad government. Slowly, crops began to increase, factories were opened, and the population grew. Nevertheless, Paraguay sadly needed leadership—the leadership of which it had been robbed by the loss of its ablest sons in the needless war of López.

Unfortunately for Paraguay, that leadership never came, at least not the kind of leadership that could prevent the country—many years later—from being dragged into another terrible war. This was the war with Bolivia (1932-1935) over the unknown swamplands of the Chaco. Although by no means as disastrous as the earlier war, it was still a bitter dose for Paraguay to swallow. Today again, therefore, the persecuted people of this little nation are earnestly trying to recover from disaster. Again they need and wish for a leader who can give them new hope.

Other wars there have been between the nations of Latin America. The War of the Pacific (1879-1883) between Chile, on the one hand, and Peru and Bolivia, on the other, is best known, but no other Latin-American people has suffered so cruelly as the Paraguayan. Serious wars, however, have been growing less frequent, and, except for the War of the Gran Chaco, there has been none since 1884. Perhaps, in Latin America, the day of cruel, ambitious dictators like Francisco Solano López is drawing to a close. The model of Napoleon's crown in Buenos Aires, therefore, is a kind of symbol of their disappearance.

CHAPTER XIV

DOM PEDRO II: NEW WORLD EMPEROR

Cannons boomed on December 2, 1825, in the little Brazilian capital of Rio de Janeiro. Again and again for several days the cannonading echoed through the hills surrounding Rio's lovely bay, and for a week gay people rollicked in the illumined parks and plazas. The *cariocas* (residents of Rio de Janeiro) of all races were celebrating the arrival of an emperor—or rather an emperor-to-be, for he was still only a newborn baby.

Within a week the baby was baptized in the National Cathedral—with water from the River Jordan. His proud father, Dom Pedro I, carried him, and his eldest sister, Maria da Gloria, although only six, was his godmother. He was given a royal name, a very long name—Pedro de Alcántara João Carlos Leopoldo Salvador Bibiano Francisco Xavier de Paula Leocadio Miguel Gabriel Rafael Gonzaga. His blood was royal, too, for he was descended from many famous persons, including Charlemagne, Alfred the Great, William the Conqueror, Louis XIV, Ferdinand and Isabel, and Emperor Charles V of Spain. Not long after his baptism the little child was legally recognized as the heir apparent to the throne of Brazil. Sooner than anyone knew, Pedro de Alcántara would become Dom Pedro II, Emperor of Brazil, fifth largest country in the world.

One day in April, 1831, when Pedro was only five, cannons were again booming around the bay of Rio de Janeiro. Brightly-clad soldiers were drawn up near the royal palace, their muskets trimmed with the green and red berries of coffee plants. *Cariocas* by the hundreds moved about the royal gardens. Everywhere in the city were to be seen the blue, green, and gold of the national flag—blue for Brazil's clear skies, green for her growing plants, and gold for her fabulous wealth in minerals. As the crowds cried out, "Long live Dom Pedro II, Emperor of Brazil!" the little boy appeared on a balcony, where he stood on a chair so that he could see, and be seen. Pedro, too, displayed the national colors—the green was in his costume; the gold was in his hair; and the blue was in his eyes. He waved a handkerchief to thank his people for their cheers, although, in that exciting moment, he would have been much less happy if he could have known that his father was already out in the harbor, on an English warship, fleeing Brazil. Pedro de Alcántara, not yet six, was emperor of all Brazil.

An emperor in Brazil? Monarchy in the New World? Yes, strange though it may seem to those of us who think of the Western Hemisphere as the home of republics, there have been attempts to create monarchies here. Our neighbors, Mexico and the Negro people of Haiti, both tried government by kings, though unsuccessfully. Only in Brazil, of all the New World nations, was monarchy for a time successful, and there it endured sixty-seven years, roughly the lifetime of Pedro II. How can we, then, explain this rare event?

Brazil, largest of all nations in the New World (even larger than the U. S.!) was the only Portuguese colony in America. Soon after Columbus' first voyage, Portugal claimed and occupied Brazil, and continued to rule it as a vital part of the empire until after 1800. Then Napoleon's invasion of Spain and Portugal—the same event which set off the independence movement in the Spanish colonies—led to a series of changes in Brazil. When the armies of Napoleon occupied Lisbon (1807), the royal family of Portugal hastily fled to their greatest possession, Brazil. Here, in Rio de Janeiro, the people greeted Prince John as "Emperor of Brazil," although he was really only regent of Portugal, ruling for his insane mother.

Regent John, upon the death of his mother in 1816, became King John VI, ruler of the *United* Kingdom of Portugal and Brazil. Meanwhile, he had been giving attention to Brazil's many needs. He permitted friendly nations to trade in Brazilian ports for the first time, and, in order that commerce might increase, he aided industry, agriculture, and transportation. He brought in printing presses, started the Bank of Brazil, and established schools, a public library, and a botanical garden which has become one of the world's finest. Nevertheless, all of these improvements were expensive, as were the wars in which John engaged. Taxes rose, and the Brazilians began to grumble about their ruler. By 1820 affairs were going badly in Portugal, too, and in April of the next year John left his son, Pedro, as regent of Brazil, and he himself sailed off to the mother country.

Dom Pedro, however, was not long to remain mere regent. Desire for complete separation speedily developed among the Brazilians, sentiment which Pedro determined to guide. He made their cause his cause, and his wife, Leopoldina, furnished inspiration. In a letter, she challenged him: "The apple is ripe. Harvest it now, or it will rot!"[1] He was equal to the challenge. On September 7, 1822, while riding along the little Ypiranga River, he suddenly reined his horse, stripped

[1] Quoted from Chapman, *op. cit.*, p. 306.

from his uniform the Portuguese emblems and shouted: "It is time! . . . Independence or death! We are separated from Portugal!"[2] It was the *Grito do Ypiranga* ("Cry of Ypiranga"), Brazil's declaration of independence. The days of Regent Pedro were over. Within a month he was proclaimed Pedro I, Emperor of Brazil. Unlike the Spanish colonies, Brazil had won its independence without war, without bloodshed, even without expense. Moreover, it was to become a stable nation without the endless quarrels over leaders and government which were so common in all the new Spanish nations.

The emperor of Brazil was to be a constitutional emperor, much like the king of England. The leaders who drafted the constitution of 1823 saw to that. Laws were to be made by an assembly of two houses. The lower house, like our House of Representatives, was to be elected—but for four years, not two. The upper house was to be made up of senators appointed by the emperor and serving for life, like the English House of Lords. Along with these somewhat democratic features, the emperor was given great powers, including those of calling the assembly, dismissing the lower house, and vetoing any bill he wished. There was to be a judicial power separate from the other branches. The Roman Catholic religion was to be state-supported, although there was toleration for all others. There were guaranties of personal liberties, much as in our bill of rights. This, in brief, was the constitution under which Brazil was to live for sixty-five years, that is, until the fall of the monarchy and the close of the reign of Dom Pedro II.

Thus, without bickering, the Brazilians settled upon lead-

[2] Quoted from Mary Wilhelmine Williams, *Dom Pedro, The Magnanimous* (Chapel Hill, University of North Carolina Press, 1937), p. 7.

ers and the type of government they wished. Other nations were quick to give official recognition to the new monarchy, the United States first of all. Brazil seemed to be moving steadily along the path toward national unity and order. Still, ruling the sprawling provinces of Brazil was no easy task for Dom Pedro I, for beneath the seeming order there were dissensions. Dissensions on the part of some provinces and political groups led to outright opposition. Gradually, Pedro found his hold on the people slipping, and, finally, when his army deserted him on April 7, 1831, he resigned his throne in favor of his young son. This was the occasion, as we have already seen, which the people of Rio de Janeiro celebrated so enthusiastically.

Dom Pedro II was only five, hardly old enough to be a ruler of five million people. Older persons, therefore, must serve as his regents until he had time to mature and to be trained in the ways of ruling. Because his father was in exile and his mother died when Pedro was only nine, teachers were placed in charge of his education. One of the first of these was Dona Marianna, a strict but kindly woman, whom he came to love almost as a mother. Pedro received most of his formal education, however, from a man, José Bonifacio de Andrada e Silva. Under this firm but sympathetic teacher, the boy had to follow a carefully regulated program. There were appointed times when he must go to mass, read, be read to, study, play, and practice conversation. Before he was fourteen he could read, write, and speak both English and French, could translate Latin, and had read some of the novels of Sir Walter Scott. He was studying German, philosophy, history, geography, and the natural sciences. With all this, there was still time for taking lessons on the piano and other musical instruments and for trying his hand at art.

Dom Pedro was also learning to be a king during these years of his regency (1831-1840). One of his textbooks contained the following advice to "kings": "Love your people as your children; taste the pleasure of being loved by them; and so act that they will never reflect upon their peace and joy without remembering that these rich gifts have come from a good king." When studying French and English, he sometimes had to copy mottoes like these: "Let us think before we speak." "Let us do unto others that which we wish them to do unto us." "Greatness includes simplicity, unity, and majesty."[3] Very early in his boyhood, therefore, Pedro was learning the principles of justice and fair play. Besides his bookwork, Pedro sometimes had to review troops, receive foreign diplomats, and dedicate public buildings. His was indeed a busy boyhood.

By the time Dom Pedro was fifteen, his closest advisers deemed it wise that he become emperor in fact. For some time the young man had been watching with anxiety the troubles of his people under the regency. He was intelligent enough to know that he was too young and inexperienced to solve all the problems that faced his country, but he knew, too, that worse troubles might come if he waited longer. On July 23, 1840, therefore, the fifteen-year-old boy became the ruling emperor of a vast nation. For the third time in his very young life he was the object of enthusiastic celebration; again there were flags, fireworks, music, and church services.

Now, as emperor, it was necessary that Dom Pedro have a wife, one who would bring him an heir to the throne. Princess Thereza of the House of Austria was selected for him, and, without ever having seen each other, they were married, she

[3] All quotations in this paragraph are taken from Williams, *op. cit.*, pp. 37, 38.

being in Naples and he in Rio de Janeiro. Even at seventeen, however, Dom Pedro knew the kind of wife he wanted, and Thereza was not exactly that kind. She was short and slightly lame, by no means as attractive as he had hoped. Yet, the marriage contract fulfilled, he remained faithful to her all his life, respecting and esteeming her character. Four children came to the royal couple, the last of whom, a boy, was named Pedro. The family was able to spend much time together, especially during the summers when they moved to Petropolis, high up in the mountains forty miles from Rio de Janeiro. Whether in the capital or in Petropolis, the emperor continued his studies, rode horseback when he could, and strolled about a great deal, talking with people or shopping in the markets. He was now, at twenty-three, a full-grown man, at least six feet and three inches tall, handsome and dignified. Now, at last, Dom Pedro II was really ready to be an emperor.

The country which the emperor now sought to unify and strengthen sprawled over more than half the continent of South America. It was a tropical country, with much of its area overrun by the crawling jungle, a jungle of rubber trees, mahogany trees, trees of many kinds. Part of the country was mountainous, with mines of gold, silver, and precious stones. The southern section was a plateau, splendidly suited to the growing of coffee, corn, cereals, and the raising of cattle. Brazil was rich, unbelievably rich. Yet it needed people who could develop its wealth; there were only seven or eight million. It needed better transportation; there were no railroads and few steamboats. It needed more schools; more than 90 per cent of the people could not read and write. Brazil needed many things, but all these would come—in due time—and, meanwhile, the Brazilians, happy and carefree, were enjoying what they had.

The Harbor of Rio de Janeiro, undoubtedly one of the most beautiful in the world. The peak at center right of picture is Sugar Loaf Rock.

Independence Monument in São Paulo, Brazil. It was on this spot that Dom Pedro I is supposed to have shouted the *Grito do Ypiranga*—"Independence or Death!"—Brazil's declaration of independence from Portugal.

Dom Pedro II, Emperor of Brazil.

It would be a little more truthful to say that most Brazilians were happy and carefree, for in some of the provinces, especially in the far north and in the far south, there were revolutionaries who did not wish to come under the rule of the young emperor. Some of these continued to make trouble for years, and not until 1848 was order established in the whole of Brazil. During the next forty years Brazil was normally peaceful within, although it fought two foreign wars. One of these (in 1851-1852) was against Rosas, the Argentine dictator; the other was the bitter struggle against Paraguay. (This we have studied in the chapter on "López.") The latter conflict was a great tragedy to Brazil, for it cost over three hundred million dollars and fifty thousand lives. There were other problems of foreign policy, too, but all were settled peaceably. In fact, after the war with Paraguay, Brazil tended to settle its international disputes by peaceful means, a tendency which Dom Pedro encouraged.

After the close of the Paraguayan War, Brazil was more united and more peaceful than it had ever been. For this reason, Dom Pedro decided that the time had come for him to see other lands, about which he had read and talked so much. The Chamber of Deputies offered to give him special funds and to permit Brazilian warships to escort his vessel, but the emperor preferred to travel as a private citizen. On this first trip abroad, in 1871-1872, he visited most of the countries of Western Europe, even going as far as Egypt. He talked with interesting people, including Pope Pius IX and Queen Victoria, and enjoyed ten full months of sightseeing.

Three years after his return from this trip, Dom Pedro got another attack of the "wanderlust." This time he wished to see the United States. For more than a year in 1876-1877, the emperor and empress traveled about the United States:

from New York to Salt Lake City and California—back to
Chicago, Washington, and Philadelphia—out to St. Louis
and down the Mississippi to New Orleans—back north to
Niagara Falls and the Thousand Islands—to Montreal, to
Boston, and again to Philadelphia. The American people
came to admire the democratic emperor and his wife. They
became accustomed to Pedro's black "Prince Albert" coat, and
autograph-seekers besieged him. People liked to see the royal
couple ride in the familiar horse-drawn hacks of that day.
The emperor came to like the United States, too, improved
his use of English, and even picked up a bit of American
slang. Once, when a newspaper man, James J. O'Kelly, commented on the extent of his travels, Dom Pedro was ready
with a reply.

"Your Majesty means to accomplish a great deal in a short
time," remarked O'Kelly.

"Yes, I am always go-ahead."

"In fact, Your Majesty is quite a Yankee."

"Yes. Certainly I am a Yankee," said Dom Pedro. "I always go ahead."[4]

The emperor had many experiences on his tour, which
countless Americans would have felt privileged to enjoy. He
met and conversed with Longfellow (his favorite American
poet), Lowell, Emerson, Holmes, Whittier, and Louis Agassiz. He was presented to President Grant and visited Congress.
He was a frequent visitor at the Centennial Exposition at
Philadelphia, the "World's Fair" of 1876, where the telephone
was being exhibited for the first time. He picked up the
receiver and put it to his ear. Someone spoke at the other end,
and the emperor exclaimed, "My God! It speaks!" When, with
his empress, Dom Pedro was ready to leave the United States,

---

[4] This incident is related in Williams, *op. cit.*, p. 189.

Brazil seemed a much more important country to Americans than it had a year earlier. One newspaper even called him "Our Yankee Emperor."

Back home from these two tours and from another which he took to Northern and Eastern Europe in 1877, Dom Pedro gave increasing attention to the security and welfare of his own people. Having learned about the rest of the world from his travels, he hoped to benefit his countrymen by transmitting to them the fruits of his journeys. He arranged the founding of normal schools to train teachers and the establishment of schools of medicine, law, pharmacy, mines, agriculture, and music. Primary education received attention, so that the number of people who could read might be increased above 10 per cent. During the last thirty years of his reign the number of primary pupils increased from seventy thousand to more than two hundred and thirteen thousand, still a pitifully small number. Sometimes Pedro visited schoolrooms and actually conducted classes himself. This he had no trouble in doing, for he knew much about a great many subjects. He could read fourteen languages, and speak at least eight. He translated several books of the Bible from Hebrew into Latin, and knew enough of astronomy, botany, history, and geography to be able to teach them. In fact, Dom Pedro sometimes seemed more professor than emperor.

Dom Pedro knew that, above all, Brazil needed men—men to till the vast lands, men to work the rich mines, and men to fell the valuable trees. Therefore, he encouraged immigrants to settle in Brazil. In 1870 only nine thousand came, but in 1888 there was a wave of one hundred and thirty-one thousand. These were largely Germans, Italians, and Portuguese, although from the United States came some Southerners. Thus, with more workers, more railroads, and more telegraph lines, it was possible to grow more coffee, more cattle, more cotton and sugar, and all the other many crops Brazil was capable of producing. Commerce increased, and with it, the prosperity of the people. In many ways, therefore, Dom Pedro was making his nation modern and progressive. The masses of the people, of course, were still poor and ignorant, but the upper classes were becoming more prosperous, better educated, and more progressive.

Nevertheless, with all his efforts to improve the lot of his people, all was not well with Dom Pedro's Brazil. Underneath the surface calm there were rumors and rumblings of discontent, which, toward the end of his reign, began to break out into the open. The main groups of dissatisfaction were four: the church, the army, the republicans, and the slaveholders. The church had been offended because it thought the emperor had not been vigorous enough in expelling Free Masons from certain men's societies in the local churches. Moreover, although the church could not question the sincerity of his religious beliefs, it was skeptical of his broad views. The army officers were hostile, because, after the Paraguayan War, Dom Pedro had become decidedly pacifist and refused to give to the army the superior position in the nation which its leaders wished. Gradually after 1870, those who favored a republic in Brazil began to speak out, and by 1889 they had formed a well-organized party.

The opposition which finally turned the tide against Dom Pedro came from the slaveholding landowners. In 1853 there were as many as three million slaves in Brazil, almost a third of the population. Through the freeing of all children born to slave mothers (Law of 1871), this number had fallen to less than a million by 1888. Slavery was well on its way out by that time. However, while the emperor was absent in

Europe, his daughter, the Princess Isabel, ruling in his place, succeeded in getting a law passed which provided complete emancipation without any compensation. This act was the final straw. The smoldering protest against Dom Pedro which had been gaining ground for twenty years now broke into the open. Leaders of the four groups—churchmen, generals, republicans, slaveholders—engineered a plot against the emperor and his monarchy.

The plot developed, discontent spread, and by November 15, 1889, the plotters felt strong enough to seize the emperor and demand his resignation. The army of Dom Pedro had gone over to the revolutionaries. There was no shooting, practically no bloodshed. Neither Dom Pedro nor his family suffered harm. They at once realized that their days of happiness in the Brazil they loved were at an end. They agreed to leave the country quietly. On the ship bound for Lisbon, the emperor passed his sixty-fourth birthday. There was no party, but from his three little grandsons he received this note:

Dear Grand Daddy: We have no flowers here to offer you on this day which is so dear to us; but, as always, we offer you our hearts.

Your little grandsons, who love you very much,

Pedro,
Luiz,
Antonio.[5]

Meanwhile, but very slowly, back in Brazil the republic was making progress. In 1891, a constitution was adopted for a federal republic to be called the "United States," that is, the "United States of Brazil." The new constitution was a very close copy of that of the United States, that is, the United

[5] Quoted in Williams, *op. cit.*, p. 357.

States of America. Brazil now, after nearly seventy years of government by monarchs, was to try government by presidents.

In Portugal and France, Dom Pedro, heartbroken at the turn of affairs in Brazil, had only a short time to endure exile. His wife died within three weeks after their arrival in Lisbon, and he, grieved and afflicted, followed her in two years. In 1920 the government of Brazil decided to have the bodies of the empress and emperor brought back to Brazil. This was done, and they were placed in a little church in Petropolis, where Dom Pedro had spent so many pleasant summers with his children and friends. There, today, loyal Brazilians pay homage to their great emperor, the greatest Brazilian, and one of the greatest men of the Western Hemisphere. They love him still because he was human, understanding, and democratic.

CHAPTER XV

PORFIRIO DÍAZ: MAN OF MILLIONAIRES AND MISERY

"Can the Ethiopian change his skin or the leopard his spots?" The manner of asking this Biblical question clearly suggests a negative answer. Without hesitation one would also say, "No," to the query, "Can a genuine patriot and a lover of his country become its dictator and the oppressor of its people?" Yet the career of Porfirio Díaz, of Mexico, goes far toward proving that it is possible. Up to a certain point Díaz' life was devoted, often at the risk of death, to supporting a system of liberal government and defending his country against foreign aggression. From that point, personal ambition and a thirst for power overcame the spirit of devotion to country, and Díaz developed into a lawless revolutionist and then a dictator—a bloody dictator who ordered the death of thousands of Mexicans and added to the misery of millions of others. Did he change his spots, or did his later career merely reveal him in his true character? The story of his life suggests the answer.

Oaxaca, the city of Porfirio Díaz' birth, lies in an elevated valley among the mountains due south of the nation's capital. Díaz' tribe was the Mixtec. Though largely Indian, Díaz possessed some Spanish blood. The infant Porfirio was baptized on September 15, 1830, the twentieth anniversary of the beginning of Mexico's war for independence from Spain. Like the stones of his Mixtecan country, Porfirio's early years were hard, since his father had very small means and died when Porfirio was an infant. The boy, when he was old enough, assisted his mother with the small inn which she kept and did odd jobs to earn a few *centavos*. He was industrious and determined in whatever he undertook. His mother had ambitions for him and made sacrifices to send him to elementary school, and later to a Catholic seminary to prepare him for the priesthood.

However, the clerical life was not for Díaz. About the time when he was to finish at the seminary and enter the priesthood, he became acquainted with the family of Marcos Pérez, a lawyer and professor of law in the non-sectarian Institute of Arts and Sciences of Oaxaca. Díaz, invited to visit the Institute, was impressed with its liberal system as compared to that of the church school in which he was studying. This was a fateful point in Díaz' life. He had never felt a genuine enthusiasm for the church career and now, after much serious thinking, he decided he could not follow it. Much to the distress of his mother, who was too wise to make serious objection, he quit his clerical studies and entered the Institute to study law. There he spent the next five years. One of his teachers was Benito Juárez, Zapotec Indian from Díaz' own section of Mexico. It does not appear that Díaz at any time applied himself very seriously to his studies. To the end of his life his grammar and his spelling were bad. (In this weakness he resembled our Andrew Jackson. Neither seems to have held with the Indianans of *The Hoosier Schoolmaster* that "the chief end of man was to learn to spell.")

During Díaz' childhood and school years, Mexico was going through a distressful period. Since its people lacked political experience and truly patriotic leaders, the government was made an instrument of personal gain and personal ambition. For twenty-five years after 1830 the most prominent man in Mexico, though by no means the best, was General López de Santa Anna. Nine times this man was president of Mexico, though he seldom served out a full elective term. Several times he was not elected, but rather *took* the office. At different times he was on every side of every important public question. Indeed, he often approached the seeming impossibility of being on both sides at the same time. He was a veritable political chameleon. No consistent progress of any sort could be made under the "leadership" of such a man. Mexico was continually in an uproar. At the worst period came the war with the United States when the country lost two-fifths of its territory. The times called urgently for a leader but, until the mid-fifties, no leader appeared. At that point Benito Juárez left the governorship of Oaxaca and stepped upon the national stage. In one of the many political overturns of the times, Santa Anna was driven from the country—and a good riddance!

Juárez was a democratic liberal and an anti-clerical. He wished to see a democratic government in Mexico, one that should manage the nation for the people and not for a small group of spoilsmen. He wanted also to secure the distribution of church lands among the landless peons. Mexico's church was perhaps the most conservative, the least social-minded, to be found anywhere in Catholic Christendom. When Díaz was born the church possessed some 40 per cent of the privately-owned land of Mexico. For more than three hundred years the church had held a highly privileged place in Mexican society and had been very influential in the government. The army vied with the church for position and privilege.

Priests and generals have been throughout Mexico's history, at any rate until very recently, the greatest obstacles to the development of political and economic democracy.

To correct this situation, Juárez and his supporters sponsored a series of laws. They deprived the church and the army of their special courts. They made marriage, burial, and the registration of births and deaths civil functions, and obliged the church to sell its lands, that is, that part of it which was not needed for buildings of the church. The content of these Laws of Reform was embodied in a constitution which was adopted in 1857.

Church and army leaders and, in general, the wealthy of the country, objected very sharply to these measures. They organized an opposition, with the Pope's blessing, and soon a civil war, the War of the Reform, broke out. It was almost as extended as, and perhaps even more terrible and injurious than, our own Civil War, which began just at the end of Mexico's war. Juárez, who had been elected president under the new constitution, was forced very early to abandon the capital. For three years he maintained a government in various cities in the northern section of the country, often close to our border. He was chased about "from pillar to post" until 1860 when, having defeated the revolutionists, he regained the capital.

In these years Díaz, a young and daring leader, performed heroic and efficient service for the liberal cause in the region south of the capital. Wounded often, at times leading his troops while suffering from malaria, he proved himself a brave and skillful warrior. At this stage his fidelity to President Juárez and the cause of reform were not in the slightest degree questioned. In this period were passed the Reform Laws of 1859, which declared confiscated the property of the church. These measures were taken because the church was doing everything in its power to aid the revolution.

When the anti-reform revolution was put down after so much waste and bloodshed, Juárez found himself back at the capital, still at the head of a liberal government. The country was in a terrible state. Disorganization and want were everywhere. Business was at a standstill. Little revenue was available to pay the necessary expenses of government. The foreign debt was large, the payments burdensome. It was found impossible to meet them, so for the time being they were declared suspended. The governments of France, England, and Spain decided to send in their bills and force Mexico to pay. They would get blood out of the Mexican turnip. This was the beginning of the French occupation and the empire of Maximilian. After Mexico had made a satisfactory adjustment, English and Spanish troops were withdrawn, but the French soldiers remained. The French ruler, Emperor Napoleon III, wanted to prove himself a worthy nephew of his "glorious uncle." French troops took the capital and occupied a large portion of the country. Juárez was forced again to set out on his travels. A clique of Mexican generals and churchmen, with the support of Napoleon and the blessing of the Pope, invited Maximilian of Austria and his wife Carlota to wear imperial crowns in Mexico. They accepted and appeared in the country in 1864 in circumstances of as much pomp and panoply as could be arranged. The imperial court was established in Mexico City. But all the while Juárez maintained a republican government in some remote section of the country.

Again the patriot Díaz performed marvels of valor and skill in leading forces against the French and Maximilian. Twice he was captured and imprisoned. By great daring he escaped on both occasions and returned to the struggle. Again his theater of operations was the southern and southeastern region, that which embraced his home state of Oaxaca. Finally, owing to a number of factors—a dangerous political situation in Europe, the insistence of the United States, inability of Maximilian to pacify Mexico—Napoleon withdrew his army. This action was equivalent to signing Maximilian's death warrant, unless he should abandon the country. He refused to do so. Carlota hastened to Europe for aid but, refused assistance by both Napoleon and the Pope, she became insane and accomplished nothing. Maximilian could not maintain himself. His army was defeated, he was captured by the forces of Juárez—and shot. The Maximilian episode was ended. Juárez resumed his office in Mexico City, and the constitution once more was the law of the entire nation.

When Maximilian was executed, Juárez had already exercised the powers of the presidency for three years beyond his constitutional term. No election could be held during the war with the French. Now he sought and received reëlection. Juárez and Díaz at this time seem to have begun to distrust each other. This was not unnatural, for Díaz, the successful general, lacked respect for civilians, while Juárez, who considered militarism a curse of the country and wanted to stamp it out, had no liking for generals. Díaz felt that the president did not show him the regard nor give him the reward which his services deserved. Perhaps here is the point where the leopard began to change his spots.

When the presidential term approached its end in 1872, there remained much to do in reconstructing the country and establishing the principles of reform. Wishing to carry on with these matters and seeing around him no able man whom he could trust to be loyal to liberalism, Juárez sought reëlection. He offered Díaz a place on the ticket as vice-president, but the general refused and announced for the presidency. Nevertheless, in a close race, Juárez was reëlected. Then Díaz arose in revolt, proclaiming his opposition to "reëlection," a matter of which it is well to take special note. But the revolt went badly. It did not arouse the popular support for which Díaz hoped, and Juárez still had energy. Even Díaz' own state did not support him. His brother Félix was captured and killed—cruelly, since he himself had been most cruel. Every center of revolt was crushed, and Díaz found it necessary to go into hiding until he could make terms with the government to save his skin. Of Díaz at this juncture, Carleton Beals writes this paragraph:

And so, in bitterness, defeat and lust for power, Díaz descended to a pathetic level; Díaz, the one-time Liberal, the leader of a great anti-clerical movement, the man who had fought hundreds of battles and had embarked on revolution presumably to preserve the 1857 Constitution and the 1859 Reform Laws, now—to reach Lozada's fastness without being killed—disguised himself as a priest to ask aid from an ignorant fanatic who had denounced and fought against those laws for fifteen years. Díaz had proclaimed his love for law; now he appealed to a man who had violated every written and unwritten law.[1]

Is this the picture of a man of principles, a true patriot? Or is it the leopard changing his spots?

Unfortunately for Mexico, just after the Díaz revolt was smothered, President Juárez died. He was succeeded by the vice-president, Lerdo de Tejada. If Díaz could only have

---

[1] *Porfirio Díaz; Dictator of Mexico* (Philadelphia, J. B. Lippincott Company, 1933), p. 184. Lozada was an Indian chief, who had been able to maintain a sort of independence in a very remote and rugged section of Mexico.

foreseen the future when he was invited to be a candidate for the vice-presidency, he might now have been an honored president without the stain of treachery. Instead he was hiding in mountain fastnesses and negotiating with Lerdo for his safety. Many of Díaz' old comrades-in-arms regretted his action exceedingly. One of them wrote to him:

> General! What has happened to the soldier of the Republic and of Liberty? Where is the chief of democracy, who so many times . . . seated himself by my side in the shade of a tree and spoke to me with a voice tremulous with emotion of the fatherland and its hopes? . . . The highest head and the brow most circled with glory are most beautiful in a democracy when they incline with respect to the law.[2]

After the president had agreed to include Díaz in the general amnesty to revolutionists, which had been proclaimed, Díaz left his mountains and went to Mexico City. Refusing to take the post of president of the Supreme Court—or any other, for he wanted the presidency—he retired to a sugar plantation. The succeeding three years he spent there, prospering with his sugar business and laying his plans for securing the presidency in the next election—or before. By promises of future gain, he rallied about him all of the discontented—churchmen, supporters of Maximilian, dissatisfied army men.

In 1873, Díaz became a candidate for the Supreme Court position which he had previously scorned, demanding in his platform "abolition of all dictatorship." How ironical in the light of later history! He was roundly defeated. The president tried to get this center of political disturbance out of Mexico by offering him the post of minister to Germany. Díaz declined. He wanted to be president of Mexico. Again he set

[2] Quoted in *ibid.*, p. 188.

himself against the constituted authorities. He was unwilling to await the election and to run as a simple candidate. So, several months before the election was to have taken place, he drew a long document of charges against President Lerdo and placed himself at the head of an army. This time his plans were well made. Lerdo lacked the leadership of a Juárez, and his position was weak. Consequently, Díaz' stroke was successful. He shortly found himself with his army in Mexico City. A provisional government was organized, and an election was arranged. Measures were taken to assure the election of Díaz. Thus, near the end of 1876, the great "General of Reform" saw the fulfillment of his long-held ambition. He was president of Mexico.

From this point the story of Porfirio Díaz is the story of the longest dictatorship any Latin-American country has known. From 1876 to 1911, except for the period 1880-1884, when another man occupied the presidential chair with Díaz watchful on the side lines, Porfirio Díaz was president of Mexico. All of his criticisms of reëlection were forgotten— though he was careful to make his neglect of that matter constitutional by having the constitution amended to permit it.

The cause of Juárez, that cause of liberal government for which Díaz earlier had fought, had stood for democratic government and economic advances. Díaz disregarded the former point completely and concentrated on the latter. No democracy existed in Mexico in the years of the Díaz dictatorship. Díaz had accused Juárez and Lerdo of dominating elections and of interfering in the internal affairs of the states. In the Díaz period there was not a single election that could be called free. In fact, parties disappeared from the Mexican scene. State governors were the tools of Díaz. Nothing in Mexico was free from his dictatorial and absolute power. The courts were his. No man's person or property was secure if Díaz, or one of his friends, wanted it. If a democracy is to be successful, the people must have enlightenment. But Díaz did very little for the cause of education in Mexico, and with the country's wealth he *could* have done so much.

As for economic development, it may be said that something was accomplished. Foreign capital was invited into the country, and it entered on very advantageous terms. Among the railroading Americans who accepted and went in avid pursuit of dollars were Gould, Huntington, and Harriman. Mining properties were secured and developed by Hearst, the Guggenheims, and the United States Steel Corporation. Millions of acres of land were acquired by cattle men. About the turn of the century the oil men had their day. Edward L. Doheny was the leader. Standard Oil, Gulf Oil, and the Sinclair interests all had their innings. Total investments of citizens of the United States in Mexico in 1912 were placed at $1,077,000,000. Railroads, street railways, mines, power plants and power lines, telegraph and telephone lines, and many other businesses were taken over by foreign capital, not all of it by any means American. Mexico, on the surface at least, assumed the appearance of a modern country. Grand boulevards and showy public buildings were constructed in Mexico City and other centers of population. But all of this was for the small element of whites and *mestizos* in the cities. The great majority of Mexico's population, the ten million Indians in the rural sections, were not reached. Their lot became more distressing than ever. It was as if, to use the figure of a Mexican scholar, "palaces were built on garbage heaps." The profits of industrial development were absorbed by the friends of Díaz. It was they who controlled the banks, who enjoyed the rich graft that was made possible by their

A Mexican market place near Mexico City. Indians like this did not share in the Díaz prosperity.

Statue of Simón Bolívar in the Plaza of Caracas. Here in 1813 he made a triumphal entry as the "Liberator of Venezuela."

A modern Argentine school boy, in dust coat, riding a llama in the Buenos Aires Zoo.

Argentine soldiers on parade.

relations with foreign capitalists and the absolute power of the Díaz government. As to Díaz himself, in justice it must be said that he made little use of his position for monetary profit. Power satisfied him. He left the "financial pickings" for his army of officials, state and national.

The powerful, the moneyed, drew into their possession more and more of the land of Mexico. The humble Indians were deprived of almost all that remained to them. If they protested, armies were sent into the hills to burn and slay. The captured were sold into slavery in the henequen fields of Yucatán or condemned to semi-slavery elsewhere. *Rurales,* mounted national police, many of them reformed bandits, were instructed to shoot out of hand anyone caught committing a crime. Many innocent persons suffered at their hands. Díaz brought peace to Mexico, a most unaccustomed peace, it must be confessed. But, as many commentators have remarked, it was "the peace of the grave."

Díaz had declared his adherence to the Constitution of 1857 and the Reform Laws of 1859. But not long after he became president he married, as his second wife, a young Spanish-Mexican of good family, Carmen Romero Rubio, a devout Catholic. Under her influence, he ignored the laws respecting the ownership of land by the church, and much that had been accomplished by Juárez and Lerdo was undone. The church returned to a position of economic and political power, being exposed thereby to the temptation to neglect its spiritual functions. The economic condition of the peon became steadily worse, despite the brilliance of the picture presented by the scene at Mexico City where Díaz and, in the years after 1890, his financial wizard, José Ives Limantour, were performing their miracles of "progress."

As has been noted above, in 1912 Americans had investments in Mexico of more than a billion dollars. At that time 58 per cent of the oil, 68 per cent of the rubber business, 72 per cent of the country's smelters, and 78 per cent of its mines were owned by American capital. Foreigners of other nationalities also had huge holdings.

More than three-fourths of the Mexican people derived no benefit from these business activities. Indeed, in many ways their sad lot was made worse. When one reflects on this fact it is not hard to see that Díaz was building up for a tremendous earthquake at the future date when his stone heart and his iron hand should no longer be strong enough to control the depressed ones.

The nation-shaking earthquake came. Díaz had killed or persecuted into silence the most intelligent and most liberal part of the Mexican people. He had corrupted another large element by giving men opportunity for dishonest gain in order to win their support. The army on which his control depended had grown weak and more corrupt than ever. And all the while the bitterness and hatred caused by his repressions were growing behind a giant dam that would some day burst. The fearful collapse came in 1910. At the age of eighty, after thirty-six years of complete dominance of the nation, Díaz still could not bear the thought of quitting power, and he again announced himself for reëlection. The nation could no longer tolerate his dictatorship, especially as it was evident that his powers were definitely waning. Then came the revolution. After trying every possible ruse to stop it, old Porfirio had to bow and to quit the country whose sum total of happiness he had done so little to increase. He retired in 1911 to Paris. There he lived four years more, dying just as the great storm of fire and blood was breaking in Europe.

In his own Mexico, the hurricane which blew him from the

country was destined to rage with fury for ten long years. And for twenty years more, other Mexicans were trying to undo the work of Díaz—to secure for the people a just share of their own wealth, to equalize somewhat the terribly distorted economy of the country, to redistribute to millions of the humble the land which Díaz had permitted his favorites to gather into their claws, and to develop a condition that would make possible a genuine democratic system for Mexico's millions, both high and low. The tragedy is that Díaz, with his great power and Mexico's resources, could have done so much good for the people. But he was blind to his opportunities. "Where there is no vision the people perish."

CHAPTER XVI

JUAN VICENTE GÓMEZ: A DICTATOR IN OIL

A half-breed Indian stood beside the statue of Simón Bolívar in the Plaza of Caracas, capital of Venezuela. It was the evening of October 26, 1899. Silently, but thoughtfully, he watched the throbbing crowds that overflowed the open square into the cobblestone streets beyond. Never before had he visited a large city, with modern buildings, horse-cars, and gas lights. Never had he worn a pair of shoes, nor seen fashionably-dressed ladies, riding about in elegant carriages. Unnoticed, but not unknowing, the Indian missed no detail.

He was much less interested than were the city people, however, in the strange parade which moved through the crowded streets. He already knew that the general who rode at the head of the parade was Cipriano Castro, now the strongest man in all Venezuela. He knew that the general's army of ten thousand ragged mountaineers had grown miraculously from a handful of sixty in barely six months. He knew that, to reach Caracas, many of the soldiers had marched and battled their way seven hundred and fifty miles, sometimes through high, dangerous passes of the Andes. He knew that the Indian women who followed the army through the streets, driving their burros and goats, carrying chickens and cooking utensils, had loyally fed the army on the march.

All these things the Indian knew, because, with relatives

214

and close friends, he had organized the original band of sixty who pledged themselves to General Castro. He had marched with the army, through mountain cold and valley heat, all the way from the borders of Colombia. His special job had been to feed and arm the soldiers on the march. He had gambled his life's savings of thirty thousand *bolívars* (about six thousand dollars) on this adventure. Now, from his vantage point beside the statue of his country's greatest hero, he was relishing the fruits of his gamble.

This half-breed Indian, dressed in the wide hat and the *ruana* (a blanket-like cloak with a slit in the middle for the head) of his people, was Juan Vicente Gómez. Only a few months before he had sold his landholdings over the border in Colombia in order to cast his lot with Castro and the budding revolution. Then he still cooked his food over an open fire and ate from gourds. He had never seen a city or sailed the sea. He could read and write but little; he knew a smattering of bookkeeping. Gómez' rise to power from this humble position was astonishing. Within eight years he was to be vice-president, commander-in-chief of the army, provisional president, and, finally, dictator of Venezuela. From 1908 to 1935, he would rule with an iron hand, master of the people and the wealth of his country. For twenty-seven years— longer than any other dictator of South America—he would keep himself in power. Only death itself would be strong enough to unseat him.

When Juan Vicente Gómez first saw the gas lights and gay ladies of Caracas that October evening in 1899, he was forty-two years old. Most of those years he had spent as a **hard**-working cattleman in the rugged mountain country of Western Venezuela and Eastern Colombia. These mountains are a part of the mighty Andes, which stretch, fortress-like, all along the Pacific shores of South America from Cape Horn to Panama. At a point on the border of Venezuela and Colombia the Andes split into a kind of Y, one wing turning northwestward toward the Isthmus of Panama, the other bending northeastward toward Caracas and the Caribbean Sea. In the mouth of the Y is the huge Lake Maracaibo, with its fabulous oil deposits.

To the east and south of Gómez' mountains stretches the basin of the Orinoco River and its branches. Much of this great valley (it occupies two-thirds of Venezuela) is composed of gently sloping table-lands, green with waving grass in the rainy season (May to October), sere and brown in the dry season. These plains, called the *llanos*, are the home of Venezuela's livestock industry, although the cattle must struggle against the perpetual heat, the dry season, the insect pests, and the deadly reptiles. On the *llanos* lived the plainsmen who furnished much of the strength in men and money which kept in power Gómez and other Venezuelan overlords.

When Columbus sailed along the coast of Venezuela on his third voyage (1498), the Indians who lived there, like those on the Caribbean islands, were mainly of the Carib family. (The Caribbean Sea was named after them.) During the next four centuries, with the settlement of the Spanish and the introduction of Negro slaves, the population of Venezuela became as thoroughly mixed as any in all Latin America. The real Venezuelan of today, therefore, may be part white, part Indian, and part Negro, or simply *mestizo*. This mixed race has produced a great artist or two, seven leading generals of the wars for independence, and the first presidents of five South American republics. It produced

Miranda and the great Bolívar. Juan Vicente Gómez, too, was a Venezuelan *mestizo*.

There are many reasons, therefore, why Venezuela, throughout the nineteenth century, was a country difficult to govern. The mountains, the flooding rivers, and the swampy jungles made troublesome and expensive the construction of roads and railroads. The mixed population, largely illiterate and widely scattered, could not easily be united under a democratic government. Moreover, no area of South America suffered such heavy losses in the struggle for independence. Perhaps three hundred thousand people lost their lives on the battlefields, in the terrible earthquake of 1812, or from disease and famine. The wars cost the exhausted people more than nineteen million dollars.

During the first century of their independence the people of Venezuela never enjoyed peace and order for any extended period. There were scores of revolutions, large and small, and at least fourteen constitutions. Dictators, one after another, paraded in and out of the presidency. Only a few remained in office long enough to establish constructive programs for their country, and most only got themselves well-hated. For the residents of Caracas, therefore, there was little new in the invasion of General Castro and his ragged horde. The scene was familiar. Only the characters were different. Castro and his lieutenant, Gómez, hoped to succeed where others had failed. Castro and Gómez! These were the men— one or the other, or both—who were to rule Venezuela for the next thirty-six years.

Cipriano Castro brought to the people of Venezuela the unhappiest days they had known. Hardly more than a savage, though fairly well-educated, this swarthy little man ruled with greed and lust. He ate and drank too much, indulged in all manner of luxury and dissipation, and treated his opponents with ferocity. He robbed the National Treasury to pay for his own pleasures and to add to his personal fortune. When he refused to pay debts owed to European nations, Germany, Italy, and Great Britain blockaded Venezuelan ports. When his political opponents threatened revolution, Gómez was sent to crush them. Gómez never failed him. It was natural, therefore, that Castro, when he went to Europe in 1908 to seek expert medical aid for his broken health, should make his aide provisional president. Gómez, of course, accepted the appointment, knowing that his days of playing "second fiddle" to Castro were ended.

Gómez was now the strongest man in Venezuela. He had led victorious armies into all parts of the country. He had commanded war vessels. He had studied men and learned from them—and about them. He understood his country and his people. To many of them he was *brujo*, the "witch doctor," who could read their minds and who never forgot a thing he saw. The president was on a ship bound for Europe. Gómez was provisional president; he knew that he could be president whenever he chose. He waited only twenty-seven days to proclaim himself.

The new president immediately began to bring order into revolution-torn Venezuela. He invited able men to join him in planning the reconstruction of the country's national life. Like Mussolini, Stalin, and Hitler, in later years, he put an end to all political parties except his own. If Venezuela were to progress, political agitation must be crushed. Soon the prisons were filled with his opponents, and hundreds were driven into exile. Gómez began to rule as a dictator; he continued to rule as one for the next twenty-seven years.

During all his private and public life, Gómez had two

consuming ambitions: to gain power and to pile up wealth. These two aims, of course, were closely related, and he pursued them with such brute force that he created enemies in all parts of the country. Therefore, he first gave his attention to the army, organizing it in such a way that revolt against him was impossible. He placed his relatives or his mountaineer friends in key positions everywhere: in the generalcies, in charge of military garrisons and prisons, as presidents of the states and chiefs of the villages. Where revolt was most likely to flame forth he stationed additional troops.

The president himself lived the life of a soldier, both in his public appearances and in the privacy of his bare, barracks-like room. He rose early and retired early. He never used liquor or tobacco. He always wore a soldier's uniform. In the years before 1914, when he greatly admired Theodore Roosevelt, he dressed like the American, with boots, khaki breeches, and hat with upturned brim. Later, with Kaiser William II of Germany as his idol, he wore a spiked helmet, carried a sword, and turned his mustache upward. The uniforms and drill of the soldiers, too, responded to the tastes of General Gómez.

The dictator used terror and exile, as well as the army, to crush any who dared challenge his will. Those who came under his suspicion were executed, imprisoned, or cruelly tortured. They might be thrown into ancient prisons, crawling with insects and filthy with the dirt of years. They might be brutally punished with leg-irons, weighing twenty or more pounds, which cut into the tender flesh of the ankles. Some were racked until their bones broke or their organs were torn out. Only the more fortunate might be left to starve to death on tasteless gruel and bananas. Thousands went or were sent into exile and became perpetual conspirators. To keep these persons from plotting against him, he organized an international spy system which cost the country far more money than it spent on its schools. No person was safe from the "witch doctor." Not even Castro, the former president who had given Gómez his chance, was permitted to return to his homeland, although he tried on many occasions. He died, in exile, in 1924. By these methods did Gómez establish "peace and order" in Venezuela.

But Gómez was also attending to his second great ambition, that of gaining money, both for himself and for Venezuela. He had inherited from Castro an empty treasury and, what was worse, huge debts. Before his death in 1935, Gómez paid off the entire foreign debt, greatly reduced the domestic debt, and left a good-sized surplus in the national treasury. He established the currency of his country on a solid gold basis and encouraged the investment of nearly a billion dollars of foreign capital. Moreover, he reduced the taxes of the people and spent millions of dollars on public works, such as road-building, drainage and irrigation projects, and in aid to agriculture and local industries. In spite of war and depression, he made Venezuela unique in the world.

As soon as he entered office, Gómez undertook this vast program of financial reform. After 1914 he was greatly aided by the World War which increased the prices of the products Venezuela had to sell—coffee, hides, cotton, and cattle. Gold was already rolling into the country, when, in 1917, an oil boom began. Foreign companies, American, Dutch, and English—the Standard Oil Company, the Sun Oil Company, the Gulf Oil Company, the Texas Oil Company, the Atlantic Refining Company, Sinclair, the Royal Dutch Shell—came in to exploit the new-found riches of Lake Maracaibo. But Gómez saw to it that Venezuela got its share. An excellent oil law (1918) guaranteed to the nation a commission on every barrel of oil produced. As the oil flowed out of the country, the gold flowed in. By 1930 the revenue from the "black gold" rose to more than twenty-five million dollars, and in the same year Venezuela paid the last penny on its foreign debt.

While the foreign companies were getting rich from Venezuela's oil, President Gómez missed no opportunity to feather his own nest. The Oil Law required that one-half of each tract of land taken up by an oil company be turned over to the government. Mysteriously, these lands became the property of a company owned by Gómez, which then sold them back to the companies at fat profits. Oil, however, was only one business among many from which Gómez and his cronies took their profits. By methods legal or illegal dozens of *haciendas* fell into his hands, until he possessed a monopoly of the rich cattle industry. Then the huge estates were turned over to relatives, to friends, or to dummy corporations that seemed to represent the "best interests" of the nation.

Gradually Gómez and his clan got their fingers into almost every profitable business in the country. Monopolies were created by government order, and the president controlled the monopolies. Among these were the cotton business, butter and milk, paper, soap, and matches. Profits from the control of the lottery and gambling, from the manufacture and sale of liquors, from the making of cement, and from the salt industry went to Gómez or his henchmen. In the cities, especially Caracas, Gómez permitted relatives and friends to control moving-pictures, automobiles, furniture, drugs, and other lines of business. To all of these persons went special favors, such as freedom from taxes and import duties. Many of them became immensely wealthy, traveled in Europe and the

United States, educated their children abroad, and stored their fortunes in foreign cities. Because the national debts were reduced and the pockets of the leaders filled with gold, the Venezuelan Congress honored President Gómez with a title—*El Benemérito* (The Well-Deserving). Foreign governments, too—France, Belgium, and Holland—together with the Pope, gave him special honors. To the downtrodden people of Venezuela, however, these honors meant nothing. They knew Gómez for what he really was—a merciless, hateful old man.

El Benemérito was never so busy with politics and profits that he had no time for personal pleasures. When he tired of living in Caracas, he moved to his *hacienda* near the village of Maracay, sixty miles up into the mountains. Here he built a small industrial center to furnish supplies for his ranch and his guests—a cotton mill, a dairy, a soap factory, a slaughterhouse. There were a club, with swimming-pool and tennis courts, and a spacious hotel—to be used only by his friends—with four hundred rooms, modern baths, lounges, balconies, and a bar. He built broad boulevards and gardens, a bull-ring, and a zoo.

Maracay was cool, breezy, and far from the noises and dirt of Caracas. It also had the advantage of easy defense, especially since Gómez stationed there a number of military planes and fifteen thousand of his best troops. *El Benemérito* took no chances with those enemies who might be plotting against his government—or against his life.

As Gómez grew older, he spent more and more of his time at Maracay. Here he had everything he wished for the entertainment of his household and his guests. Here he could easily defend himself, if need should arise. From Maracay orders went to all parts of the nation—to put down a revolt, to torture a political prisoner, to build a new road, or a new hotel. To Maracay, over paved roads, came tourists and foreign dignitaries who saw only the good and realized little of the evil of the dictatorship. His children and grandchildren came to visit him. Although never married, he was the father of eighty or more children. Maracay became the capital of the nation, as well as the home of Gómez.

President Gómez was well into middle age when he came to power. He had said he wished to live and rule until he was a hundred. He did rule twenty-seven years, although, when he died in 1935, he still lacked twenty-two of reaching the age he wished. He died on the anniversary of the death of his hero, Bolívar, as he had been born on the birthday of the Liberator. (Both dates were probably falsified.) It was two days before the people could realize that the dictator was really gone. Then they danced into the Plaza of Caracas and, beside the statue of Bolívar, shouted, "The Catfish is dead! Viva la Libertad!" They tore his pictures from public places, destroyed his homes, and wrecked the theater and other buildings he had constructed. Scores of his relatives and his friends were driven from the country. The *brujo* was gone. The people were happy.

Nevertheless, Juan Vicente Gómez, the "Well-Deserving," had left his mark upon the country. He was not a drunkard or a show off, nor did he create troubles with other nations. He brought his people peace, that is, freedom from serious revolts and international wars. He paid off the external debt, placed the nation on a sound financial footing, and attracted foreign investors. He improved roads, sanitation, agriculture, and industry. Yet against these benefits must be charged great costs. The people had lost their political liberties, their freedom of speech, and their freedom of movement. Many had lost their lives or been forced into exile. The public works had been largely confined to the section of the country around the capital or to those areas into which Gómez wished to send his troops. Public instruction and higher education had been almost completely disregarded.

Gómez had worked to satisfy his own greed for power, not to contribute to the happiness of his people. With all the wealth of Venezuela at his command and with all the power he wielded, he could have made himself beloved by all. Like Dom Pedro II in Brazil, Gómez might have become a national hero. Instead, the Venezuelans revelled in his death.

PART FOUR

TOWARD A BETTER FUTURE!

INTRODUCTION

"We Latin-Americans do not wish the United States to feel toward us as a big brother. We would prefer being left alone to stew in our own juices." This declaration of an intelligent Latin-American expresses an attitude that is widely held in all parts of Latin America. If this attitude does not prove that the other Americas have reached maturity, it at least reveals their conviction that they are becoming mature. In actual fact, many of the Latin-American nations have every right to claim that they have attained full-grown stature.

A factor of the past that has opposed the achievement of maturity was the lack of capital for the development of their own resources. In this they were in a situation very much like our own at the end of the Civil War. Because they had little capital of their own, they permitted the entry of capital from abroad, usually on very liberal terms. The presence of much foreign capital usually meant foreign influence exerted on local political affairs. In many cases this was an evil for the Latin-American nations, since foreign capitalists did not always consider the best interests of the countries to which they went. Just as we, in the later years of the nineteenth century, began to take over our own capital market, so the Latin-Americans are taking over theirs. The recent experiences of American oil companies in Mexico and Bolivia and of British-owned railways in Argentina are cases in point. The Latin-Americans will eventually gain control of their own internal economic affairs, and, though that fact may not benefit the foreign capitalist, there is little doubt that it will benefit the countries themselves.

Communications, sadly lacking until comparatively recently, are now being rapidly improved. Not only are the nations building auto roads to connect their own population centers, but they are coöperating in the promotion of better international communications. The Pan-American Highway, about which so much has been written in recent months, is the most remarkable example of this coöperation. Shipping lines are also being developed by Latin-Americans. Recently they have felt the necessity for this development, because the European war has badly dislocated their seaways.

Another sphere in which the Latin-Americans tend to become self-sufficient is that of technical and professional education. Their medical and engineering schools are not yet the best in the world by a great deal, but there are in several of the countries universities that are very good ones. A half century ago there was not a single really good agricultural school in Latin America. That cannot be said at the present time. Many of the nations have excellent schools of this type whose faculties are composed of native citizens rather than foreigners. Still, many of their students go abroad for additional scientific studies, as we went to Germany and other European countries before 1900. Latin-American nations have always had a plentiful supply, perhaps over-plentiful, of law schools and divinity schools. Their schools of liberal arts and of fine arts are growing in number and excellence. A proof of this is the fact that American students in increasing numbers are traveling to Mexico, Peru, Chile, and Argentina, and elsewhere to study.

Many Latin-American nations are devoting serious thought

and much money to general education, and some possess excellent systems of public instruction. Most have compulsory education laws, though, it must be confessed, only a few are now able to supply the facilities necessary for educating all of their people. Nevertheless, these efforts have already borne excellent fruit, and there is no reason to be pessimistic about their future in this connection. As general intelligence and information increase, the people will demand a greater share in government, and genuine democracy should be the eventual result.

The existence of great numbers of Indians and Negroes in the population of some of the Latin-American nations has been a hindrance to progress. This is not because the Indians and the Negroes, given an opportunity, cannot take an education. Rather, it is because the whites, a minority in number, have insisted on keeping for themselves control of the government and control, likewise, of the economic benefits of society. This has meant that the people of color must be kept down. Now, with the entry of the Negro and the Indian into the life of their countries, there are signs that this difficulty is to be removed. Although Mexico is the only one that has gone very far in the movement, it has shown the way, and others may well follow.

Latin America's artists, poets, and writers have been in recent years gaining greater foreign recognition. Art exhibits from Latin America travel about in our country and arouse much interest. North American publishers hold contests in novel-writing for Latin-Americans and publish books written by them. Works of Latin-American authors are to some extent being translated into English, while English books are being translated into Spanish and read in Latin America.

Attention was first called to the archeological wealth of

Latin America by foreign scientists and investigators. Important work is still being done in Mexico and Peru by foreign institutes and missions. But Latin-American scientists are more and more entering the field. It may be expected that here too, in time, the Latin-Americans will become self-sufficient.

This tendency to become self-sufficient which can now be widely observed is the most important current development in Latin America. It is an historical process through which many regions of the world have passed. In many lines we ourselves have become self-sufficient only recently. It may be said that we had a start of half a century on our Latin-American friends. They are now at the point which, probably, we had reached just before the Spanish-American War. They are rapidly developing their own manufactures, and each month new products from them reach our markets. In scientific and intellectual matters they are making noticeable progress. Their musicians and musical compositions, both popular and classical, find eager listeners throughout the civilized world. Thus, in countless ways the people of the other Americas are moving toward a better future.

Politically, Latin America gained international recognition as a result of the First World War. More than half of the nations were represented at the peace conference, and most of them joined the League of Nations. Individuals from various Latin-American nations have filled important posts in the machinery of the League—Bustamante, Cuba; Alejandro Álvarez, Chile; Mello Franco, Brazil; Saavedra Lamas, Argentina. Perhaps the greatest gain by Latin America in international politics is the recent action of the United States in accepting, in fact soliciting, their collaboration on a basis of complete equality. No more do we consider them as inferior and try to dictate to them in matters that are of common concern. Our relations with them are now on a partnership basis.

The nations of Latin America are no longer immature children who must be looked after solicitously by someone older and stronger. Many of them are already husky adults, able to care for themselves quite well. They have become nations with whom we should do well to be on friendly, coöperative terms. Our welfare demands it; their welfare will best be served by it. As a people, we should turn much more of our attention toward Latin America. We ought to learn who and what they are. We must understand them. When we do so, we shall be able to admire them for many things and to sympathize with them in the many problems which they have yet to solve. Only thus can the Americas become united in the pursuit of worthy common ends. Only thus can they play the important role in world civilization which they are entirely capable of playing—which, in fact, they ought to play.

CHAPTER XVII

DOMINGO F. SARMIENTO: EDUCATOR AND STATESMAN

Domingo Faustino Sarmiento is a big, mouth-filling name. But it is no bigger than the man who bore it through a long and exceedingly vigorous life. Nor does the pronouncing of it fill the mouth more completely than the fame of its possessor fills the memory of his countrymen. In fact, that fame is too big for the Argentine Republic, the land of his birth. It spills over into Chile and Uruguay and other parts of South America which have felt the influence of his activities.

Like our own Abraham Lincoln, Sarmiento was big also in body, though his bigness did not run quite so much to height as Lincoln's did. Like Lincoln, too, he was homely—with a rugged, massive sort of ugliness. Again like Lincoln, he was born on the frontier of his country. San Juan, in the year 1811, was nothing more than a small village, isolated in the foothills at the eastern edge of the Andes Mountains. It slept, cradled among its hills, at a distance no less than eight hundred miles west of the city of Buenos Aires, the New York of Argentina. It was scarcely the place from which one would expect a great man to emerge. But neither was Central Kentucky, where Lincoln had been born but two years before Sarmiento.

Late in life, Sarmiento wrote that the two men he most

loved were Lincoln and Horace Mann, the great Massachusetts educator. However, the first North American whose acquaintance he made was Benjamin Franklin. Far out there beyond the *pampa*, the great Argentine plain, in some manner, a biography of Franklin came into his hands. He read it with the greatest interest, for he found in Franklin a splendid example for himself. Later, remembering this period, he wrote:

I felt myself Franklin. And why not? I was exceedingly poor as he was; I was studious like him and giving myself free rein and following in his steps, I should be able some day to make myself like him, to be an honorary doctor like him, and to make myself a place in letters and in American politics.[1]

It is not surprising to find Sarmiento declaring, many years later, that the life of Franklin ought to be found in every primary school library.

Educational opportunities in San Juan during Sarmiento's boyhood were few. However, he secured a few years of primary schooling—enough for one of his high intelligence to enable him to carry on with his own education. He was nominated by the school authorities of his home town for a fellowship at a school in Buenos Aires, but was disappointed when the final choices were made. This was a severe blow to his ambitions, but he was not discouraged. Sarmiento as a man always exhibited a tremendous power of determination— *stubbornness*, his enemies called it. With an uncle, a well-educated churchman in San Juan, he continued his studies stubbornly and, on the whole, effectively.

Throughout his life Sarmiento was a patriot, though not in a narrow sense, and a sincere believer in democracy. This

[1] Quoted in Alberto Palcos, *Sarmiento, la Vida, la Obra, las Ideas, el Genio* (Buenos Aires, 1929), pp. 29, 30.

was to be expected, as he was born but a few months after his country had begun its revolution against the mother country, Spain, and he was growing up, an impressionable youngster, while the struggle was in progress. Of course he heard continuous talk of the war, of the problems of independence, of the advantages of self-government, of types of government. When the Spanish authorities were expelled, Argentina did not at once settle into an organized, peaceful existence. Instead, there was a great deal of argument, indeed much fighting, between different groups on the question of the form that their government should take. Sarmiento, young, intelligent, hot-blooded, did not restrain his feelings or the expression of his views. Consequently, at the time when the dictatorship of Rosas was developing, his position was so dangerous that he had to leave the country in order to save his life. This was in 1831. He sought a haven in Chile, just over the Andes—though he had to do some good climbing to get there as the road crosses the mountains at an altitude of 12,500 feet. Pike's Peak is not much higher!

When he arrived in Chile, Sarmiento was entirely without means—except for his undaunted youth and his iron determination. He must earn his bread. His first way of doing so was by teaching a primary school. Though the young Argentine was but twenty years old, he already had some decided theories about what a school should be. He was a "progressive" educator; he experimented. He was liked by his pupils and their parents. But, unfortunately, the governor of the district was not advanced in his ideas on education. He criticized Sarmiento and, when the latter defended his methods and refused to alter them, he was dismissed. Sarmiento then went to the port city of Valparaíso where for a time he clerked in a store. In his spare hours, he studied English. He next took a place as foreman in the copper mines at Copiapó, in North Central Chile. Sometimes he would rise in the middle of the night to work at his English. His health broke down because of overwork and, on the advice of his friends, he returned to San Juan to recover. There, after recovering, he continued his studies—French, Italian, philosophy, history.

Already greatly interested in education, and believing that before a society could be genuinely enlightened its women, as well as its men, must be educated, Sarmiento founded a school for girls, the High School of the Inmates of Saint Rose. In all of Latin America at the time no attention was given to formal education of girls. Primary schools for boys were few and poor, most of them operated by the church. Such schools as existed were not free, so that children of the poor could seldom attend them. It follows that only a fraction of the people could read and write. Often in families of means and some social standing, the girls and women were illiterate. Sarmiento's school was badly needed. He also founded a newspaper in San Juan, and was the prime mover in a literary society where liberal political reforms were discussed. All of this was much too advanced for the arbitrary and suspicious provincial authorities at San Juan. Soon Sarmiento was in their bad graces, and another crisis developed. Finally, he decided it was high time that he again cross the Andes. In 1840, Sarmiento was back in Chile.

At first he thought of establishing a *colegio* in the city of Rancagua, that is, a private school of which he would be director and one of the teachers. Chile, in matters educational, was in no better case than Argentina. Illiteracy was equally as great, schools were as scarce. However, before Sarmiento got his school set up, an article that he had written attracted the attention of the director of the Chilean newspaper *El Mer-*

curio (*The Mercury*). Sarmiento was offered and accepted a place on the paper's editorial staff. Later, he wrote for or edited a number of other Chilean newspapers. Through them he attacked Rosas and his dictatorial system in Argentina, becoming a bothersome thorn in the flesh of that arbitrary person. It was in this period that he wrote his classic, *Facundo, Civilization or Barbarism*. The book was a study of Facundo Quiroga, a semi-barbarous military despot of the Argentine region in which San Juan is situated. The book is a social study of the people of that place and time.

Sarmiento continued to maintain (as was the case throughout his life) his interest in educational matters. His writings on this subject attracted so much attention that he was commissioned by the national authorities of Chile to draw a plan for a normal school. When the school was established—the second such school in the Western Hemisphere, that of Horace Mann in Massachusetts, founded two years earlier, being the first—Sarmiento was invited to be its first president. This was in 1843. For two years he taught several courses in the school, wrote a number of textbooks for use in them, and at the same time continued to write a great deal for the local press. It was never an unusual matter for Sarmiento to discharge the tasks of two or more full-time jobs.

An enlightened and progressive man, Manuel Montt, was at this time responsible for the educational system of the nation—if what they then had may be dignified by the name "system." Some of the larger cities had high schools, though they were not very good, and there was a college at Santiago. There was great need of hundreds, of thousands, of elementary schools. Teachers for them were needed. A start in supplying them was being made at the Normal School. There was need, if a literate citizenry was to be developed, that elementary education should be free. Montt felt keenly that the education of the masses was one of Chile's serious problems. In some of the European countries and in certain states of the United States there were systems of primary education that had caused much comment and news of which had reached even to remote Chile. As a means of finding firm ground on which to build a genuine system of national education, Montt decided to send a commissioner to these foreign countries to learn what they were doing. Sarmiento was offered the commission. He accepted without hesitation. He left Chile in 1845 and spent the greater part of the three succeeding years abroad—first in Europe (Spain, Italy, France, Prussia, England), then in the United States. When he was in London, Sarmiento came across a book written by Horace Mann. Mann had been in Europe two years earlier on a mission like that of Sarmiento, and the book was his report to the Massachusetts Board of Education. Sarmiento said that after he had read that book he had "a fixed point" to which to direct himself in the United States. So he crossed the Atlantic Ocean to our country.

In Massachusetts, the Chilean commissioner spent three days with Mr. and Mrs. Mann. They were thrilling days for him, devoted to deep discussion of educational matters with a master of such things. His study of English had not made him able to speak or understand that language well, for he states in his *Viajes* (*Travels*) that Mrs. Mann, who spoke French fluently, as did Sarmiento, acted as interpreter for the two schoolmen. Sarmiento was greatly impressed by the advance in education which our country had made. It particularly amazed and delighted him that, apparently, almost everyone could read, whether laborer or banker. Sarmiento traveled westward through the Central States and descended to New Orleans on an Ohio-Mississippi River steamer. While he observed certain crudities in manners, he frankly liked our people, forming an opinion of them which, as Mrs. Mann thought, was somewhat idealized.

Back in Chile, Sarmiento made his report. It was published in 1848 under the title *Concerning Popular Education*. In it he stressed the need of normal school training for teachers. He recommended that Chile train women as teachers of the young. He insisted that there ought to be schools for everyone from the grades through college, free on most levels. He declared that Chile must have special buildings, especially equipped for the schools, and that special funds for their support should be raised by general taxation. Though all of these recommendations were not immediately put into practice in Chile, the principles set forth in this report were the basis of many subsequent years of Sarmiento's work in the field of education in Chile and Argentina. Eventually, all of the measures recommended became law and practice. The result is that the school systems of those two countries are the best organized and most advanced in all of Latin America.

In the early 1850's, Sarmiento returned to his country, believing that he might be able to assist in the overthrow of the dictator, Rosas. But he saw no place for the exercise of his abilities, so he returned to his foster-country.

In the meantime, Manuel Montt had become president of Chile. He made Sarmiento director of primary education and entrusted to him the editing of a monthly periodical, *School Monitor*. This editorship gave Sarmiento an opportunity to print and distribute widely his views on school matters. And the directorship of education enabled him to effect some improvements in the educational field. He initiated the practice of having periodical meetings of teachers in order that he might instruct them in modern teaching ideas and methods. He wished to establish public libraries in all centers of population. Though he was not immediately successful, his work later bore fruit. He also wrote another book, *Common Education*, which contained many admirable suggestions for the improvement of Chilean schools and society.

In all of his years of exile, Sarmiento lost none of his love for his homeland and was always waiting for the time when he could return and have a part in building a better country. Rosas was overthrown in 1852, and the country returned to constitutional government. Early in 1855, Sarmiento felt that he might venture to return. So he closed up his business affairs in Chile and crossed the mountains to Argentina.

The exile had been elected by the Argentine province of Tucumán as a delegate to the national congress and he directed himself toward the city of Paraná, where the congress was then sitting. But, because of certain frank criticisms that he had written, he was suspected of conspiring against the government. This angered our patriotic Sarmiento, and he immediately sought out the governor of San Juan and gave him a severe tongue-lashing. The governor listened smiling, and when Sarmiento had finished, remarked, "What a don Domingo! Always the same." When one of Sarmiento's friends afterward asked him how in the world he had dared to speak so to an official, who controlled the lives and many of the great estates of the province, he replied dryly, "From fear, of course." But President Urquiza, too, was unfriendly to Sarmiento, so instead of going to Paraná, where he saw he would be unable to do anything worth while, he resigned his seat and went instead to Buenos Aires.

When Sarmiento returned from Chile, nearly everyone in Argentina had pretty clearly taken a position on the question of centralism or federalism in the nation's government. This was the old debate on the centering of all power at Buenos Aires or leaving some in the hands of the provinces. All wondered what Sarmiento's position would be and awaited his decision with great interest. He had earlier written, "When I am in the provinces I am a Porteño, when I am in Buenos Aires I am a provincial, but everywhere and all the time I am an Argentine." This attitude he was able to maintain for some time after he returned and he did not mix very definitely in the centralist-federalist struggle. He stood first of all for the nation.

At Buenos Aires, Sarmiento was quick to begin his efforts to educate and improve his countrymen. He became the editor of a leading newspaper, El Nacional (The National), the editorship of which had just been quitted by Bartolomé Mitre, another of Argentina's great men. It was not long until Sarmiento, with his inexhaustible energy, was in addition filling these offices: member of the Consultative Council of the Province of Buenos Aires, councilor (or alderman) of the city of Buenos Aires, and chief of the Department of Schools of the province. In the last capacity he began in 1858 to publish Annals of Common Education, an important monthly periodical. Moreover, he was three times elected provincial senator, or, as we should say, state senator. Idleness had no place in the life of Domingo Faustino Sarmiento!

Early in 1862, as a consequence of political developments that need not be described here, Sarmiento was made governor of his home province, San Juan. In the new office the "returned native" immediately resumed his earlier task of educating and advancing his home people. His was one of the most progressive governments the province has ever known. His accomplishments can be indicated only briefly.

He founded a model farm school to further scientific agriculture. He got under way a movement to found a preparatory high school, which was completed shortly after the end of Sarmiento's administration and did a splendid work as the Sarmiento School. He reorganized the administration of justice in the province. He provided a much better building for the public hospital. He caused the making of a new election law which surrounded the ballot with safeguards designed to prevent fraud and produce a more democratic system. Many other excellent measures were effected. The governor proved himself a very able executive.

Then, in 1864, Sarmiento was appointed minister of Argentina to the United States. He said later that the reason for the appointment was the desire to get him out of the country to prevent his becoming a candidate for president in the next election. Whatever the motive for the appointment, Sarmiento accepted. He was especially attracted by the instructions given him to study and make a report on education in the United States.

Having stopped en route in Lima, Peru, to attend an international conference of Latin-American states, the new minister did not reach the United States until May, 1865—one month after the assassination of President Lincoln. The president's death caused the new minister great sadness, for now both of those men whom he said he most loved were no more, Horace Mann having died in 1857. Nevertheless, Sarmiento passed three very happy years in the United States. He renewed his friendship with Mrs. Mann and paid a visit to a recently unveiled statue of Mr. Mann in Boston. Sarmiento and Mrs. Mann exchanged many letters on literary and educational matters. Sarmiento wrote a book, *The Schools, Basis of Prosperity and the Republic in the United States.* This was the report which his government had instructed him to make. Mrs. Mann made an English translation of Sarmiento's *Facundo*. Sarmiento founded a quarterly, *Both Americas*, to carry scientific information throughout South America. He attended national educational conventions and made public addresses. He was awarded the honorary degree of Doctor of Laws by the University of Michigan. This pleased him greatly, for Franklin also had been awarded the honorary doctorate. The event gave him a feeling of intellectual kinship with one of his boyhood heroes.

And then a most interesting thing occurred. While still abroad, Sarmiento was elected president of Argentina. How surprised must have been those persons who had managed to get him out of the country to prevent this very thing! He had, of course, many eminent and influential friends in Argentina and he had himself kept in close touch with political developments there. It may even be said that from his distant post he campaigned for the election—and effectively! He had started home before he learned the result of the election. When his boat stopped at Rio de Janiero, he was told that he was his country's president-elect.

His six years as president of Argentina, 1868 to 1874, were full years. Sarmiento's years could not be otherwise. Education, immigration (which he felt Argentina greatly needed), industrial and agricultural development, and national union were his great concerns. At his request, Mrs. Mann selected a score of young women and a few men who went to Argentina to staff normal schools (one was founded at San Juan), agricultural schools, and schools of other types. Sarmiento founded an astronomical observatory at Córdoba, the first such institution in the Southern Hemisphere, and brought Dr. Benjamin A. Gould down from an American university

Modern school children of Buenos Aires. Sarmiento would have approved of the dust coats which all Argentine school children are required by law to wear. These coats not only protect the clothing of the children, but also—and more important—prevent class distinctions arising from differences in dress.

(Left) Obelisk in Buenos Aires commemorating the 400th anniversary of the founding of the city in 1536. It stands on the Avenida Nueve de Julio, named for the important date July 9, 1816, when the national declaration of independence was made. (Right) Domingo Faustino Sarmiento, great Argentine patriot and educator.

A group of modern Peruvian Indians, high in the Peruvian Andes, who have come to watch the arrival of a train on the Oroya railroad, originally projected by Henry Meiggs.

Native thatched-roof huts in the high Peruvian Andes. These are to be seen at 15,000 feet above sea level on the Central Railroad built by Henry Meiggs.

to be its director. Of course, being Sarmiento, he continued to have his controversies, result of his enthusiasms and his pugnacity. Some of them resulted favorably for him, some did not. But when he retired from his high office, he was greatly respected by most of his countrymen and had a name well-known in all of South America.

The years from the presidency to his death in 1888 were by no means idle ones, though, because of advancing age, his activities proceeded at a slower tempo. He occupied for some years the post of national director of schools and did valuable work in that position. As president, he had caused the creation of many hundreds of elementary schools and many high schools in the larger cities. Now, as director of schools he had an opportunity to provide for their continuance and improvement. He worked hard at the task, but his accomplishments fell short of his desires. Money was lacking, and a great many of the people with whom he had to deal did not have his vision of what education could mean to Argentina. When he left this office, he was greatly disappointed at the amount of progress in education which his country had made.

With everything else that he did, Sarmiento continued to write for the press. So voluminous are his writings, principally in the newspapers, that when collected they filled some fifty volumes. Of all Argentines, only Mitre comes near to equaling his output.

Sarmiento died in Asunción, Paraguay. He had gone there for the warm climate, as we would go to Florida. The cause of his death was heart disease. For the return journey to Buenos Aires, his body was wrapped in four flags—those of Argentina, Chile, Paraguay, and Uruguay—the flags of the countries he had most greatly served.

Sarmiento was not the only great man that Latin America

had produced. Indeed Argentina alone has bred two or three others who deserve to be placed near him, perhaps with him. It may well be claimed that he was South America's greatest educator. He was a truly great man in many ways—in honor and honesty, in intellect and industry, in his immense desire to make his people and the world better.

CHAPTER XVIII

HENRY MEIGGS: MAN OF MILLIONS

In natural wealth Latin America is one of the richest regions of the globe. Mexico, Peru, Brazil, Bolivia have long been noted for their mines of the precious metals. The emeralds of Colombia and the diamonds of Brazil have been famous for many years in the markets of the world. In recent decades petroleum has been discovered in widely distributed areas. Chile and Peru are richly endowed with copper. And for a time, strange to say, Peru (and to a less extent Chile) had great wealth in bird manure, called by the Spaniards *guano*. It is the product of the flocks of countless *guanays* which for thousands of years have roosted and made deposits, in some places sixty feet deep, along the desert coasts of Peru and Northern Chile.

With all of this wealth, however, the nations which contained it remained for a long time relatively poor. Among the most important reasons were the lack of ready money with which to finance expensive developments and the lack of men with sufficient technical training to carry them through successfully. Perhaps, too, there was with some of the Latin-American people a lack of that drive that South Americans have sometimes called "Yankee go-ahead." Furthermore, the absence of good government made foreign capitalists hesitate to enter some countries, lest lack of governmental protection cause failure and financial loss.

It is not difficult to see that in these rich but undeveloped countries there were great opportunities for the men of money or technical skill (or perhaps merely of daring) who should venture to break this virgin soil. The first who dared to do it in a big way was an American, Henry Meiggs, who might almost have stepped from the pages of *Arabian Nights*.

This man's life began in the village of Catskill-on-Hudson, New York, in the year 1811. By the time he had reached his thirty-sixth year, he had married his second wife (the first having died) and had failed more than once in the lumber business. But failure never seemed to discourage Henry Meiggs very much. He was always able to find another opportunity which, in his opinion at any rate, offered him a chance to make a million dollars. His daring spirit drove him to California in 1849, when so many "gold-rushers" were heading in that direction. His nose for profits led him to charter a vessel for the trip and to load it with lumber. His luck carried him and his family safely around stormy Cape Horn and to feverish San Francisco. There, in that lumber-hungry city whose size was doubling every six months, his business sense enabled him to sell his lumber at a profit of fifty thousand dollars. Thus Henry Meiggs was brilliantly launched upon the second phase of his remarkable career.

Very soon Meiggs formed a company (of which he, of course, was president) to get out timber in the forests on the other side of San Francisco Bay. The timber was sawed and transported to the booming city where it was sold at very good prices. In a short time Meiggs went into real estate. He bought a sizeable acreage in the North Beach section of San Francisco where he anticipated there would soon be a building boom—with some skillful persuasion on his part. He also became active in street building and other operations. Unfortunately, he had miscalculated about the demand for North Beach property. Nobody seemed to want it. Meiggs had borrowed money to buy and develop this property, and now he was forced to borrow much more to keep it and his other interests going.

To secure money in San Francisco in those days was not very difficult—particularly if one had a reputation such as that of "Honest Harry" Meiggs—but interest rates were very high. At length Meiggs had got all that he could lay his hands on—and still it was not enough. Then he made the greatest mistake of his life. He forged, or had an employee forge for him, many pieces of city paper. The city was running on credit in those days. When a contractor did a job for it, such as opening a new street, he would be given, properly signed by the city officials, a certificate of indebtedness. The holder could then use this paper as a security for borrowing money from a bank or a money-lender. It was such paper as this that Meiggs forged, filling in large amounts, signing with the names of the officials, and then using it for making loans. No doubt he expected to sell some of his property and take up the paper before anyone ever learned what he had done. In San Francisco in those days one absorbed the spirit of daring with every breath he drew. But Meiggs's luck played him false, for a business depression made it impossible to sell his lots, and the time came when the danger of exposure became very great.

No doubt "Honest Harry" spent many hours wrestling with his terrible problem, trying to decide whether he should remain in San Francisco and face the consequences of his act or fly to other parts. Should he decide to remain, it was highly probable that, when his forgeries were discovered, he would be hanged. That was the punishment of many wrong-doers of that rough frontier town. Meiggs decided to save his neck and continue to live elsewhere. Living, he might some day be able to make money enough to pay back what he had "borrowed." He would "cut the Gordian knot" of his difficulties by fleeing. In preparation he bought a small ship, the *America*, and employed a captain whom he knew very well to equip it for sea and command it for him. When all was in readiness, at three o'clock on the morning of October 4, 1854, he slipped aboard the little boat with his wife and three children and a brother, John Meiggs, and they put out to sea. Eventually, the San Franciscans discovered the flight and the cause thereof and organized a pursuit. But they were too late, and Meiggs and his party—and ten thousand dollars in gold which he had managed to secure—were safe on the high seas. After six months of wandering about in the South Pacific, the fugitives decided to steer for a port in Chile. Early in the following March, the *America* cast anchor in the port of Talcahuano. Turning the boat over to the captain and the crew, Meiggs and his people went ashore to face a new life in a new country. Since most of the gold had been spent during the months of wandering, they were practically penniless.

The first years must have been very difficult for all of them. But they managed to live, and at length Meiggs was entrusted with some small contracts connected with the building of a railroad in Southern Chile. He did his work so well, so rapidly, and handled the Chilean laborers so skillfully that he was soon given other and larger contracts. Then, in August, 1861, the national government gave him a contract for finishing the railway, which for almost ten years had been under construction from Valparaíso, the chief seaport, to Santiago, the national capital. This road had been the cause of great distress to the government and people of Chile. One chief engineer after the other (most of them English) had met obstacles that they could not surmount. Several had died on the job. The road was costing a great deal more than the original estimate. It seemed that there was no one who could handle the undertaking. And then Meiggs came forward. Having sufficiently proved his ability to fulfill his contracts, he was given this difficult task.

With the greatest speed, Don Enrique (Mr. Henry), as he was now generally called, got together eight thousand Chilean *rotos* and a staff of trained engineers, most of them from the United States. They literally made the dirt fly. The great reason for Don Enrique's desire for speed was that under the terms of his contract he was to be paid a large bonus for every month less than three years which he could save in finishing his big task. By dint of driving his engineers and superintendents and being unceasingly active himself the road was completed, and a big inaugural celebration was held exactly *two years* from the signing of the contract. No wonder that Meiggs was now famous all over South America as a successful railway contractor. No wonder that he should have considered undertaking the immense task of building a railway across the Andes to Buenos Aires. Nor is it any wonder that the Peruvians should have begged him to come up and build railways for them.

But the great contractor was not yet ready to leave Chile. He had made a million dollars on his last contract. Part of it he sent by agents to San Francisco to pay some of his debts there. He spent three hundred thousand dollars to build a palace-like house in Santiago. Entirely cut and fashioned in the United States, it was sent to Valparaíso complete in one boat. It needed only to be freighted across to the capital on the recently completed railway and put together—by the men who had built the railway and, according to a Santiago legend, free of charge. There can be no doubt that at this time the Chilean *roto* thought a great deal of Don Enrique. The style of the house was unusual. The floor plan was in the form of a cross, the lines crossing at a little less than right angles. At the point of crossing, there was a great circular hall, marble-paved, off which opened the doors of four magnificent rooms—the "Red Room," the "Blue Room," the "White Room," and the dining room of natural Douglas fir. Over the circular hall rose a dome three stories high and glass-covered, and a massive mahogany stairway curved gracefully up to the second floor. The house was equipped with plumbing and hot-air heat and a system of speaking tubes. Though of frame throughout, the house was built so well that it remained standing in good condition, and was occupied until late in 1940 when it was torn down to make room for modern business buildings. The city long since had built out and surrounded it. Some of the great dinners and balls that Don Enrique gave for his friends in this mansion were talked of throughout the country. On one occasion a fine supper was laid in the stables at the rear of the garden. Some Chileans say that Meiggs taught them to live graciously and sanitarily. Don Enrique had become a highly respected man and moved in the best social circles of Chile.

He built other railways and, as usual, bought land, much land. After a tragic fire that burned down one of Santiago's leading churches in the midst of a Christmas program and took the lives of two thousand women and children, Meiggs became one of the leaders in organizing a system of volunteer fire-fighters. He ordered a fire engine from Boston and stored it for a time in the basement of his mansion.

But at length, perhaps in part because his business affairs

were not going too well in Chile, Meiggs decided to go up to Peru. He may have thought there was gold there for a modern Pizarro. He made the move early in 1868.

At that time there was great rivalry between Peru and Chile. Each country felt that it could rightfully claim to be the leading Pacific power among the South American countries. Chile was developing its nitrate and *guano* beds and gaining much wealth from them. Peru was getting out and marketing abroad thousands of tons of *guano* each year. And now Chile had a grand railway running from the coast to the capital. Peru, anyone could see quite easily, needed a railway as badly as Chile, perhaps even worse. Railways for Peru had been for some years a subject of discussion by the more thoughtful Peruvians, including the half-German engineer, Federico Blume, whose home was now in Peru. It was felt that the wise course for Peru was to use the income from *guano* to build a system of railways, to construct something permanent before the *guano* was exhausted. Railways would, as it were, "level" the Andes somewhat, enable the country to develop its great mineral and agricultural wealth, and bring the widely separated elements of the population closer together. The railway was regarded as a civilizer. Much was said of the effects of railways in the United States where at the moment the Union Pacific was nearing completion. Peru *must* have railways. This was the state of Peruvian opinion when Meiggs decided to go there.

Just before Meiggs's arrival, a revolution had brought to the presidency, temporarily, General Pedro Diez Canseco, a native of Arequipa. Arequipa, Peru's second city, lies about a hundred miles from the sea at an elevation of some 7,500 feet. Diez Canseco was determined that his city should have a railway, and he immediately contracted with Don Enrique to build it—for the sum of twelve million dollars. There was talk of corruption, of bribes given by Meiggs to persons in influential positions. Don Enrique was busily at work fulfilling the terms of his contract when, a few months later, an election brought to the high office Colonel José Balta. The new president, as a Peruvian friend said of him, had a mania for building railways and public works. He did not long delay in making with Meiggs, "the Messiah of the Railway," as the same Peruvian called him, contracts to build a half dozen roads in various parts of the country. The combined length of these roads was about 1,050 miles; the combined cost something more than one hundred million dollars. All of them were to run from the coast inland. The two most important were the road from Arequipa to Cuzco, a continuation of the road from the sea at Mollendo to Arequipa, and the Oroya Railway, which was to run from Lima across the Cordillera to tap the copper and silver mines and the agricultural region of the high tableland. Meiggs was an unequaled competitor for these contracts. He had great fame as a successful railroad builder. He had immediately available a corps of skillful engineers and construction superintendents along with much construction machinery. Besides he had money which he used without too many scruples where it would do the most good. So, he came out victor in all of the bidding for contracts.

Meiggs was not himself a trained engineer. But he was a daring and able contractor, and he knew how to choose able lieutenants and how to keep them up to the mark on the job. Not long after he took the Arequipa contract, he brought his brother, John, from New York and made him general superintendent of all of his railway building operations. As there was not enough labor in Peru, Meiggs imported from Chile

many thousands of the *rotos* who had formerly worked for
him—and brought their families with them. Hundreds of
Bolivian Indians were employed to work on the roads in
Southern Peru. Later thousands of Chinese were used. When
yellow fever and malaria and other diseases attacked the
workmen and when Don Enrique had trouble in meeting
his payroll, the Chileans became very troublesome. They
rioted on the line; they fought with the Peruvian workmen
—and usually put them to flight. The others were less hard
to manage.

Despite great natural difficulties, the Arequipa Railway was
finished in record time—and another bonus was gained. Now
there must be rejoicing, loud enough to echo along the giant
chain of the Andes and be heard in Santiago. A great two-
weeks celebration was carried through. The president and
almost the entire national government with eight hundred
guests made the two-day boat trip down the coast from Callao
to Mollendo. There, after eating a fine dinner and dancing the
greater part of the night to the music of a military band, they
spent the remainder of the night as Don Enrique's guests
in improvised dormitories—the railway offices and shops. Then
they journeyed on up to Arequipa, the first official run on
the new railway. How exciting it all must have been! Southward they ran along the sea for some miles (wondering
whether the waves might not some day roll up on the shore
far enough to destroy the track); up through the terrible
Cahuintala canyon (where the trains had to circle around
like birds to gain height); across a great desert of sand,
covered with golden dunes (ever drifting slowly toward the
high mountains, driven by the constant force of the winds);
and finally, arriving at Arequipa where an immense crowd
(all of the inhabitants of the city and everyone for many

miles around) had been for hours impatiently awaiting the arrival of the wonderful new locomotives and their eminent cargo. And for eight days that crowd of guests remained there at the foot of El Misti, one of the most perfect and most beautiful volcanic cones in the world, rejoicing and celebrating in every imaginable kind of ceremony or activity the completion of the first big Peruvian railway. It was all capped off by a splendid dinner and ball which Don Enrique gave for the president and the eminent ones of Peru.

On January 1, 1870—exactly a year before the Arequipa inauguration—work was begun on the Oroya Railway. This beginning was celebrated, too, with much enthusiasm. In a number of respects the Oroya road is more remarkable than the Arequipa. The engineering problems were greater and more numerous, for the road follows the wild, deep-cut canyon of the Rímac River. At places, so great is the river's fall, it was necessary to run up side canyons for some miles or build "zig-zags" in order to gain elevation without exceeding the legal grade. At times the road runs through tunnels cut inside the solid rock side-walls of the canyon. In one spot, it emerges from a tunnel such as this, crosses the river by a two hundred foot bridge one hundred feet above the rushing water and plunges into another tunnel on the opposite side. The difficulties of construction here were so great that the workmen named the spot the *Infiernillo*—in English, "Little Hell." The road crosses the Andean summit through the mile-long Galera tunnel which passes under Mt. Meiggs at an elevation of 15,610 feet. It is the highest standard gauge railway in the world. Hundreds of mules and thousands of llamas were used as pack animals. It can be imagined how hard were working conditions among the snows and extreme cold of these high altitudes. It was almost impossible to keep the Indian working crews up to the desired strength. Though he finished the grade to Oroya and dug the tunnel, Don Enrique was able to lay track no farther than some ninety miles up the canyon from Lima.

Meiggs went ahead with his several railways but, after 1872, with more and more difficulty. The government had floated great loans abroad, in England and France chiefly, to pay for the roads. The loans were all secured by *guano*. But *guano* began to be exhausted, the better quality all taken out, and other kinds of fertilizer came into competition with it. Prices in general (*guano* not included) rose to unheard of levels in Peru. Financial distress seized the government and everyone in the country, not passing over Don Enrique. In 1874 work on the roads had to be suspended for want of funds. Without money it was impossible to secure from abroad rails, ties, locomotives, and other necessary supplies, even food for the workers. And, of course, payrolls had to be met if the men worked.

Meiggs used every possible means to get money. He had early gone into real estate again. He organized a big concern, the Public Works Company, and tried to sell stock. He finally made an arrangement with the government for working the silver and copper mines of the great Cerro de Pasco deposits. All to no avail! The country was faced with bankruptcy and a war with Chile, and Meiggs himself was just at the end of his resources. All that saved him from a complete financial crash was his death. It occurred at the end of September, 1877.

The only one of Meiggs's Peruvian railways that was finished was the Mollendo-Arequipa road. Track was laid on less than ninety miles of the famous Oroya road. The line from Arequipa to Cuzco was carried by Don Enrique only as far as Puno on the shore of Lake Titicaca. Even Meiggs's ambitious plan for the building of a series of wide boulevards in Lima was abandoned when only partly finished.

Meiggs had never returned to the United States. In Chile he had lived what seems to have been an honest and useful life. In Peru he used methods not above reproach in his business affairs. Many discreditable things are said there of his personal life. Only in his vigor, courage, and resourcefulness is he a figure for emulation. But it ought to be borne in mind that he was a product of that era which in the United States was producing the Goulds, the Vanderbilts, the "Diamond Jim" Bradys. The swollen fortunes of those men were gained by means no more admirable than those employed by Henry Meiggs.

Chile undoubtedly profited from Meiggs's years there. Perhaps Peru gained in the long run, though the gain was greatly delayed. Very shortly after Meiggs's death, Peru was at war with Chile. The country's efforts to build railways had exhausted it financially before the war was begun. Small wonder that Chile was victorious and was able to take some valuable sections of Peru's territory. The capitalists who furnished the money for building Chile's roads fared very well. Those who paid for Peru's have been trying ever since to recover on their investment.

Nevertheless, it is true that these activities brought much foreign capital into these countries and caused a great increase in their foreign trade. Some capital came from Europe, but Great Britain furnished most of it. Most of the rails that were laid on the iron roads were imported from Great Britain; the ties to which they were nailed were secured chiefly in California. Lumber, wheelbarrows, much other construction material, were bought in the United States. At first Don Enrique purchased in France and Great Britain the iron for his bridges. Later, he learned that the American product of this type was superior and turned to our manufacturers for his needs. Most of the engines and other rolling stock with which the roads were equipped were likewise secured in the United States. All of this meant a strengthening of economic ties between these industrial countries and Peru and Chile. With the passage of time and the gradual increase of foreign investments and foreign trade, these two Pacific nations have been able to do a great deal in developing their natural wealth. A similar development, it must be understood, was going forward in many other Latin-American countries.

All things considered, it can be said that Peru and Chile and, to a certain extent the United States and Great Britain, gained something through the remarkable activities of that daring and somewhat unscrupulous son of North America, Henry Meiggs.

CHAPTER XIX

RUBÉN DARÍO: POET OF THE AMERICAS

Nicaragua is an obscure Central American country whose area is not much more than that of the state of New York, and whose population numbers scarcely a tenth that of New York City. Yet Nicaragua gave to the world Rubén Darío, the father of Modernism in poetry, who is recognized in three continents as one of the great masters of the Spanish language. Darío was too big to be monopolized by any single country. However, it is probable that the unimportance of his country of origin made it easier for all the Americas to claim—and acclaim—him.

This great artist is scarcely known in the United States. This is owing in part, of course, to the fact that few of our people know the Spanish language, a beautiful and highly adequate medium, particularly for literary expression. In part it is owing to a long-existing tendency to center our attention on Europe at the expense of other parts of the world, some of which are perhaps equally important to us. Many of our people can read in the original language the novels of the great Frenchman, Victor Hugo, for whom, incidentally, Darío had a tremendous admiration. Moreover, those novels have been translated into English and widely read. A much smaller number of us can read in the original Spanish the perfect poems of Rubén Darío, and, unfortunately, very few of them

Memorial to Ricardo Palma. This bust of one of Latin America's literary masters is in Miraflores, a suburb of Lima, Peru, where Dr. Julio Tello also has his home. Palma, as director of the National Library, gave Tello a minor position there.

Henry Meiggs, an American who helped develop Latin America by building railroads through the mountains.

A Navajo silversmith at work. The art of silversmithing was one of those taught the Navajos by Father Kino.

Navajo silver jewelry. The necklace is called a squash blossom necklace, but the large beads are really conventionalized pomegranates. The two bracelets at the left are old, the one on the right modern.

have been rendered into our language. We appear still to find it difficult to believe that any worthy literary work can come out of Latin America. Until after the Civil War, it was customary for us snobbishly to feel the same way about our own artists of pen and brush. Happily, we have recovered from that mistaken notion. And now it seems possible to hope that we may before long give just recognition to the artistic productions of our friends of the other Americas.

There are few educated North Americans who would not recognize the name of Diego Rivera. After having covered with brilliant and striking mural paintings thousands of square feet of wall space in the public buildings of his native Mexico, Rivera was given rich commissions in our country. His astonishing productions can now be seen and enjoyed in many parts of the United States. His fellow-countryman and fellow-artist, Orozco, is also known by us, though not so well. José Sabogal and Julia Codesido, Peruvian artists of great ability, are becoming known among us, as are certain other artists of Latin-American countries. In the field of music, Carlos Chávez of Mexico and Heitor Villa-Lobos of Brazil—not to mention that other beautiful Brazilian, the supple, flaming Carmen Miranda—are well known to us. We know fewer of Latin America's literary masters. The works of Güiraldes and Hernández of Argentina have been translated and read to some extent, chiefly, perhaps, because they pictured the life of the *gaucho*, the Argentine counterpart of our vanishing cowboy. We know something of the writings of Rufino Blanco Fombona of Venezuela and Manuel Ugarte of Argentina and others who shared their way of thinking, because they were severe critics of the United States and its former policy toward the Latin-American countries.

But, as a rule, it is only the specialist in Spanish language and literature who knows anything of the greater number of Latin America's literary masters, such as Uruguay's José Enrique Rodó, Mexico's Manuel Gutiérrez Nájera, Peru's José Santos Chocano and Ricardo Palma, Cuba's José Martí and José María Heredía, and Nicaragua's Rubén Darío. Our general ignorance of the works of these writers is regrettable, for they contain a treasure of beauty and inspiration of which we should take advantage. Furthermore, our failure to know the best that is produced by our "Good Neighbors" leaves us unappreciative of their true merits, and makes it hard for us to arrive at a mutual good understanding.

The life of Rubén Darío was as remarkable, if not as beautiful, as the poems he wrote. If any man's life could be called "novel-like," his could. It alternated between the glowing mountain tops and the unhappy, shadowy depths. At times he had money, which he spent freely. At other times he was reduced to what would have been beggary but for the timely assistance of faithful friends. It was no uncommon thing for him to abandon his living quarters when hopelessly behind with his rent, simply leaving his household effects as payment to the landlord. Spiritually, he went through extremes just as great. Sometimes he was optimistic, happy, careless of religion and morals. Often he was haunted by distressing dreams and terrible fears of the hereafter. For extended periods he would live healthfully and decently, then he would plunge into a long debauch of drunkenness, accompanied by delirium and followed by desperate illness. He had successively two wives. The first died quite early, leaving a son to whom Darío gave little thought; the second he deserted. Another able Latin-American writer, an intimate friend of Darío's through many years, wrote of him this paradoxical, but probably true, statement, "Never in a body so sinful was there lodged a soul so pure."[1]

Darío was born in a little village in Nicaragua in 1867. This event has its poetic association, since it was in this same year that Nicaragua made a treaty with the United States concerning the possible later construction of a canal through Nicaragua. And many years later Darío wrote an "Ode to Roosevelt" which severely criticized the president's activities in the building of the Panama Canal. The blood in Darío's veins was a mixture, according to his own statement of "Spanish, Indian and, perhaps, even African."[2] This mixture has also its "poetic" aspect, for the "Poet of the Americas" ought, logically, to represent the white, the red, and the black.

Darío's name actually was Félix Rubén García Sarmiento, the Darío by which he is known having been the name of an ancestor of local fame. His mother and father lived together but a short time, and for that reason the boy was reared by his relatives, the Ramírez, a family of some means, a fact which was not true of his own parents. Rubén was exceedingly precocious, being able to read at the age of three. It is probable that he was not much older when he began to write rhymes. At any rate by the time he was five or six he was writing verses quite readily and at twelve he was known throughout Central America as "the boy poet." Darío himself has said that he never *learned* to write poetry, but that he was born with the ability. It is odd that his first local fame as a poet came from the rhymed epitaphs which he wrote for

[1] Vargas Vila, as quoted in Isaac Goldberg, *Studies in Spanish-American Literature* (New York, 1920), p. 121. (Actually in Goldberg the quotation appears as "Never in a soul so pure was there lodged a body so sinful," which is evidently inverted.)

[2] Francisco Contreras, *Rubén Darío, su Vida y su Obra* (Santiago de Chile, 1937), p. 49.

deceased persons among the families of his friends. He was much in favor, too, with the ladies because of his skill in writing suitable verses to be painted on their fans, a fad of the time.

The youngster was almost as precocious in love as in poetry. His first love perhaps is not known, but when he was about twelve he fell in love with an American circus performer and tried to join the circus in order to be near the "goddess." By the time he was sixteen, he had been on the editorial staff of a newspaper, had taught grammar (at fourteen!) in a high school, had been appointed to a position in the National Library at Managua—and had been for a brief time the rival in love of the president of the neighboring republic of El Salvador. While he was in the library, he was paying devoted attentions to "a green-eyed, chestnut-haired maiden of a gentle pallor." All his life Darío was enraptured, and tortured, by love.

In 1886, a particularly bitter disappointment of a romantic nature caused Darío to resolve to quit Nicaragua. He thought of coming to the United States, but a friend persuaded him to go instead to Chile. Arrived at Valparaíso, he read in a newspaper, which had been brought aboard, news of the death of an eminent Chilean, Benjamín Vicuña Mackenna. On the instant, he sat down and in twenty minutes had written an article on the subject. It was published in the newspaper *El Mercurio*, and immediately Darío had a place in the intellectual group in Chile. What brilliance he must have had! Pedro Balmaceda, son of the president of Chile, became one of Darío's best Chilean friends. Darío wrote for a number of newspapers. But for various reasons he got into difficulties with his superiors, and before his two and a half years in Chile were ended he had descended to a job of no importance in the customs house at Valparaíso. In matters of money, men, or morals, Darío possessed nothing of what we usually call "common sense." In Valparaíso he became badly addicted to drink, but despite that unhappy fact he continued to write.

It was in Valparaíso that some of his friends managed the publication of his famous little book with the odd title *Azul* . . . (—and don't forget the three periods, for they are a part of the title, *Blue* . . .). It was a collection of poems and prose-poems touching on idealistic subjects. The book was immediately recognized as the work of a master of Spanish, and of Spanish used in a new manner. Its most notable characteristic was its spirit of cosmopolitanism, that is, its breadth, its universal character, its lack of any narrow loyalties or narrow prejudices. Latin-American writing (in fact European letters as well) needed this spirit to jolt it out of its provincialism. The little book had a truly revolutionary effect on literary history. "It was," says Goldberg, "the spark that ignited the modernist conflagration."[3]

Darío returned to Nicaragua in 1889 more famous than when he left it. A marked characteristic of the author of *Azul* . . . , whose brilliant mind, one would think, ought to have held him above such pettinesses, was a liking for the trappings of diplomatic office. He had a childish respect for anything connected with government service of this sort. In 1892 he had his first diplomatic post when he was appointed to represent Nicaragua at the Colombian Celebration, which was in that year being held in Spain to mark the four hundredth anniversary of the discovery of America. (We, too, it will be remembered, were having at Chicago our celebration of that event.)

Nicaragua made frequent call on his diplomatic services,

[3] *Op. cit.*, p. 130.

the appointment which most delighted him being that of minister plenipotentiary (so big a title for the small job it proved to be) to Spain. About the only satisfaction he got from any such post was that which came from wearing the showy uniform and receiving the honors that go with such offices. Financially they were of small worth. But, in truth, no sum of money was ever of more than temporary help to Darío —he always spent just as rapidly as possible every *peso* that he got from whatever source. Returning from Spain, Darío stopped off in Colombia to visit that country's aged great man and former president, Rafael Núñez. Through the influence of Núñez, the Nicaraguan was appointed consul of Colombia in Buenos Aires.

Darío made a "tour," en route to his new office at Buenos Aires, visiting the United States and Europe, where he felt he *had* to see Paris. In 1893, in New York, José Martí and other Cuban patriots were in the midst of their preparations for revolt in Cuba. They received Darío with much warmth, Martí addressing him as *hijo* (son). The poet made a journey to see Niagara Falls, America's great natural wonder, which all visitors must see. Darío's lively imagination had formed such an exaggerated picture of what he would see that the reality left him only faintly impressed. He did not write the "obligatory ode" to the Falls which was expected of him.

The Buenos Aires period saw the publication of two of Darío's best works, *Prosas Profanas* (*Worldly Prose Pieces*) and *Los Raros* (*Rare Spirits*). Both added much to his reputation. The latter was a collection of impressions of several eminent persons, published originally in newspapers. Most of them appeared in *La Nación*, the eminent daily for which Darío wrote regularly for almost a quarter century. These works again demonstrated Darío's command of his mother tongue and marked developments in his skill in both prose and poetic forms.

The diplomatic office at the Argentine capital did not last long. When the Spanish-American War was begun in 1898, *La Nación* sent Darío to Spain as a special reporter. From that year on, the poet lived almost continuously in Europe, sometimes in Spanish cities but usually in his great love, Paris. His income, such as it was, came from his books, from journalistic activities, and from occasional periods of service as a consul for Nicaragua or some other Latin-American country. His writing, considering his great abilities, brought inadequate returns. Literary agents took advantage of his lack of business sense and cheated him. The consular jobs paid little and that quite irregularly. He was often in want.

Darío's health was never robust and, of course, his periods of excessive drinking further weakened it. In his early years, he had been a "night-hawk," frequently talking and drinking with friends the night through. If he were not out with friends, he often passed the entire night reading. His was a most irregular life in almost every respect, judged by ordinary standards. As his years increased and the state of his health grew worse, he became something of a recluse, going out little, passing his days in reading and writing. Fits of melancholy were frequent, and at those times he was not considerate of the feelings of those around him. Francesca Sánchez, the kind but unlettered Spanish woman who was his faithful companion for many years and the mother of one of the two sons that survived him, had often to suffer from his bad humors.

Francisco Contreras, the Chilean biographer of Darío, who knew him well, has written this description of Darío's character:

This extraordinary poet was a man fundamentally good and highly cultured, but he had strange weaknesses and was not exempt from worries. He abominated intrigues, was unacquainted with envy, was enthusiastic for everything that he thought beautiful or noble, but at the same time he showed an absurd timidity, a childish respect for dignities and was obsessed with fear of the beyond, which induced him to treat his enemies gently, to bow himself before diplomatic titles, and to live in a sombre obsession with death. Nevertheless, at bottom he was sensual, a good liver, was proud, and somewhat punctilious. He loved elegance, he enjoyed a good table, did not disdain incense, and attacks affected him profoundly. . . . Amado Nervo . . . has written of him that he was "a child—a child egotistical or tender, capricious or serene—jealous of his caresses, as susceptible as a violet . . . a great, nervous child." Exactly: that is what he was.[4]

A briefer, and perhaps a better, estimate of Darío is that of the eminent Spanish man of letters, Valle-Inclán. "Rubén," he declared, "is a genius. His observation is not comparable to that of common writers, like Blasco Ibáñez, for example. He perceives the mysterious relationship of things."[5]

Some idea of this power of insight may be gained from one of his poems. Here is his "Slings," as translated by Alice Stone Blackwell:

> I dreamed a slinger bold was I,
> Born 'neath Majorca's limpid sky.
> With stones I gathered by the sea
> I hunted eagles flying free,
> And wolves; and when a war arose,
> I went against a thousand foes.

[4] *Op. cit.*, pp. 122, 123.
[5] *Op. cit.*, p. 129.

A pebble of pure gold one day
Up to the zenith sped its way,
When in the heavens blue and wide
A huge gerfalcon I espied,
Attacking in the fields of air
A strange, bright bird, of plumage rare—
A wondrous bird; its flight on high
With ruby streaked the sapphire sky.

My stone returned not; but to me
The cherub-bird flew fearlessly.
Straight to my side it came, and said:
"Wounded, Goliath's soul has fled.
I come to thee, from out the sky:
Lo, David's radiant soul am I!"[6]

Only twice after 1898 did Darío return to Nicaragua. One of these returns was made in 1907 when he was at the height of his career and fame. His country made the most of his visit, for in honoring its famous son it was calling attention to its own worth. The government declared the returned native a guest of honor for the entire period of his stay, and his friends and admirers gave him all manner of attentions. In Corinto where he landed, and in Managua and Léon, both large cities, he was given triumphal entries—palms and laurels everywhere. The sound of bells and cheers "made the heavens tremble." The people were delirious with enthusiasm. Darío, though filled with emotion, conducted himself with dignity and discretion. The visit was climaxed with his appointment as minister plenipotentiary to Spain. Nothing could have pleased Darío more, and he left the country in 1908 in a glow of satisfaction and happiness.

[6] *Some Spanish-American Poets* (Philadelphia, University of Pennsylvania Press, 1937), pp. 189-90.

The last return was made in 1915. Late the previous year, the poet had left Paris for the Americas on a business venture in the course of which he was to lecture at widely separated points. He was again in New York briefly. He went to Rio, then to Colombia. He had been quite ill when he left Paris, and finally he found himself compelled to abandon his tour. It was then that, as he said, he "returned to Nicaragua to die." After an illness of some months, during which he was not too well cared for, the tuberculosis from which he suffered brought death. This was early in 1916, when he had almost reached his forty-eighth birthday.

Rubén Darío's ignorance of practical life, his lack of foresight, his timidity, his addiction to drink, his many weaknesses, contributed to making a life which, as life merely, was very painful, probably very unsatisfactory to Darío. But this poet should not be judged on material grounds alone. He never prospered, if by that word we mean to get ahead financially. But he did prosper decidedly in making a great name for himself in literature. And he left a treasure created in his sensitive and brilliant mind that has made the world his infinite debtor.

CHAPTER XX

JULIO TELLO: PERUVIAN SCHOLAR AND
SCIENTIST

Perched on a narrow backbone of rock, which lies within a hairpin bend of the roaring Urubamba River in Peru, are the lichen-spotted ruins of the ancient Indian city of Macchu-Picchu. To the eye of the tourist they seem to be balanced there rather nervously. The almost perpendicular walls of the needle-like peak of Huayna-Picchu, at the extremity of the backbone, soar up three thousand feet above the rushing river. The ruins themselves are not less than two thousand feet above the water. All about, in a giant circle, rise steep mountains, green-clad except where thousand-foot cliffs rise sheer from the margin of the river.

No wilder, more isolated spot could well be imagined. Yet here, as the extensive ruins prove, once lived a people who must have numbered several thousands. The city was a marvel of planning and skillfully built masonry. Water was brought down from heights above in stone conduits and led about the streets and the passages among the buildings. Special quarters, particularly well-built, housed the families of chiefs and priests. Other larger but less well-built sections provided accommodations for the humbler elements of the population. Terraces a few feet in width, built up securely with stone, where the inhabitants grew corn and other food crops, lean at dangerous angles against every possible slope in the vicinity. They even blanket the precipitous sides of Huayna-Picchu. The visitor of today marvels at the determination and the bee-like industry which must have been necessary to build the city in the first place and to sustain life there afterward. It must have required months, even years, to shape some of the huge stones that lie among the ruins. Many questions concerning the city's ancient inhabitants come to one's mind, but a great many of the facts which we should like to know about the mysterious men who lived there are unknown. It is not even certain when the remarkable structures were built, though it is clear that the most powerful motive of the builders was defense. To pass a night in the little guest house which the government maintains near the ruins is an interesting experience. It is an awesome experience to gaze at night upon the gray ruins bathed in pale moonlight, and to try to imagine the history of the dark-skinned men who lived there a thousand years ago.

The clearing up of mysteries such as this is the work of that class of patient scientists known as archeologists. They have no written records to guide them in their investigations. They can only dig patiently among the ruins, hoping to find fragments of tools or weapons which will help them to solve the puzzle. What they find they study, comparing, recording, adding a bit here and a bit there, until at length, if they have been fortunate in their discoveries, a hazy picture of former reality begins to appear. Bit by bit the canvas of Peru's ancient history—a history covering many hundreds of years before the Spaniards came—is being painted. Many parts of the canvas yet remain to be covered, but already large sections have been in some manner filled in.

The early work of archeology in Peru (omitting mention

of the sketchy, unscientific records made by Spaniards of the colonial period) was done mainly by foreign scholars. About 1850, a Peruvian, Rivero, and an Austrian, Von Tschudi, published a book on Peruvian antiquities. In the early 1870's an American diplomatic official, E. G. Squier, spent eighteen months clambering about all over Peru, examining and measuring the known ruins. His findings, along with accurate drawings of the plans of the ruins, were later published. The German, Max Uhle, somewhat later added very important investigations, as did the American, Adolph Bandelier—after whom Bandelier National Forest in New Mexico is named, in recognition of his contributions to archeology in our own country. More recently still, the former Yale professor and United States senator, Hiram Bingham, made expeditions that uncovered in 1912 the Macchu-Picchu ruins. Philip Ainsworth Means and Edgar L. Hewitt have written books concerning ancient Peruvian life. But the Peruvian government finally awakened to the importance of its ancient treasure, and Peruvian scholars have largely taken over the task of developing the country's pre-Spanish history. Among those Peruvians who have done work in the field, the most eminent is Dr. Julio C. Tello.

It is most fitting that this Peruvian archeologist, who has a world reputation, should be a full-blood Quechua Indian. In studying the early history of Peru, he is studying the history of his own ancestors whose achievements in many lines may well cause him pride. This famous man was born in Huarochiri, a small, isolated Indian village far up in the high Andes of Peru. His father was the mayor and the leading man of his village. His mother, unlettered as were perhaps 99 per cent of the villagers, was of a family of weavers and raisers of llamas, two of the most essential occupations of the Peruvian Indians for hundreds and hundreds of years. The young Julio took an active part in the native fiestas, those which celebrate planting, harvesting, and the other activities which are of great importance to a people living an agricultural or pastoral life. The village must have been in many respects much as it had been before the arrival of the Spaniards. It furnished an excellent starting point for a Peruvian archeologist.

A curious fact of young Julio's childhood had a direct effect on his turn to archeology. The ancient Peruvians were known to have performed bone operations on the skull. A scientist of Lima, who was studying this matter, wanted a collection of Indian skulls, and he appealed to Julio's father to assist him. The young Julio saw the skulls which his father gathered and, boy-like, was much interested in them.[1] We shall presently see where the skulls reappear in his life.

Julio's mother had little appreciation of the need of "book-learning," but his father was ambitious for him and felt that he must have an education. His superior intelligence, in comparison with his twelve brothers and sisters, must early have been noticeable. The father, therefore, determined that Julio should go to Lima to be educated. Though the family had some wealth when compared with the other families of the village, it was largely in flocks and land and could not be turned into money without depriving the family of its living. The only possible means of finding money to send Julio to school in the national capital was to sell a fine collection of colonial silver that had been in the family for a long time. This was done, and the youngster, at the age of twelve, was taken down to Lima and placed in school. Shortly thereafter,

[1] Blair Niles, *Peruvian Pageant* (Indianapolis, Bobbs-Merrill Company, 1937), p. 74.

the devoted father died. Other members of the family aided Julio for a time, but soon became unable to continue. The boy was left on his own, in the old American tradition. Again in the good American tradition, this lack of support did not frighten or discourage the youngster. He managed, though with some difficulty, to sustain his life and continue his education.

Among the people of Lima who assisted Julio at this time was the great Peruvian *tradicionista*, Ricardo Palma, the writer of the traditions of the country. "Don Ricardo" was director of the National Library. He gave Julio a small position there. Looking through some books in the library one day, Julio came across one which contained pictures of the skulls which his father had sent to the scientist some years before. He seems immediately to have decided that his life work should be to learn more about those skulls and the ancient life of his ancestors. Thenceforth, he aimed all his education in that direction.[2] He studied the Indian language of his people as well as Spanish and foreign languages. He earned in his university, the old Greater University of San Marcos, the degrees of Bachelor of Medicine, Doctor of Medicine and, several years later, Doctor of Science. One of his theses was written about the skulls. In the meantime, he went abroad on fellowships which his brilliance had won and took the degree of Master of Science from our Harvard University. He then spent a year studying at the University of Berlin.[3] (This was in the days when the University of Berlin was a great school.)

For the past twenty-five years Dr. Tello has had employment in the educational life of his country, all of his posts

[2] *Ibid.*, p. 76.
[3] *Who's Who in Latin America*, P. A. Martin, ed. (Stanford University, 1940), p. 502.

more or less directly associated with his particular field of interest. He is now professor of archeology in the University of San Marcos and director of its museum of archeology. He is also director of the important National Museum of Anthropology. From time to time he goes abroad to represent his country in conferences or congresses that have importance for archeology.

One feature of Dr. Tello's work is the discovery of ancient ruins. If these ruins are in the mountains, they are usually well concealed with dense vegetation; if they are on the seacoast, the covering is sand. When the concealing materials are removed, the plan of the settlement and the materials and form of houses can be learned. Among the ruins, pottery, weapons, and tools may also be found. When studied by an expert, all of them yield some bit of information. Another important phase of the work is the discovery of burial places. Dr. Tello has located many ruins and ancient cemeteries.

Among the most valuable burial places was that at Paracas, a spot near the coast in South Central Peru not far from the modern town of Pisco. Paracas was a rich find. In deep beehive-shaped burial rooms scores of mummies were found. In addition to the materials buried with each mummy, there were many specimens of pottery.

The early Peruvians preserved the body much as did the ancient Egyptians. The first Spaniards who entered the great Indian religious center, the Temple of the Sun at Cuzco, must have had quite a start when they learned that the cone-shaped objects seated all about the sides of the main hall of the temple were the preserved bodies of former emperors. But the Egyptian and Peruvian methods differed somewhat. The Egyptian mummy was wrapped in hundreds of yards of narrow strips of cotton and linen and deposited in a prone posi-

Ruins at Tiahuanaco, near Lake Titicaca, Bolivia. These ruins are believed to be of a large city or sanctuary of Pre-Inca days. The carved head in the center of the gate represents the Creator of the Universe, to which surrounding figures are bowing.

Ruins of Macchu-Picchu. This ancient Indian city was once a well planned home of several thousand people. Isolated as it was, it had well built stone conduits to bring water from the heights above, and housing accommodations for all the classes. The Incas grew grain and other food on terraces like these.

Home of Julio Tello, Miraflores, Peru. Dr. Tello, whose life's work has been to learn about his Indian ancestors, their life and art, has used Inca motifs in the construction of his home.

Castle of Chapultepec, Mexico. This is the official presidential residence in Mexico City used by Díaz. Cárdenas refused to use this pretentious building, with its associations with corrupt Díaz.

tion in painted wooden coffins. The Peruvian mummy also was wrapped in cloth, but of various sorts—belts, squares, whole mantles—and disposed in a sitting position in a basket. The magic phrases and signs that were painted on the Egyptian coffin were replaced in the Peruvian mummy by little figures of gods and other religious objects. After the Peruvian *difunto* was completely swathed in his vestments, a false head was attached to the top of the cone to give him a somewhat human appearance. The real head was bowed on the knees and wrapped within the cone. The Egyptian mummy had a tomb which possibly was more imposing and more durable. But it was probably not drier than that of the Peruvian mummy, for it is to be remembered that the Peruvian coast is desert and that it hardly ever rains there. A body so wrapped and deeply buried in the sand would remain dry through the centuries. Hence, the Peruvian mummy is almost as well preserved as the Egyptian. When a discovery is made, the mummies are removed to Lima where they await study and classification.

It is illegal in Peru for a private individual to dig for mummies or other ancient deposits. Nevertheless, private persons do dig up these treasures, which have, of course, a monetary value when a purchaser can be found before the law catches up with the seller. There is, in actual fact, in Peru a small business in "bootleg" mummies. Not only the textile wrappings are sold, but the body itself. Of course this type of illegal activity distresses the archeologist for he loses the opportunity to study the mummy and its wrappings.

When Dr. Tello sets about the work of unwrapping a mummy, he requires the assistance of at least three persons. One performs the actual work of removing the layers one by one. Dr. Tello observes closely the material of the cloth, its color, patterns, and other qualities, and the objects that are brought to light, figurines, tassels, fans, religious objects of various sorts. The data regarding all of these matters he dictates to a stenographer or helper. A photographer is present, for from time to time a picture must be made of some particularly valuable find or of the mummy itself at various stages of the unwrapping. Several hours are needed for each mummy. When the work is finished, the poor mummy is exposed in his unlovely, dark-brown, shriveled nudity, and the workers are covered with the dust of ages. But in the pictures and the notes Dr. Tello has another store to add to his archeological treasure. Everything is carefully numbered and filed, and eventually the mummy and the materials will be classified and placed in the showcases or on the shelves of some museum. More important, the new store of scientific data will be fitted into its place in the history of the former inhabitants of Peru. It is a tribute to our scientific age that the farther we get, in point of time, from the ancient people, the more we know about their life. The scientific study of archeology is, of course, a fairly recent development.

When the Spaniards arrived in Peru four hundred years ago, they found many ruins, ruins that already had been for centuries famous with the native Indians. One such ruin is that of Pachacamac, beside the sea some twenty miles south of Lima. It was a place of ancient religious pilgrimage. Chan-Chan, three hundred miles north of Lima, also on the coast, had been, centuries before, a great city of at least a hundred thousand inhabitants. On the edge of Lake Titicaca, at an elevation of 12,500 feet, lay the gigantic, pinkish stone figures, presumably of gods, that had been there for centuries on centuries. They were the ruins of Tiahuanaco. These and others were well-known. But at scores of other places in Peru were extensive ruins that the jungle had invaded and taken for its own to the extent that even the Indians had lost sight and knowledge of them. Of that class was Macchu-Picchu. These ruins are now being sought for, and from time to time the report comes from the mountains that another has been found. Such an incident occurred late in 1940 when a party of explorers identified another large series of ruins not far from Macchu-Picchu. Dr. Tello and his fellow scientists are, of course, deeply interested in these discoveries. As soon as money is available, they will be studied. And thus another chapter will be added to American pre-history.

Peru is not, of course, the only rich archeological field in the Americas. Our own Southwest has its Chaco Canyon, its Mesa Verde, its cliff dwellings, and pre-historic ruins in many other places. Mexico has its marvelous Mayan ruins of Yucatán and the less rich but scarcely less important Aztec ruins in the neighborhood of Mexico City. In some parts of Central America and in Colombia are ruins that have not yet been carefully studied. All of these, along with Peru's treasures, are the laboratory, the library, of the archeologist. Archeologists are fond of saying that "only the surface has been scratched." Nevertheless we now know a great deal more about our predecessors and ancestors on these continents than we knew a few decades ago. There are many, many facts yet to be learned. But it is not entirely foolish to imagine that some day the riddle of the early American will have been solved. While now we merely *guess*, some day we may actually *know*, that man came to the Americas from Asia across a narrow land bridge at what is now Bering Strait, or across the strait itself. Similarly, the estimated time of his arrival may be much more definitely established than the wide range now presented between the estimates of five thousand and twenty thousand years ago.

If, or when, we arrive at this definite knowledge, it will be because of the devoted labors of men such as Dr. Tello, the humble Indian boy of the Andes, who became a world authority on Peruvian archeology. Dr. Tello has been a very busy man; his publications are many. Aside from what he has accomplished in the field of archeology, his life has been of value in disproving effectively the theory held in some quarters in Peru and other Indian countries of the Americas, that the Indian cannot be educated and that it is not wise to attempt it. Dr. Tello's life history also aids in destroying the notion which many of our people have that the Latin-Americans are essentially backward countries. Dr. Tello is only one native scientist of Peru. Men of like intelligence and high attainments are to be found in almost every Latin-American country. Those countries are developing their own scientists and scholars, their own engineers and agricultural experts, their own schools of medicine and the other sciences.

Dr. Tello's work specifically has been of importance in advancing the science of archeology, in Peru and in a wider theater, and it has elevated the standing of Peru internationally in matters intellectual.

CHAPTER XXI

LÁZARO CÁRDENAS: MEXICO'S "NEW DEAL" PRESIDENT

Suppose sixty million inhabitants of the United States lived on an unvaried diet of pancakes, beans, pepper, and whisky—and seldom had enough to satisfy their hunger. Suppose most of that number had never owned a pair of shoes, that they wore patched and insufficient clothing, had no medical service, and lived in miserable, insanitary huts. Suppose most of them could not read and write, and that they had pagan or medieval notions about religion. Suppose, moreover, that the great majority of the prominent men of the country were interested in "feathering their own nests" rather than in helping their miserable fellow-citizens. Suppose also that the greater part of our oil resources, public utilities, and millions of acres of our land were owned and operated by foreign capitalists who sent their profits out of the country. Suppose all of this and much more equally undesirable, and you will have some idea of the gigantic, almost hopeless task that confronted Lázaro Cárdenas when he became president of Mexico on December 1, 1934.

President Roosevelt has often declared that one-third of our people are "ill-clothed, ill-housed, and ill-fed." But the condition of that one-third is a great deal better than was the condition of more than one-half of the people of Mexico in

279

1934. And the task of President Cárdenas in bringing his "New Deal" to Mexico was correspondingly more difficult than that of President Roosevelt in bringing the "New Deal" to the citizens of the United States.

In the earlier chapter on Porfirio Díaz it was seen that, while foreign capital in great amount entered the country and a beginning was made in the development of its natural resources, nothing was done to improve the condition of Mexico's humbler citizens. The lives of the Indians, in fact, were rendered more miserable while the number of wealthy Mexicans increased and many foreigners grew rich exploiting the country's resources. The developments of the period are bitterly characterized in the Mexican saying that Díaz made Mexico "the mother of the foreigner and the step-mother of the Mexican."

The movement to readjust Mexican economic and political life in favor of the great mass of population began with the uprising which overthrew Dictator Díaz. The movement was led by the diminutive, squeaky-voiced idealist, Francisco Madero, an admirable and capable person. This was the beginning of the Mexican Revolution. Its watchwords became *libertad y tierra*, "liberty and land." The Revolution has been in progress since 1910 and, from the point of view at least of the Mexican liberal, it is yet far from completed. After years of storm and bloodshed the Constitution of 1917 was drawn and adopted. In its clauses on social and economic matters it is one of the most liberal to be found anywhere. But, unfortunately, not all of Mexico's leaders have been true to its principles. Carranza, president at the time of its adoption, did little to make it effective. In the succeeding decade, which was comparatively peaceful and orderly, Presidents Obregón and Calles made some advances.

The best yardstick for measuring the achievements of the revolution is that of land distribution. The Constitution of 1917 (still in force) provides for distribution of land to all the peasants of Mexico. As most of the fertile land was owned by a comparatively small number of great landowners, or *hacendados*, land for the peasants could be secured only by cutting up those great holdings. The owners could not see the justice of taking land from them to give it to the ignorant, inefficient peon. They were forced, however, to acquiesce. Obregón and Calles did not distribute land so rapidly nor in such great quantity as the liberals thought desirable. Calles and his relatives and friends became, themselves, wealthy men and the owners of landed estates. With this development their zeal for parceling out the land grew less. But Calles in particular did effect the distribution of some millions of acres.

Calles went out of office in 1928. For the following six years the presidency was occupied by a succession of three men who took their orders from Calles, the *Jefe Máximo*, the "Supreme Chief." As the election of 1934 approached, *El Jefe* looked about for a candidate whom he could control. The man must be a liberal and identified with the Revolution. He thought he had found his man when he chose General Lázaro Cárdenas.

The blood of Lázaro Cárdenas, as of that other great Mexican, Benito Juárez, is largely Indian. His people are the Tarascans, of the state of Michoacán, which lies west of Mexico City. Cárdenas was born in the village of Jiquílpan, on May 21, 1895. When he was old enough, his father, owner of a small grocery store, sent him to the village school where he learned his three "R's" and perhaps a bit more. It has been said that as Lázaro grew older and continued to learn, it seemed to him that the history of his country was a story of unending warfare between Indian and Spaniard, between farm laborer and plantation owner.[1] As he was of Indian blood and of the poorer class, it was quite natural that his sympathies should have been with the Indian, the laborer. The leaders of Mexico's war for independence and of the later wars of social revolt became his heroes. He was particularly interested in books about Napoleon and those of Victor Hugo which described phases of the French Revolution and the burdens of life among the poor of France of a century earlier. He grew ambitious to become a general and to do something to better the condition of Mexico's millions of poor.

Throughout the period of Cárdenas' youth the condition of those millions had grown steadily worse as the friends of Díaz became millionaires, as grand buildings were erected and gorgeous boulevards built in Mexico City, and as more and more land was taken from the Indians to make richer the favorites of Díaz. The great economic inequality that existed in Michoacán is suggested by these facts:

In Michoacán 97.3 per cent of the rural families owned no land, and there were only 4,500 small farm owners in a state with about a million inhabitants. Five large haciendas monopolized more than 1,340,000 acres of land.[2]

While still a boy, Lázaro became interested in political questions; he and his companions debated them earnestly. They came to understand fully the distressed condition of the agricultural class of Mexico, a class that constituted much more than half the population. So, when the Revolution came, Lázaro felt immediate sympathy for it. In the crisis

[1] Nathaniel and Sylvia Weyl, *The Reconquest of Mexico* (New York, Oxford University Press, 1939), p. 21.
[2] *Ibid.*, p. 23.

year of 1913 he was holding the job of keeper of the village jail and was caring for its one occupant. He released the prisoner, and they set out together to join the nearest band of revolutionists. Thus, at the age of eighteen, Lázaro Cárdenas began the public career which was to lead him far.

Cárdenas' cool head and his cold courage made him an excellent leader of soldiers. One promotion followed another until before the end of a decade he had become the general of his earlier dreams. As a revolutionary leader, he did some very unusual things—unusual, that is, for a Mexican revolutionary commander. On one occasion, when in need of funds to care for his men, he levied a loan on the citizens of a certain town. He was careful to give each "lender" a receipt, promising to repay the sum. This was the usual procedure, but no one was ever repaid. In this case, however, when the campaign was ended and other resources were available, to the great astonishment of everyone, Cárdenas sent agents to repay the loans. At another time, when he was sent out in command of a body of troops to perform a certain mission, he was furnished one hundred thousand dollars for "extraordinary expenses." He was not expected to return the money; no questions would be asked. It was simply a form of bribery, the customary means of encouraging a general to remain loyal. After General Cárdenas had successfully completed his mission, he returned to the treasury ninety thousand dollars, the unused balance of his extraordinary fund. Surely this was an *extraordinary* type of man. By such actions General Cárdenas proved his honesty and his incorruptibility.

In still other matters this general did not run true to form. He did not permit his soldiers to loot private property. He did not shoot or torture his prisoners. He forbade his men to molest women and punished them if they disobeyed. He did not hold civilians for ransom. The fact that he showed respect for human life made him famous throughout Mexico. Perhaps it was these qualities, as well as his military skill and courage, that earned Cárdenas promotion to the rank of major-general at the early age of twenty-nine years. There was but one higher rank in the army.

In 1928 Cárdenas was urged to become a candidate for the governorship of his home state, Michoacán. He hesitated, for the state was in a distressing condition—disorderly, almost bankrupt, riddled with political corruption. He doubted the wisdom of meddling with such a hornet's nest of difficulties. But his loyalty to the Revolution and to his people triumphed, and he became a candidate. As a candidate for political office, Cárdenas' procedure was again unusual. Ordinarily a candidate went merely to the big centers of population and made a few speeches filled with the usual pledges of loyalty to the Revolution and expressions of interest in the welfare of the "dear people." Cárdenas went to every village in the state. And here, as in every stage of his public life, Cárdenas permitted the people to approach him freely. He was friendly and unassuming. He got acquainted with them, learned their needs, and convinced them of his interest in their welfare. The result was his election by a large majority.

As governor, Cárdenas did notable work. He cleared the corruptionists out of office, eliminated extravagance, and reformed taxation. He paid the salaries of public officials, much in arrears when he entered office. He gave especial attention to education, in which he saw the sole means of making the Revolution a success. During his first two years in office he increased the number of schools from about three hundred and fifty to one thousand, and increased correspondingly the number of teachers and pupils. As an aid to the health of the undernourished children, he established school restaurants to provide them with free breakfasts. In the second year of his administration, almost half of the state's budget was devoted to the service of education. Land distribution was carried forward in accordance with the provisions of the Constitution and many other reforms were effected. As a governor, Lázaro Cárdenas was a great success.

Later, on his way to the presidency, this able man occupied several national offices. He was president of the National Revolutionary Party, the only political party of Mexico. He occupied successively two ministries in the president's cabinet, the second that of minister of war. In all of them he displayed firmness, honesty, and efficiency. Moreover, he was unwavering in his loyalty to the national government, refusing to associate himself with any revolutionary activities. Since President, and later Former President, Calles was the dominant figure in Mexico in this period of Cárdenas' life, it was no wonder that Calles should have chosen him for the presidency in 1934.

In the late 1920's and the first years of the following decade the Revolution was moving less swiftly. Calles, the *Jefe Máximo*, was losing his enthusiasm for reform. But shortly before the election of 1934 the National Revolutionary party produced its "Six Year Plan," a restatement of the revolutionary platform. Cárdenas studied it and found that it could be made to harmonize with the liberal features of the Constitution, and that it would afford an excellent basis for the reforms which he wished to carry through. Therefore, he made himself master of its provisions, and in the course of the campaign toured every section of the nation, explaining the plan to the people and pledging himself to carry out its terms. Since the government was back of his candidacy and since he was most

favorably known all over Mexico, Cárdenas found no difficulty in winning the election.

Shortly after the new president was installed in the official
residence, the Castle of Chapultepec, the *Jefe Máximo* was
rudely awakened from his dream of dominating successive
Mexican presidents. When Cárdenas showed by his early acts
that he intended to carry out his pledges to make the Revolution effective, Calles moved to "put on the brakes." But Cárdenas refused to be slowed down and exhibited such political
skill that Calles very shortly found himself aboard a plane—
at Cárdenas' "invitation"—bound for the United States. This
incident proved Cárdenas' political ability and gained for him
a free field to carry on the Revolution.

In the matter of President Cárdenas' achievements, our
attention will be confined to three which have been much
commented upon—land distribution, education, and oil ex-
propriation.

Under the Indian governments of the pre-Spanish period,
landholding in Mexico had been communal. The individual
did not *possess* land, but the group of which he was a member
enjoyed the use of an acreage sufficient to supply its needs.
With the Spanish conquest, the land passed into the possession of the conquerors and their friends, the Indians becoming, in effect, slaves. Generally speaking, the only land which
continued in the possession of the Indians was that in isolated
regions of the country. Throughout the nineteenth century
and the dictatorship of Díaz, the concentration of land into
large, privately-owned holdings, continued. The previously-
mentioned fate of the Yaquis in Sonora is an example. The
largest single factor in the Revolution of 1910 was this matter
of land. The Constitution of 1917 provided for the breaking
up of large estates and the formation from the land thus freed

of communal areas—*ejidos* is the Spanish word—for the use of peasant villages. Presidents Obregón and Calles and their successors down to Cárdenas had distributed to communities altogether some nineteen million acres. But when Cárdenas entered office much more than half the agricultural population were still without land. Cárdenas at once set about changing this situation.

The *hacendados*, it can readily be understood, opposed this work of distribution. Being in most cases influential men, they had been able to cause delay in many places. There was also an immense amount of "red tape" involved in parceling out the land. And the peasants, as they had not for centuries lived under a communal land system, were ignorant of what they should do. Moreover, they had no money to buy the necessary tools and machinery. They did not know how to market their surplus, if they were lucky enough to have one. They lacked engineering skill to plan and execute irrigation works which were necessary for many communities. This list of difficulties is sufficient to indicate the great size of the task that Cárdenas faced, when he set out to speed up and complete the land program of the Revolution. But he did not allow himself to be dismayed by the immensity of the problem.

He established government banks to furnish credit for the purchase of tools and seeds and to give advice. He provided engineers to assist in surveying and building irrigation ditches. He built agricultural colleges to train experts to assist the ignorant peons. In extreme cases he armed the peasants with rifles that they might defend themselves against the "strong-arm squads" of *hacendados* who opposed land distribution. He organized coöperative marketing groups. The president himself often went into a community where things were not going well and took personal charge. And he got results. In his first four years in office Cárdenas distributed almost twice as much land to the landless as had been distributed by all of his predecessors since 1917. During his last two years, economic and foreign troubles slowed up the work, but it proceeded nevertheless. Now Mexico has several millions of communal landholders.

In the field of education President Cárdenas' work was equally significant. Little attention had been paid to education under the long dictatorship of Díaz. The Constitution of 1917 had taken education entirely out of the hands of the church which had been from the beginning strongly opposed to the revolution. When Cárdenas became president, almost 60 per cent of the people were illiterate. Cárdenas, like Thomas Jefferson before him, was convinced that a democratic government could be successful only with an enlightened people. Much more effort was needed in this field.

As early as the presidency of Obregón (1920-1924) a new direction had been given to public education in Mexico. Educators had come to the conclusion that if the Indians were ever to be educated and made into good citizens a strong motive must be provided. They hit upon the plan of appealing to the Indians' own past history. Instead of representing as unworthy of respect everything associated with the Indian and his past, these new men encouraged the Indian to feel pride in the work of his ancestors. The beauties of Indian art were discovered. The unrivaled skill of the Indian artisan was pointed out. Moctezuma and the other ancient Indian heroes were "re-discovered." In every possible way the Indian was encouraged to feel pride in his "Indianism." This was a new approach, and it brought results. The Indian rediscovered his pride, took a new interest in himself and his surroundings.

Cárdenas speeded up this movement. New normal schools were founded. Thousands of new rural schools were built, and teachers provided for them.

The teachers became in a real sense missionaries of enlightenment. In some districts they worked against dangerous odds. The church was angered at being excluded from the educational field and at having its property nationalized. It branded the new education as atheistic, and in some districts priests encouraged the ignorant, but fanatically religious, Indians to attack the schools. Not a few teachers lost their lives, and it was quite common for them to lose their ears. But they stuck to their jobs. In Mexico the teacher is much more than a classroom teacher. He is an adviser and an assistant to the members of the village in everything that concerns them. He campaigns for sanitary improvements. He aids in forming coöperative groups, whether of farmers or industrial laborers.

This work is getting results. In 1932 workshops, baths, outhouses, and libraries were lacking in more than half the rural schools. Eighty-one per cent of Mexico's more than seventy thousand peasant communities had no school; less than one-third of the two and a half million rural children were in school. What was accomplished by Cárdenas' campaign to make possible political and economic democracy in Mexico, is suggested by this statement:

According to government records, illiteracy in Mexico decreased from 59 to 45 per cent during the 1930-1938 period. Eight thousand federal rural primary schools grew to 21,158 between 1934 and 1938. The 17 regional agricultural schools which Cárdenas inherited increased to 33. In 1938, Mexico had 50,000 teachers, and total school attendance (including workers and peasants in night classes) had risen to 2,124,000. If these figures are correct, from one-half to two-thirds of the rural population of school age is enrolled in the primary schools.[3]

Since March, 1938, our newspapers and periodicals have given much space to one of President Cárdenas' dramatic domestic actions—that of expropriating Mexican oil properties owned by foreigners. In order to understand this action, one must recall that Díaz had invited foreign capitalists to Mexico and had given them very rich concessions for developing its natural resources. For decades these foreign concerns operated, paying low wages to workers, who lived miserably, and sending rich dividends to their stockholders abroad. The oil industry in Mexico came into being around 1900, and shortly a number of United States, British, and other foreign concerns had pretty well monopolized the petroleum resources of the country, on very liberal terms and usually on ninety-nine-year leases.

President Cárdenas was as deeply concerned to better the condition of the Mexican industrial laborer as he was to assist the Mexican peasant. He encouraged the formation of labor unions and showed himself a friend in their drives for better wages and working conditions. In 1937 the union of oil-field workers demanded an increase in wages and a share in the management of operations. The companies refused the demand and used every resource of Mexico's courts in their opposition. In every case the decision was against them. But still they refused to make the concessions which commissions and courts had decided they could make and still draw a reasonable profit from their operations. It was at this point that President Cárdenas stepped in and declared the oil industry to be the property of the Mexican nation. To expro-

[3] *Ibid.,* p. 319.

A village in the state of Michoacán, Mexico. Cárdenas was born in just such a village in that state, of which he later became governor. As governor, he did much to improve conditions for the rural population which, in Díaz' day, lived in great poverty.

Sarape Market in Mexico. Cárdenas encouraged the Mexicans to take pride in their Indian history and art. Here in the sarapes we see some ancient Indian motifs and designs.

When Sir Eric Drummond, secretary of the League of Nations, made an official tour of South America, he was met in Brazil by Mello Franco, Brazilian Minister of Foreign Relations. Here left to right, are Mello

Facade of Old Senate Building, Lima, Peru. This building, originally the Hall of the Inquisition, is now the Inquisition

priate does not mean to confiscate. Mexico promises to pay
the oil companies—what *Mexico* believes is due them, and
in the manner determined *by Mexico*. In every country in the
world the right of eminent domain exists—the right to seize
private property for public good. With the refusal of our
liberal government to interfere with the free action of a
neighboring, liberal government, the initial outcry in this
country has died down. It is probable that eventually an adjustment more or less satisfactory to the evicted capitalists
will be made. In the meantime, Mexico has asserted and supported its right to regulate its internal affairs without undue
interference from outside influences, whether private or public—and, incidentally, has made a great step forward in
securing control of her own resources.

The presidential term of Lázaro Cárdenas came to an end
on December 1, 1940. The Constitution provides that no
president may succeed himself. Many friends of the Revolution urged Cárdenas to ignore the Constitution or have it
amended to permit his reëlection. But, despite the fact that
there was in Mexico no man of his own caliber to succeed him
(perhaps he was too modest to believe this) and to continue
at the same speed the work of the Revolution, the president
refused. In doing so he gave the country another much-needed
lesson in respect for the law. He was not a candidate nor did
he insist, in the usual Mexican fashion, on dictating the choice
of his successor. An election—not entirely quiet but much
more so than had been generally feared—chose the successor,
and, at the close of his constitutional period, Lázaro Cárdenas
stepped down from his high office. He retired to private life
with the confidence and the gratitude of the humbler people
of Mexico, as well as of the upper classes.

In the measures which Cárdenas carried through, Mexico

has given a lesson to the other Indian countries of Latin America. Half of the Latin-American nations may be called Indian. All of these, if they are to achieve the political and economic democracy which they profess to desire, must learn the lesson of Mexico. Otherwise they face the danger of a tragic period of revolution such as Mexico had. Will they learn it? If there were in all of them a few leaders like Lázaro Cárdenas, we might hazard an affirmative answer. As it is, the answer must be left to history.

CHAPTER XXII

AFRANIO DE MELLO FRANCO: FRIEND OF INTERNATIONAL PEACE

It was Christmas Eve, 1938. The hall of the Peruvian Senate in Lima was crowded with the diplomats of the twenty-one American republics. Cordell Hull, the quiet but forceful secretary of state of the United States, had just finished speaking and resumed his seat. The last sounds of the prolonged applause were still echoing through the chamber, when a distinguished Brazilian rose to ask the privilege of speaking. Precisely-dressed, every inch of his small, slender figure held with dignity, he edged toward the platform and passed close to the seat of his friend, Mr. Hull. Pausing for a moment, the little man smiled warmly, shook hands with the secretary of state, and congratulated him. At this simple but dramatic gesture, the diplomats broke out in spontaneous applause. It was applause for two friends, the one North American, the other South American, and for two friends of peace, peace in the Western Hemisphere and in the world.

The Brazilian gentleman was Dr. Afranio de Mello Franco, chairman of the Brazilian delegation to the Eighth Pan-American Conference. For thirty years he had been prominent in the intellectual and political life of his country, and for twenty years he had been a familiar figure in international gatherings in America and Europe. Like Cordell Hull, he had labored long and faithfully for the ideal of international peace. Now he was addressing the men and women who had gathered in Lima to try to guarantee that peace for the Americas. He spoke in the soft, lyrical rhythm of the Portuguese language, his speech as pleasant as the harmony of a sonata. His slowly turned phrases were easily understood by the Spanish-speaking delegates, and even the Americans and the French-speaking Haitians who could not understand him were impressed by his language. Mello Franco spoke, as Cordell Hull had spoken, in tribute to the Declaration of Lima.

For many days the members of the conference had toiled to draft this Declaration. They had come to Lima early in December under the shadow of dangerous threats to their democratic institutions. The armies of Germany had recently occupied Austria and a part of Czechoslovakia. Japan was invading China. Propaganda from all the dictator countries was penetrating every American republic. The Declaration of Lima was the answer to this foreign menace. It was the unanimous announcement of the determination of the American republics to make common cause in face of any threat to their peace, security, or territory. Mr. Hull, always popular and respected at the Pan-American meetings he has attended, called the Declaration an evidence of unprecedented solidarity in the Western Hemisphere. Dr. Mello Franco, soft-spoken but convincing, said it was really an agreement of the American nations to come to the assistance of each other whenever their institutions are threatened. When the document was first read, all the delegates rose to their feet and cheered.

Since 1938 many persons have come to speak of the Declaration of Lima as a "streamlining" of the Monroe Doctrine. They say that now *twenty-one* nations have agreed to do what the United States alone promised in the Monroe Doctrine. When in 1823 President Monroe stated his now famous principles, he pledged the United States to resist any European attack upon the territories or democratic governments of American nations, and to prevent the transfer of any land in the New World to European countries. On several occasions in the nineteenth century the United States intervened, or threatened to intervene, to prevent such aggression. Gradually the Doctrine gathered prestige and came to be respected by the world powers. Usually the Latin-American republics appreciated the protection which the Doctrine gave them, although there were occasional critics who thought the United States was seeking to dominate their affairs.

Near the end of the nineteenth century the United States initiated a second policy with reference to the Latin-American nations. James G. Blaine, secretary of state, had the idea that, if representatives of the various countries could meet together, they might come to know one another better, and trade between their countries might increase. Upon the invitation of the United States, therefore, the first such conference was held in Washington in 1889-1890. Since that time eight of these general conferences have met in the various capitals of the American republics. In addition, nearly a hundred special conferences have been called from time to time to deal with such subjects as highways, health and sanitation, the Red Cross, arbitration of disputes, radio communications, copyrights, and education. These conferences are officially known as International Conferences of the American States. More commonly, however, they are called Pan-American conferences, and the entire movement has come to be known as Pan-Americanism. In general, Pan-Americanism has had three main purposes: (1) the peaceful settlement of all disputes; (2) the encouragement of inter-American trade; and (3) the strengthening of cultural bonds.

Afranio de Mello Franco first came in close touch with the Pan-American movement in 1906, when the third general conference met in Rio de Janeiro. In that year he was elected a member of the national congress of Brazil from his state of Minas Geraes, where he was born on February 25, 1870. His education had been broad, although mainly in the field of law. He had been a professor of psychology, logic, the history of philosophy, and the history of religions, but his special work was in public international law. The meeting of a great international conference in Rio, therefore, gave Mello Franco a fine opportunity to observe diplomats at work in the making of international law.

Of all the statesmen who attended the Rio meeting none was greater than Elihu Root, distinguished American lawyer and secretary of state. Then, and on several later occasions, he exercised a profound influence on the life and career of Mello Franco. The Brazilian lawyer, himself later to become a world figure, was aware that Root had secured a postponement of the Second Hague Conference in order that the Third Pan-American Conference might be held. Moreover, he had succeeded in getting invitations for all the Latin-American republics to the meeting at The Hague, whereas only Mexico and Brazil had been invited to the first Hague meeting in 1899. These actions of the secretary of state Mello Franco understood and appreciated, for they tended to increase the prestige of Brazil and the other countries. Mello Franco never lost his admiration for Elihu Root.

After 1906 Mello Franco's reputation grew gradually but consistently from that of a local figure, known only in Brazil, to that of a truly international statesman. For the next twenty-three years the people of his native state elected him again and again to the Brazilian congress, where he served as a member of various parliamentary committees. On one occasion he was appointed secretary of finance of his state, and on another was minister of communications and public works in the Brazilian cabinet. The public and the leaders alike trusted him, and he was almost continuously a public servant. From state and national politics he directed his talents to diplomacy, centering his attention first on the American continents. In 1917 he was sent as special ambassador to represent Brazil at the inauguration of a new Bolivian president. Two years later he was in Washington as the Brazilian delegate to the First International Labor Conference. At Santiago, Chile, in 1923, he was president of the Brazilian delegation to the Fifth Pan-American Conference. Everywhere he went, whether among Brazilians, Spanish-Americans, or Anglo-Saxon-Americans, his personal charm and his gentlemanly approach to individuals won him the respect and admiration of all.

However, the talents of Mello Franco were far too great to be confined to one country or even to one hemisphere, especially in a disturbed world like that which followed the close of the World War in 1918. World diplomacy now commanded his services. His country had joined the League of Nations soon after its foundation, and the representatives from Brazil had been invited to sit as members of the League Council. In 1923, just after his return from Santiago, Mello Franco was sent to Geneva as special ambassador and head of the permanent Brazilian delegation to the League. For almost three years he loyally served the League, twice as president of the council.

Mello Franco's activities at Geneva were manifold. His colleagues were soon aware of his great understanding of public affairs. They respected his humanitarian approach to questions in dispute. Often he was requested to conduct an investigation and to make a special report. He concerned himself especially with the delicate problem of population minorities within the new boundaries created at the close of the World War, such as the German minorities in Poland and the Jewish minorities in Hungary. He regarded "the impartial and calm solution" of these questions as indispensable to the strengthening of peace among the nations. Because he thought they would contribute to raising the standard of living of people in Latin America as well as in the rest of the world, he strongly commended the Health Organization of the League and the campaign against the use of opium.

Naval and military disarmament Mello Franco advocated with all his zeal. Even before the signing of the Kellogg Peace Pact he argued that war ought to be declared a crime and all disputes between nations settled by arbitration or other peaceful means. "The right to security," said he, ". . . is the sacred right of all the peoples of the earth. . . ." Always, in his approach to disarmament, he would hold up the example of the nations of the Western Hemisphere. There, he would say, the foundations for a universal system of peace had already been laid. But continental treaties were not enough; they must become world wide.

Unfortunately, however, for Mello Franco—and for the world—Brazil in 1926 threatened to withdraw from the League. Brazilian leaders felt that Brazil, or another of the seventeen American members of the League, should have a *permanent* seat on the council. There was danger, they feared, that the League would grow into one of great non-American powers. But Brazil's request was refused, and her threat to withdraw was carried out. Mello Franco, however, continued until 1929 to serve in the judgeship on the Permanent Court of International Justice at The Hague, to which he had been appointed in 1923.

The venerable Brazilian returned to permanent residence in his homeland. He was close to sixty now, his black hair sprinkled with gray, his body frail, but his mind more powerful than ever before. The keenness of his interest in the welfare of humanity had been sharpened. By his work in the League and on The Hague Court he had contributed his share, a very great share, to the world's efforts to establish a system of enduring peace. He had become a truly great international statesman, recognized as such both in America and in Europe. With this experience and reputation he was in a position to renew his services to Brazil and to the Americas. Almost at once, therefore, he was appointed to the position of minister of foreign affairs.

These were the years when the foreign policies of the United States toward Latin America were changing sharply. Since 1889 the United States had courted the Latin-Americans with little success. The Spanish-American War, the methods used to secure the right to build the Panama Canal, the sending of marines into the Caribbean republics—all these policies had aroused fear in the minds of the Latin-Americans. They were suspicious of us; they sought security for themselves, security even against the United States. Under Presidents Coolidge and Hoover, however, and even more under President Roosevelt and Secretary Hull, there was a gradual change in our policies, a change for the better. We treated Mexico with greater wisdom. We withdrew our marines from the Caribbean. We promised to be a "good neighbor," instead of merely a big one. Slowly the Latin-Americans began to lose some of their suspicion, began to place confidence in our promises. The ideal of Pan-American-ism began to grow into something real and workable.

The Seventh Pan-American Conference, therefore, met at Montevideo, Uruguay, in 1933, in an atmosphere more cordial than that of any previous meeting. Cordell Hull, recently appointed secretary of state, himself went to the conference as the chief of his country's delegation. He was determined to make friends with the Latin-American leaders and to break down, if possible, the barrier of distrust which had grown up between his country and the other republics. By his simple and gentlemanly approach and by his willingness to discuss any problem, he gradually won their respect, then their confidence and admiration. Whenever he entered the senate chamber of the imposing legislative palace of Uruguay, there was a soft rustling as all turned to see him. When he addressed an audience in his quiet, soft-spoken manner, even though in English, every ear was attentive.

Like Mr. Hull, Mello Franco was head of his country's delegates at Montevideo. A few days before the conference he had entertained the secretary of state in Rio de Janeiro, presenting him to President Vargas and conducting him on a sightseeing tour. Like Mr. Hull, too, he was one of the prominent leaders of the conference. He was chairman of the important committee on Problems of International Law, and was one of those who worked most earnestly to bring about an armistice in the war between Bolivia and Paraguay. No delegate was more enthusiastic than he when Cordell Hull made the dramatic announcement that never again would the United States send its marines to intervene in the affairs of the other American republics. Mello Franco, like all the other delegates, knew that this was the most significant moment in the history of the Pan-American conferences. At last it seemed certain that the United States really meant what it said about being a "good neighbor." The Montevideo conference had turned out to be more successful than the Brazilians and many of the other delegates had hoped.

Immediately upon his return to Rio de Janeiro, Mello Franco resigned from the office of minister of foreign affairs, which he had held since 1930. Approaching sixty-four years of age now, he was no longer as strong as he had been. Moreover, he desired to devote more time to his writings in the fields of history and law. But Mello Franco's contributions to the cause of peace were by no means yet concluded. His services were to be commanded many times more. The first of these came in 1934 when he was called upon to aid the settlement of a boundary dispute between Colombia and Peru. In 1932 Peru had seized Colombia's port on the Amazon river at Leticia. Both nations prepared for war, there were border clashes, and for a time open war threatened. However, diplomats of the two countries were prevailed upon to meet in Rio de Janeiro to discuss their differences. Under the chairmanship and the wise counsel of Mello Franco, a settlement, satisfactory to both parties, was worked out and signed on May 24, 1934.

For his contribution to this settlement Mello Franco was given many honors. From his friend, Cordell Hull, he received the following message:

Recalling your great interest in the cause of peace at Montevideo, it gives me especial pleasure to extend my warmest congratulations on the statesmanlike role which you played in the peaceful solution of the Leticia conflict.[1]

The Brazilian Press Association nominated Mello Franco as

[1] *New York Times*, May 23, 1934, p. 15.

a candidate for the Nobel Peace Prize, awarded each year to the statesman who has contributed most to the cause of international peace. Diplomats of Colombia and Peru, as well as the congresses of Peru and Brazil, voted in favor of his nomination. But perhaps no one of these recommendations meant as much to Mello Franco as that which came from one he admired so deeply—Elihu Root. The great American judge, himself awarded the Nobel Prize in 1934, recommended Mello Franco for the 1935 award. When the Brazilian came to Washington in 1937 as chairman of the Committee of Experts on the Codification of International Law of the Americas, he made public testimonial of his appreciation of Elihu Root.

In December, 1938, as we have seen at the beginning of this chapter, Mello Franco attended the Pan-American conference in Lima. He went to that meeting, as he had gone to so many others, a staunch believer in democracy. He believed that the American republics could not tolerate the institutions of the Nazis or Fascists, and that the unity of the Western Hemisphere could survive only under democratic principles. At Lima he became chairman of the most important committee, that on the Organization of Peace. One of the many duties of his committee was to frame the Declaration of Lima, the document cheered so lustily when it was first announced. Cordell Hull and millions of other persons in the American republics were thankful for the work of Mello Franco at Lima.

The Declaration of Lima, it will be recalled, committed the twenty-one American republics to stand solidly together in defending their democratic institutions against all foreign attacks. This new unity was soon put to severe test. Upon the outbreak of war in September, 1939, the foreign ministers of all the American nations met in the city of Panama to take immediate action. Without a dissenting vote they agreed upon a measure known as the Declaration of Panama. This act established a zone of safety, a kind of "safety belt," around the Americas south of Canada, averaging in width three hundred miles. The nations at war were asked to avoid all fighting in this area. The Inter-American Neutrality Committee was created to sit throughout the war as a guardian of American neutrality. It was agreed that the committee should meet in Rio de Janeiro.

The first session of the new committee was held in the Municipal Building on January 15, 1940. A large crowd of Brazilians had gathered in the plaza before the building to cheer the opening ceremonies. The hall was filled with diplomats, newspaper correspondents, and public officials. On the platform were President Vargas and Oswaldo Aranha, minister of foreign affairs and, like Mello Franco, a close friend of the United States. Near the front of the room were the seven members of the committee, including Dr. Mello Franco and Professor Charles Fenwick, the representative of the United States. After the preliminary speeches, Mello Franco was elected permanent chairman, and the committee set itself to the task of safeguarding the right of American nations to free commerce with other neutrals.

Thus, Afranio de Mello Franco works today, as he has worked during much of his life, for the cause of international friendship in the Western Hemisphere. As he has said,

I see no reason why the principle of continental solidarity should not be stimulated. On the contrary, I think that it is the duty of the governments to coöperate by every means in their power so that America, diverse as are her states, shall stand forth in the world with majestic unity. This will make her great, without sacrificing the individual countries of which she is composed.[2]

In his lifetime, Mello Franco has visited Paris, Geneva, The Hague, Washington, Montevideo, Santiago, Lima, and other capitals, in his eternal quest for peace among the nations. Unhappily today, however, he can contribute little to peace in the Old World, the idea for which he labored in his years in the League of Nations and on The Hague Court. If the governments of Germany, Italy, and Japan were in the hands of men like Dr. Mello Franco, the world might not now be torn by war. This venerable Brazilian gentleman has become a statesman, not only of Brazil, but of the Americas and of the world.

[2] Quoted from his paper read before the American Society of International Law at its thirty-first annual meeting in Washington, May 1, 1937. (*Proceedings* of the American Society of International Law, 1937, p. 218.)

STUDY AIDS

PART ONE

I. Discussion Questions

1. Explain why Spain and Portugal were better prepared for careers of colonial expansion in the New World than England.

2. Would you say that the Spanish colonizers were confronted with greater obstacles than the English in the settlement of the New World? Consider such factors as Indians, climate, harbors, mountains, natural resources, animal and vegetable life, and deserts.

3. Compare the policies of Spain and England toward their colonies on the following points: (a) treatment of the Indians; (b) form of government in the colonies; (c) restrictions on trade.

4. Compare life among the Incas (or the Aztecs) when the Spaniards came with life among an Indian group which once lived in your community. Try to decide which had reached the higher level of culture.

5. Show how the civilization of the Aztecs and the Incas was changed by contacts with the Spaniards. Do you think the civilization of the Spaniards was changed by the Indians?

6. Do you approve the methods used against the Indians by Cortés, Pizarro, and Valdivia? Do the results which they obtained for Mexico, Peru, and Chile justify their actions?

7. Was Viceroy Toledo wise in the reforms he undertook in the viceroyalty of Peru?

8. Compare the social life and opportunities of the ruling classes in the Latin-American colonies with the position of the Indians and *mestizos*.

9. Using Potosí as a typical example, point out the part played by a frontier mining town in the development of a new country.

10. What part do natural resources play in the growth of a nation? Illustrate by reference to the abundance or lack of gold and silver in Mexico, Peru, Bolivia, Chile, and the Thirteen Colonies.

11. The inauguration of a president of the United States is a colorful ceremony. Compare the arrival of a viceroy in Lima, Peru, with the inauguration of one of our presidents.

12. Which do you think were the more important in spreading Spanish culture in the New World, the government officials or the padres working in their missions?

II. Activity Suggestions

1. Make a time chart of the leading events in Spain's conquest of the New World. Show the following events: discovery of America; Columbus' later voyages; Balboa's discovery of the Pacific Ocean; Cortés' conquest of Mexico; Pizarro's conquest of Peru; Valdivia's march to Chile; death of Cortés; and any other events which interest you.

2. Imagine you were a soldier in the army of Cortés. Write a letter to a friend in Spain describing your feelings as you first looked out over Tenochtitlán from the mountain pass. Describe also the entry of the army into the city and the first meeting of Cortés with Moctezuma.

3. You were a soldier in the army of Pizarro. Upon your return to Spain you were asked to speak to a group of friends about Pizarro's meeting with Atahualpa, capture of the Inca treasures, and the conquest of Peru. Prepare such a talk and give it to your classmates.

4. Read one of the following stories on Peru in the days of the Spanish conquest: Edith J. Craine, *Conquistador* (New York, Duffield and Green, 1931); Craine, *The Victors* (New York, Duffield and Green, 1933); Alice C. Desmond, *For Cross and*

King (New York, Dodd, Mead, 1941); Desmond, *Soldier of the Sun; a Story of Peru in the Days of the Incas* (New York, Dodd, Mead, 1939). In an oral or written report show how the story you read is based on historical events.

5. On an outline map of the Western Hemisphere lay out the routes of the Spanish explorers responsible for the following achievements: (a) the discovery of the Pacific Ocean; (b) the conquest of Mexico; (c) the conquest of Peru; (d) the exploration of Florida and the southern part of the United States; (e) the conquest of Chile. Make a key explaining the routes. You will need to look up some of these routes in other books.

6. The Spanish conquerors brought many things to the New World and the New World gave many things to the conquerors. Prepare a pictorial chart of two columns upon which you paste pictures of (a) Old World contributions to the New and (b) New World contributions to the Old.

7. Plan and arrange an exhibit of Indian objects from Latin America. Perhaps you can borrow pottery, clothing, dolls, pictures, and curios.

8. Develop a topic for presentation to the class on "The Boom Town of Potosí." Be sure to make comparisons with the California "gold rush" and the "gold rush" to the Klondike (Alaska).

9. Imagine you were a secretary of the Viceroy Toledo on his inspection tour of the viceroyalty of Peru. Make a diary of ten or a dozen entries, including dates, in which you describe the activities of the viceroy. Be sure to mention the problems which confronted Toledo and his solution of them.

10. Make a collection of pictures of Spanish missions. Arrange a bulletin board display of them, together with a map showing their location. You may find pictures in old issues of the *National Geographic Magazine*, other magazines, or in travel folders of railroads.

11. Pretend that you are Padre Kino and that your classmates

are monks who have recently arrived at the mission to take up their work. Prepare a talk for them in which you tell them of the things you have tried to do for the Indians. Tell them also of the duties they will be expected to perform in the mission.

12. Perhaps you know someone in your community who has visited the Spanish missions in New Mexico or California. Invite him to speak to your class on the missions as they are today.

13. On an outline map of the world, color in red Spain and all her colonial possessions at the time of their greatest extent. In another color indicate the route by which silver was shipped from Potosí to Madrid, Spain. Also locate the following places: Madrid, Havana, Vera Cruz, Mexico City, Panama City, Lima, Potosí, Santiago, several of Padre Kino's missions, and your home town.

III. Further Readings

Banks, Helen Ward, *The Story of Mexico, including "The Boy's Prescott."* New York, Stokes, 1926. 435 p.

See pp. 1-319 for the conquest. The remainder of the book brings the story of Mexico to the present day.

Brady, Cyrus T., *South American Fights and Fighters and Other Tales of Adventure.* New York, Doubleday, Page, 1910. 342 p.

There are chapters on Cortés and Pizarro.

Davis, Emily C., *Ancient Americans; the Archaeological Story of Two Continents.* New York, Holt, 1931. 311 p.

See pp. 171-239 for descriptions of the Mayas, Aztecs, and Incas.

Eells, Elsie Spicer, *South America's Story.* New York, McBride, 1931. 366 p.

On pp. 19-51 and 87-113 there are accounts of the religion, legends, life, and conquest of the Incas.

Embree, Edwin R., *Indians of the Americas; Historical Pageant.* New York, Houghton Mifflin, 1939. 260 p.

There are chapters on the Indians of Mexico and South America.

Gilbert, Henry, *Conquerors of Mexico, retold from Prescott's "Conquest of Mexico."* New York, Thomas Y. Crowell [1914]. 284 p.

Gilbert, *The Conquerors of Peru, retold from Prescott's "Conquest of Peru."* London, George G. Harrap, 1913. 286 p.

Both of Gilbert's books are written in conversational style.

Goetz, Delia and Fry, Varian, *The Good Neighbors: The Story of the Two Americas.* Headline Book No. 17. New York, Foreign Policy Association, 1939. 96 p.

See pp. 16-35 for a summary of the colonial period of Latin America.

Hallenbeck, Cleve, *Spanish Missions of the Old Southwest.* Garden City, N. Y., Doubleday, Page, 1926. 184 p.

There are many illustrations and maps.

Lummis, C. F., *The Spanish Pioneers and the California Missions.* Chicago, McClurg, 1929. 343 p.

See pp. 149-69 and 295-343 for descriptions of missions in general and those in California and New Mexico in particular.

Mead, C. W., *Old Civilizations of Inca Land.* 2d ed. New York, American Museum of Natural History, 1932.

Ober, Frederick A., *Hernando Cortés, Conqueror of Mexico.* New York, Harper, 1905. 292 p.

Ober, *Pizarro and the Conquest of Peru.* New York, Harper, 1906. 296 p.

Outhwaite, Leonard, *Unrolling the Map; the Story of Exploration.* New York, Reynal and Hitchcock, 1935. 351 p.

On pp. 67-119 there are maps and descriptions of the explorations of Cortés, Pizarro, Valdivia, and many other Spaniards.

Prescott, W. H., *Conquest of Mexico.* New York, Junior Literary Guild, 1934. 594 p.

This is an excellent version of the original Prescott.

Zimmerman, Arthur F., *Francisco de Toledo, Fifth Viceroy of Peru, 1569-1581*. Caldwell, Idaho, The Caxton Printers, Ltd., 1938. 307 p.

This is an adult biography, parts of which may be read by young students.

PART TWO

I. Discussion Questions

1. All parts of the Western Hemisphere were once controlled by countries of Europe. Today the Hemisphere is composed mainly of independent nations. They became independent through revolutionary movements which occurred between 1775 and 1825. Explain the importance of the part each of these revolutions played in the final independence of the Hemisphere.

2. Do you think the Spanish colonists were justified in revolting against Spain? Give half a dozen reasons to support your answer.

3. Compare Bolívar's plans for governing the new Spanish-American nations with those of San Martín. Which do you think had the more practical ideas for meeting the difficult problems of government?

4. Why did the Latin-American wars of independence last so much longer than the American Revolution?

5. The Thirteen Colonies won independence in one revolutionary movement led by one man. In Latin America there were many revolutionary movements led by many men. How do you explain this difference?

6. In many ways the Latin-American wars for independence were similar to the American Revolution. What Latin-American groups, persons, or publications correspond to the following in the American Revolution: (a) Loyalists; (b) Patriots; (c) Patrick Henry; (d) Thomas Paine; (e) George Washington; (f) Lafayette; (g) *Common Sense?*

7. Show why the Brazilian Revolution against Portugal was "practically bloodless."

8. Francisco de Miranda is called a "forerunner" of the revolution in Latin America. Explain how his travels in the United States, England, and France aided him in planning the independence of Venezuela.

9. Which do you think was the more important in bringing independence to the people of Latin America: (a) the planning, writing, and speaking of men like Miranda and Moreno, or (b) the military leadership of men like Bolívar and San Martín?

10. Compare the life and activities of Negro slaves in Haiti in the time of Toussaint L'Ouverture with the life and activities of slaves in our own South before and during the Civil War (War between the States).

11. Why was Cuba called "The Pearl of the Antilles"? "The Ever-Faithful Isle"?

II. Activity Suggestions

1. Draw a cartoon in which you show the injustices of Spain against her colonists in the New World. Some of these injustices were (a) high taxes, (b) cruel treatment of the Indians, and (c) strict control of colonial trade. Perhaps you can think of others.

2. Write an editorial for Mariano Moreno's newspaper, *The Gazette of Buenos Aires*, in which you describe Spain's abuses of her colonies. Argue, as Moreno did, for a reform of Spain's policies.

3. Write an account for a New York newspaper of 1825 of the military exploits of Bolívar and San Martín. You might compare their activities with those of George Washington.

4. Make a number of entries for a diary such as Friar Beltrán might have kept during his years of aid to San Martín's army. You might describe the work in Mendoza, the crossing of the Andes, and the battles against the Spaniards.

5. Divide the class into two equal groups. Debate the question: Resolved, that the accomplishments of San Martín were greater than those of Bolívar. Debate their achievements in (a) crossing the Andes, (b) in giving independence to peoples, and (c) in creating new nations. Try to be fair to both men.

6. Read a novel on the wars of independence in Chile, such as George A. Henty's *With Cochrane the Dauntless* (New York, Scribner's, 1898) or Frederic A. Kummer's *Courage over the Andes* (Philadelphia, Winston, 1940). In an oral or written report show how the story is based on historical events.

7. Make a speech to the class such as Toussaint L'Ouverture might have made to the people of Haiti as he tried to rouse them to drive out the French. Describe the evils of French government in Haiti and the plans of Toussaint for improving the lot of the Negroes.

8. On a map of the New World show in different colors the territory controlled by England, France, Spain, and Portugal in 1775. On a second map show in the same colors the territory controlled by each in 1825. On the second map locate the sites of the battles of Yorktown, Boyacá, Carabobo, Chacabuco, Maipú, and Ayacucho.

9. Make a time line of the wars of independence of the American republics in the period from 1775 to 1825. Indicate the following events: battle of Lexington; Declaration of Independence of the United States of America; battle of Yorktown; inauguration of President Washington; insurrection of Negroes in Haiti; independence of Argentina; battle of Boyacá; battle of Chacabuco; interview at Guayaquil of Bolívar and San Martín; battle of Ayacucho; founding of Bolivia.

10. José Martí has just arrived by boat in New York City. As a newspaper reporter, you are sent to interview him about his activities for the independence of Cuba. Write an article about your interview.

11. Debate the question: Resolved, that the United States acted

wisely in fighting the Spanish-American War to free Cuba from Spain.

12. Both the United States and the Latin-American republics fought for independence from their mother countries in Europe. Make a chart of two parallel columns in which you compare the American Revolution with the Latin-American wars for independence on the following points: (a) names of mother countries; (b) the years of fighting; (c) names of military leaders; (d) names of other leaders; (e) names of foreigners who assisted; (f) grievances of colonists; (g) handicaps to be overcome; (h) new nations created.

III. Further Readings

Butterworth, Hezekiah, *South America; A Popular Illustrated History of the Struggle for Liberty in the Andean Republics and Cuba*. New York, Doubleday and McClure, 1898. 266 p.
This is an old book, but there is much material on the wars for independence on pp. 1-153, 230-45, and 248-58.

Davis, H. P., *Black Democracy*. New York, Dodge, 1936. Rev. ed. See pp. 36-86 for material on the revolution in Haiti. This book is suitable for advanced students.

Eells, *South America's Story*.
See pp. 207-55.

Goetz and Fry, *The Good Neighbors*.
See pp. 35-44.

Lansing, Marian Florence, *Liberators and Heroes of South America*. New York, Page, 1940.
A fine, new book, with chapters on Miranda, San Martín, Moreno, O'Higgins, Bolívar, Sucre, and other liberators.

Marschall, Phyllis and Crane, John, *The Dauntless Liberator, Simón Bolívar*. New York, Century, 1933. 306 p.
An excellent biography for students.

Olcott, F. J., ed., *Good Stories for Great Birthdays*. Boston, Houghton Mifflin, 1922. 483 p.

This is an elementary book, but it contains some excellent material not easily available elsewhere. There are sections on San Martín, Miranda, Bolívar, and O'Higgins.

Rothery, Agnes, *South America Roundabout*. New York, Dodd, Mead, 1940. 242 p.

Pp. 216-227 deal briefly with Bolívar.

Rourke, Thomas, pseud. for D. J. Clinton, *Man of Glory: Simón Bolívar*. New York, William Morrow, 1939. 385 p.

An adult biography which can be enjoyed by many high school students.

Schoellkopf, Anna, *Don José de San Martín, 1778-1850. A Study of His Career*. New York, Boni and Liveright, 1924. 142 p.

A brief, though not difficult, biography on an adult level.

Shepherd, W. R., *The Hispanic Nations of the New World*. New Haven, Yale University Press, 1919. 251 p. (Vol. 50 in the Chronicles of America.)

See pp. 12-79.

PART THREE

I. Discussion Questions

1. After the American Revolution the Thirteen Colonies welded themselves into a united nation. In Spanish America, however, many independent nations have grown up. Account for this difference by describing the obstacles which prevented unity in Spanish America.

2. Explain why the people of the Latin-American nations have often accepted the government of dictators.

3. Are the people of Latin America ready for democratic government as we think of it in the United States? Try to illustrate your answer from specific countries, especially Argentina, Brazil, Chile, and Mexico. Do some countries seem to be more democratic than others?

4. What immediate factors led to the development of dictatorships in each of the following countries: (a) Argentina; (b) Paraguay; (c) Mexico; and (d) Venezuela?

5. Contrast the life of Dom Pedro II with that of Juan Vicente Gómez on the following points: (a) parents; (b) education; (c) travels; (d) methods of government; and (e) attitude toward the people.

6. Explain why Porfirio Díaz may be called a "Man of Millionaires and Misery."

7. Would you say that the dictators mentioned in Part III were better or worse than present-day dictators in Europe? Try to compare and contrast them on the following points: (a) methods of securing power; (b) methods used to control their own people;

(c) methods used against other nations; and (d) benefits or evils brought to their nations.

8. In the United States the movement of the people into the frontier aided the growth of democracy. Many of the Latin-American countries have also had frontiers, especially Argentina, Brazil, Chile, Peru, Colombia, and Mexico. Try to discover if the frontier in one or more of those countries has aided the growth of democracy.

9. Would you say that immigration has affected life in the Latin-American countries as it has in the United States? Support your answer with specific illustrations.

II. Activity Suggestions

1. Make a chart on the Latin-American dictators mentioned in Part III. Across the top of the paper head the columns with the following items: (a) name of dictators; (b) nationality; (c) contributions to his country; (d) evils inflicted on his country; (e) estimate of his character. On the left side of the paper list the dictators. Then fill in the columns.

2. Conduct a panel discussion on the subject, "The Outlook for Democracy in Latin America." Appoint a chairman and three members of the panel. Let each of the four make a report of four minutes on one of the following topics: (a) reasons for dictatorship in Latin America; (b) handicaps to be overcome before democracy is possible in Latin America; (c) progress already made toward democracy; (d) things the United States can do to aid the growth of democracy in Latin America. Then permit the members of the class to ask questions of the panel.

3. Make plans for and carry out a mock impeachment and trial of one of the following dictators: Rosas, López, Díaz, Gómez. Draw up a list of offenses which the dictator committed against his people. Appoint a judge and members of the jury. Choose prosecuting and defense attorneys. Proceed with the trial.

4. Divide the members of the class into two equal teams. Alternate opinions from the teams on the question, Resolved, that dictatorship in Latin America is inevitable.

5. Draw a cartoon on one of the following topics: (a) "Man of Millionaires and Misery"; (b) "Cowboy Dictator"; (c) "Dictator on Horseback"; (d) "A Dictator in Oil."

6. Read a book on life among the *gauchos* of Argentina, such as W. H. Hudson, *Far Away and Long Ago; a History of My Early Life* (New York, Dutton, many eds.), or Thames Williamson, *The Last of the Gauchos; a Boys' Tale of Argentine Adventure* (Indianapolis, Bobbs-Merrill, 1937). Develop an oral topic on "Cowboy Lore and Customs among the Argentine Gauchos."

7. Only one empire, that of Brazil, has endured for any length of time in the Western Hemisphere. Make a chart of two parallel columns comparing the constitutions of the empire of Brazil and the United States of America on the following points: (a) kind of executive; (b) term of executive; (c) kind of legislature; (d) terms of legislators; (e) kind of judiciary; (f) policy toward religion; and (g) policy toward personal liberties.

8. Make entries for a diary of Dom Pedro II during his visit to the United States. Describe what you think may have been his feelings about the United States, its people, the cities he visited, and the World's Fair of 1876.

9. Make a bar graph to show the amount of oil produced in 1940 (or any recent year) by the following countries: the United States; Mexico; Colombia; Venezuela; Peru; Russia; and Roumania. Try to discover if the United States imports oil from any of the Latin-American countries.

10. Write a letter to a student in Brazil (or any country you choose) telling him why you like your democratic way of living in the United States. Be honest, but not boastful. (You may secure the name of a Latin-American student who would like to correspond with you by writing to Student Letter Exchange, Waseca, Minnesota. Be sure to give your age.)

11. Develop an oral report on one of the following topics: (a) the difficulties which faced the Latin-American republics after independence; (b) the Paraguayan War and its effect on Paraguay; (c) Díaz and the Mexican revolution of 1910.

12. Make a bar graph to show the comparative sizes of the following countries: the United States of America; Canada; Brazil; Argentina; Mexico; Cuba; Panama; Spain; Portugal. (You may find the areas of the countries in any recent issue of the *World Almanac.*)

III. FURTHER READINGS

Banks, *The Story of Mexico.*
See pp. 371-413 for references to Santa Anna, Juárez, and Díaz.

Barrett, W. E., *Woman on Horseback. The Biography of Francisco López and Eliza Lynch.* New York, Stokes, 1938. 360 p.
An adult biography to be enjoyed by the more advanced students.

Eells, *South America's Story.*
See pp. 256-83 for brief sketches on Dom Pedro II, Rosas, and López.

Goetz and Fry, *The Good Neighbors.*
See pp. 38-54 for a brief discussion of Latin America in the time of the dictators and their relations with the United States.

Harding, Bertita, *Amazon Throne; the Story of the Braganzas of Brazil.* Indianapolis, Bobbs-Merrill, 1941. 353 p.
An adult biography of Dom Pedro and his family, parts of which may be read by students.

Lansing, *Liberators and Heroes of South America.*
See pp. 243-48 for a sketch on Dom Pedro.

Olcott, *Good Stories for Great Birthdays.*
See pp. 108-22 for Dom Pedro.

Rothery, *South America Roundabout.*
Pp. 149-57 give a brief and elementary account of *gaucho* life.

Rourke, Thomas, *Gómez, Tyrant of the Andes*. New York, William Morrow, 1936. 320 p.

A biography for older students.

Shepherd, *The Hispanic Nations of the New World*.

There is a chapter on "The Age of the Dictators."

Williams, Mary Wilhelmine, *Dom Pedro the Magnanimous, Second Emperor of Brazil*. Chapel Hill, N. C., the University of North Carolina Press, 1937. 414 p.

A fine biography, most of which can be read by older high-school pupils.

PART FOUR

I. DISCUSSION QUESTIONS

1. Try to justify the Latin-American point of view in the assertion, "We would prefer being left alone to stew in our own juices."

2. Since the United States is a leading center of modern culture, why is it that the Latin-Americans have not been willing to look to us as a "big brother"?

3. Justify the statement that the nations of Latin America are gradually growing more mature.

4. Most of the Latin-American countries were settled before the English colonies in North America. Why, therefore, should the task of education in Latin America be such a difficult one?

5. The first North American whose acquaintance Domingo Sarmiento made through a biography was Benjamin Franklin. Give reasons why Sarmiento in his later life declared that the life of Franklin should be found in every primary school library.

6. Do you think it has been to the advantage of Mexico (or other countries) to have so much foreign capital invested there? Is the United States acting wisely today in lending more money to the nations of Latin America?

7. Compare the kind of literature written by the Latin-American writers with that written by our authors. (See *Compton's Pictured Encyclopedia*, VIII, 67s-67x.)

8. Explain why we in the United States know so little about Latin-American authors. Why would it be well for us to know

more about them? Read and discuss some Latin-American poems. (See Blackwell, *Some Spanish-American Poets*.)

9. Explain why the Latin-Americans in general have been so backward in scientific fields.

10. Estimate the value of Lázaro Cárdenas' efforts to improve the conditions of Mexico's millions of poor people.

11. In what ways is the United States trying to improve relations with the other American republics? Do you believe the "Good Neighbor" policy toward Latin America is wise?

12. What characteristics and actions of Cordell Hull have helped to win for him the respect and friendship of Latin-American leaders?

13. Explain the statement, "Our relations with Latin America are now on a partnership basis."

14. Suggest some ways in which the members of your class may help to promote friendly relations with the people of Latin America.

II. Activity Suggestions

1. Imagine you are a prominent Argentine speaker. You have been invited to speak to a group of students in Buenos Aires on the birthday of Sarmiento. Prepare and give a speech on "Sarmiento, the Schoolmaster."

2. Make a chart comparing the building of a railroad in Peru (or Chile) with the building of the Union Pacific Railroad, covering such topics as cost, time, labor, distance, value, obstacles.

3. Write an account which might have appeared in a Peruvian newspaper of the inauguration of Meiggs's Arequipa railroad (or in a Chilean newspaper of the completion of the road from Valparaíso to Santiago).

4. Conduct a Latin-American music period. The following are some of the records which may be obtained:

"A Festival of Brazilian Music." (Musical Masterpiece Album, No. M-773. By the Brazilian Festival Orchestra. Works by Villa-Lobos. $5.50.)

"Sinfonía India," "Sinfonía de Antigona," and "Chacona." (Album No. M-503. By Carlos Chávez y la Orquesta Sinfónica de México. $4.50.)

"Folk Songs of the Americas." (Victor Album No. P-55. $2.50. Includes lullabies and other folk songs of South America, Mexico, and Canada.)

"The Other Americas. Album of Typical Central and South American Songs and Dances." (Ed. B. Marks Music Corporation, 1940. By Xavier Cugat. $1.)

5. Develop an oral report on one of the following topics: (a) the Pan-American Highway; (b) recent archaeological investigations in Latin America; (c) the contributions of Mr. Hull and Mr. Mello Franco to Pan-Americanism.

6. Write an editorial for one of the leading newspapers of Mexico City expressing your approval of the reforms of ex-President Cárdenas. If you prefer, write an editorial opposing the reforms.

7. Conduct an imaginary radio program in which you interview Mr. Mello Franco upon his arrival in New York. Have some well-planned questions to "lead him out."

8. Make a time line of the period from 1823 to 1941, showing some of the events in the relations of the United States with the other American republics. Include the following: Monroe Doctrine, Mexican War, Pan-American Conference at Washington, Spanish-American War, Pan-American Conference at Rio de Janeiro, Pan-American Conference at Montevideo, Pan-American Conference at Lima, Pan-American Conference at Panama.

9. Conduct a panel discussion on the subject, "The Work of the Pan-American Union in Building Better Relations between the United States and the Latin-American Republics." (Write to the Pan-American Union, Washington, D. C., for materials.)

10. Imagine that all the members of the class are Latin-Americans. Pretend that you are a Mexican, a Brazilian, or of whatever nationality you choose. Present arguments to show why you believe the Monroe Doctrine has been good (or bad) for your country. (You may secure information in the booklet, *The Good Neighbors*, by Goetz and Fry.)

11. Prepare a special program for Pan-American Day, which is celebrated each year on April 14th. (Materials may be obtained from the Pan-American Union, Washington, D. C.)

12. On an outline map of the Western Hemisphere show in lines of different colors the chief land, air, and water communications between the United States and Latin America. (To help your work, write for travel folders to such firms as Pan-American Airways, Grace Line, or the Moore-McCormack Company, New York.)

13. Imagine that you have been appointed by an airplane or steamship company to design an artistic picture map of Latin America. Your map will be used in a travel folder to attract people to visit Latin America. On an outline map of the Western Hemisphere mount cut-out pictures to advertise the attractive features of the Latin-American countries: styles of architecture, native life, strange animals, products, landscapes, etc.

14. Perhaps you know someone in your community who has recently visited Mexico, Cuba, or South America. Invite him to speak to your class on historical sites, native life, beautiful cities, or other topics.

15. Make a bar graph comparing the population of the twenty-one American republics, including the United States.

16. Arrange an exhibit of articles which originated in Latin America.

III. Further Readings

Blackwell, Alice Stone, ed., *Some Spanish-American Poets*. Philadelphia, University of Pennsylvania Press, 1937. 559 p.

Compton's Pictured Encyclopedia and Fact-Index. Chicago, F. E.
  Compton and Company, 1941. 15 v.
  Under the topic "Latin America," there is an excellent summary of the people, leaders, culture, recreation, education, economic and social developments, and international relations.
  There are other articles under South America and the names
  of the individual countries and important cities. Some of these
  articles have been issued in a pamphlet form, which may be
  obtained from the publishers.

Davis, *Ancient Americans.*
  On pages 3-27 and 272-91 there is a description of what
  archaeology is and how the archaeologist works.

Eells, *South America's Story.*
  On pp. 291-353 there are references to Sarmiento, to other
  leaders, and to the recent history of South America.

Goetz, Delia, *Neighbors to the South.* New York, Harcourt,
  Brace, 1941. 302 p.
  A recent book, somewhat elementary. There are many illus-
  trations.

Goetz and Fry, *The Good Neighbors.*
  An excellent summary of our relations with Latin America is
  to be found in pages 55-94.

Lansing, *Liberators and Heroes of South America.*
  Sarmiento is discussed on pages 297-311.

McCulloch, J. I. B., *Challenge to the Americas.* Headline Book
  No. 26. New York, Foreign Policy Association, 1940. 64 p.
  A readable account of the current dangers to the Western
  Hemisphere resulting from Hitler's victories.

Morris, Ann Axtell, *Digging in Yucatán.* New York, Junior Literary Guild, 1931.
  A description of archaeology in Yucatán.

Pan American Union, *American Nation Series.*
  A pamphlet on each of the nations published by the Pan

American Union, Washington, D. C., for five cents each.
There are other pamphlets on the cities and chief products of
Latin America.

Peck, Anne Merriman, *Roundabout South America.* New York,
Harper, 1940. 359 p.
A good account of some of the South American countries as
they are today.

Peck, Anne Merriam and Méras, E. A., *Spain in Europe and
America.* New York, Harper, 1937. 312 p.
There are chapters on "Spanish America Today" and "Creative
Arts in Spanish America."

Raushenbush, Joan, *Look at Latin America.* Headline Book No.
27. New York, Foreign Policy Association, 1940. 64 p.
A pamphlet filled with useful maps and charts.

Rothery, *South America Roundabout.*
See pages 51-81 for descriptions of the ruins of Peru and of
the *guano* birds.

Sanchez, Nellie van de Grift, *Stories of the Latin American States.*
New York, Crowell, 1935. 406 p.
A splendid summary of each country, with maps, brief history,
area, population, and many other facts.

PRONOUNCING GLOSSARY

Abbé Raynal, Ah-bay' Rye-nahl'
adobe, ah-tho'bay
Afranio de Mello Franco, Ah-frah'nyo they May'lo Frahn'ko
Aguilar, Ah-gee-lahr'
Alcántara, Ahl-kahn'tah-rah
Alejandro Álvarez, Ah-lay-hahn'-dro Ahl'bah-race
alpaca, ahl-pah'kah
Andrés Bello, Ahn'drace Bay'yoh
Antonio Maceo, Ahn-to'nyo Mah-say'oh
Araucanian, Ah-rau-kah'nyan
Arequipa, Ah-ray-key'pah
Asunción, Ah-soon-seeon'
Atacama, Ah-tah-cah'mah
Atahualpa, Ah-tah-wahl'pah
audiencia, ow-theain'seeah
Ayacucho, Ah-yah-koo'cho
Aztecs, As-tex'
Azul, Ah-sool'

Bayou de Libertas, Bah-you' der Lee-bare-tahs'
Benito Juárez, Bay-nee'toe Hwah'-race
Benjamín Vicuña Mackenna, Bane-hah-meen' Bee-koo'nyah Mah-ken'nah
Bernal Díaz, Bare-nahl' Dee'ahs
Bernardino Rivadavia, Bare-nahr-thee'no Ree-bay-thah'beeah
Biassou, Bee-ah-soo'

Bio-Bío, Bee-o-Bee'o
Blancos, Blahn'kos
Blasco Ibáñez, Blahs'ko Ee-bah'-nyace
Bogotá, Bo-go-tah'
bosques, bos'case
Boyacá, Bo-yah-kah'
Bréda, Bray-dah'
brujo, brew'ho
Buenos Aires, Bway'nos Eye'race
Bustamente, Boos-tah-main'tay

Cajamarca, Kah-hah-mahr'kah
Callao, Kah-yah'o
Calles, Kah'yace
Campeche, Kahm-pay'chay
Carabobo, Kah-rah-bo'bo
Caracas, Kah-rah'kahs
Carib, Kah-reeb'
Cariocas, Kah-reeoh'kahs
Carlos Chávez, Kahr'los Chah'-base
Carmen Miranda, Kahr'men Mee-rahn'dah
Cartagena, Kahr-tah-hay'nah
Caseros, Kah-say'ros
caudillos, cow-thee'yos
Caupolicán, Cow-poh-lee-kahn'
centavos, sane-tah'bos
Cerro de Pasco, Say'ro they Pahs'ko
Chacabuco, Chah-kah-boo'ko

329

Chaco Canyon, Chah'ko Kahn'-yon

Chan-Chan, Chan'Chan

Chapultepec, Cha-pool-tay-pake'

Château de Joux, Shah-toe' der Zhou

Cholula, Choh-loo'lah

Chuquisaca, Choo-key-sah'kah

Cipriano Castro, See-preeah'no Kahs'tro

colegio, ko-lay'heeo

Colorados, Ko-lo-rah'thos

Concepción, Kohn-sep-seeown'

conquistadores, kohn-kees-tah-tho'race

Córdoba, Kor'tho-bah

Cornelio Saavedra, Kor-nay'leeo Sah-bay'thrah

Cucurpe, Koo-koor'pay

Cuyo, Koo'yo

Diego de Almagro, Deea'go they Ah-mah'gro

Diego Rivera, Deea'go Ree-bay'-rah

difunto, dee-foon'toe

Domingo Faustino Sarmiento, Dough-meen'go Faus-tee'no Sahr-meeain'toe

Domingo de Monteverde, Dough-meen'go they Moan-tay-bear'-they

Don Enrique, Doan Ain-ree'kay

Doña Clara, Dough'nyah Klah'-rah

Doña Marina, Dough'nya Mah-ree'nah

ejidos, ay-hee'thos

El Apóstol, Ail Ah-pos'toll

El Benemérito, Ail Bay-nay-may'-ree-toe

El Diablo, Ail Deeah'blo

El Mercurio, Ail Mayr-coo'reeo

El Misti, Ail Mees'tee

El Nacional, Ail Nah-seeo-nahl'

El Precursor, Ail Pray-koor-sore'

El Supremo, Ail Soo-pray'mo

encomendero, ain-ko-main-day'ro

encomiendas, ain-ko-meain'dahs

Ercilla, Air-see'yah

Eusebio Francisco Kino, Aoo-say'-beeo Frahn-sees'ko Key'no

Extremadura, Ace-tray-mah-thoo'-rah

Facundo Quiroga, Fah-koon'-dough Key-ro'gah

Félix Rubén García Sarmiento, Fay'leeks Rue-bain' Gahr-see'ah Sahr-meeain'toe

Francesca Sánchez, Frahn-sayce'-kah Sahn'chase

Francisco Madero, Frahn-sees'ko Mah-they'ro

Francisco de Miranda, Frahn-sees'ko they Mee-rahn'dah

Francisco Pizarro, Frahn-sees'ko Pee-sah'ro

Francisco Solano López, Frahn-sees'ko So-lah'no Low'pace

Francisco de Toledo, Frahn-sees'ko they Tow-lay'tho

Gaceta de Buenos Aires, Gah-say'-tah they Bway'nos Eye'race

Gallo, Gah'yo

Gaou Guinou, Gah-oo' Gi-noo'

gauchos, gow'chos

Gila, Hee'lah

Godines, Go-thee'nace

Gran Chaco, Grahn Chah'ko

Grito do Ypiranga, Gree'toe tho Ee-pee-rahn'gah

guanays, wah-nice'
guano, wah'no
Guaraní, Wah-rah-nee'
Guatemala, Wah-tay-mah'lah
Güiraldes, Gooee-rahl'dace
Guzmán Blanco, Goos-mahn' Blahn'ko

hacendados, ah-sen-dah'thos
Heitor Villa-Lobos, Aee-tor' Vee'-lah-Low'bos
Hernández, Air-nahn'dace
Hernando Cortés, Air-nahn'do Kor-tace'
Hernando de Luque, Air-nahn'do they Loo'kay
hijo, ee'ho
Huayna Capac, Way'nah Kah-pahk'
Huayna-Picchu, Way'nah Pee'-chew
Humaitá, Oo-mahee-tah'

Imperial, Eem-pay-reeahl'
Inca, Een'kah
Inés Suárez, Ee-nace' Swah'race
Infiernillo, Een-feeair-nee'yo
Ismaelillo, Ees-mah-a-lee'yo

Jauja, How'hah
Javier, Zhah-veeay'
Jean François, Zhah Frahn-swah'
Jefe Máximo, Hay'fay Mock'-see-mo
Jiquílpan, Hee-keel'pahn
José Balta, Ho-say' Bahl'tah
José Bonifaco de Andrada e Silva, Ho-say' Bo-nee-fah'seeo they Ahn-drah'thah ee Seal'bah
José Enrique Rodó, Ho-say' Ain-ree'kay Ro-tho'

José Gaspar Rodríguez de Francia, Ho-say' Gahs-pahr' Ro-three'-gace they Frahn'seeah
José Ives Limantour, Ho-say' Ee'-base Lee-mahn-tour'
José María Heredia, Ho-say' Mah-ree'ah A-ray'theeah
José Martí, Ho-say' Mahr-tee'
José Sabogal, Ho-say' Sah-bo-gahl'
José de San Martín, Ho-say' they Sahn Mahr-teen'
José Santos Chocano, Ho-say' Sahn'tos Cho-kah'no
Juan Manuel de Rosas, Hooan Mah-nuail' they Ro'sahs
Julia Codesido, Hoo'leeah Koh-they-see'tho
Julio Tello, Hoo'leeo Tay'yo
junta, hoon'tah
Justo José de Urquiza, Hoos'toe Ho-say' they Oor-key'sah

La Araucana, Lah Ah-rau-kah'-nah
La Guayra, Lah Gwahy'rah
La Nación, Lah Nah-seeown'
la noche triste, lah no'chay trees'-tay
La Serena, Lah Say-ray'nah
Lautaro, Lau-tah'ro
Laveaux, Lah-voe'
Lázaro Cárdenas, Lah'sah-ro Kar'-they-nahs
Le Clerc, Ler Klerk
Lerdo de Tejada, Layr'tho they Tay-hah'thah
libertad y tierra, lee-bare-tath' ee teeay'rah
Lima, Lee'mah
llama, yah'mah
llanos, yah'nos

López de Santa Anna, Low′pace they Sahn′tah Ahn′nah

Los Raros, Los Rah′ros

Louis Agassiz, Looee′ Ah-gah-see′

Macchu-Picchu, Mah′chew Pee′-chew

Maipú, Mahee-poo′

Malinche, Mah-lean′chay

Manuel Gutiérrez Nájera, Mahnuail′ Goo-teeay′race Nah′hay-rah

Manuel Montt, Mah-nuail′ Moant

Manuel Ugarte, Mah-nuail′ Oogahr′tay

Manuelita, Mah-nooay-lee′tah

Maracaibo, Mah-rah kahee′bo

Maracay, Mah-rah-kahee′

Marcos Pérez, Mahr′kos Pay′race

María da Gloria, Mah-ree′ah dah Glo′reeah

Mariano Moreno, Mah-reeah′no Mo-ray′no

Martínez y Vela, Mahr-tee′nace ee Bay′lah

maté, mah-tay′

Máximo Gómez, Mock′see-mo Goh′mace

Maya, Mah′yah

Mazorca, Mah-sor′kah

Mendoza, Main-do′sah

mestizo, mace-tee′so

Mexitli, May-seet′lee

Michoacán, Mee-cho-ah-kahn′

Misiones, Mee-seeoh′nace

mita, mee′tah

Mixtec, Mees-take′

Moctezuma, Moke-tay-soo′mah

Mollendo, Mo-yain′do

Montejo, Moan-tay′ho

Montevideo, Moan-tay-bee-they′-oh

Nuestra Señora de los Dolores, Nuays′trah Say-nyo′rah they los Tho-low′race

Nueva Extremadura, Nway′bah Ace-tray-mah-thoo′rah

Oaxaca, Wah-hah′kah

Obregón, Oh-bray-goan′

Orozco, Oh-ros′ko

Paita, Pahee′tah

pampa, pahm′pah

Paraná, Pah-rah-nah′

Pedro Aguirre Cerda, Pay′thro Ah-ghee′ray Sair′thah

Pedro de Alcántara, Pay′thro they Ahl-kahn′tah-rah

Pedro de Alvarado, Pay′thro they Ahl-bah-rah′tho

Pedro Balmaceda, Pay′thro Bahl-mah-say′thah

Pedro Diez Canseco, Pay′thro Dee-ace′ Kahn-say′co

Perú, Pay-roo′

peso, pay′so

Pimería Alta, Pee-may-ree′ah Ahl′tah

Playitas, Plahee′tahs

Popocatepetl, Po-po-kah-tay′paytl

Porfirio Díaz, Pohr-fee′reeoh Dee′ahs

porteños, por-tay′nyos

Potosí, Po-toe-see′

Prosas Profanas, Pro′sahs Pro-fah′-nahs

Puerto Cabello, Pwear′to Kah-bay′yo

puna, poo′nah

Quetzalcoatl, Kate-sahl-kwatl'

Rafael Núñez, Rah-fah-ail' Noo'-nyace
Ramírez, Rah-mee'race
Raynal, Rye-nahl'
Ricardo Palma, Ree-kahr'tho Pahl'mah
Rímac, Ree'mock
Río de la Plata, Ree'o they lah Plah'tah
Rivera, Ree-bay'rah
Rivero, Ree-bay'ro
roto, row'toe
Rousseau, Roo-sow'
ruana, rwah'nah
Rubén Darío, Roo-bain' Dah-ree'oh
Rufino Blanco Fombona, Roo-fee'no Blahn'ko Foam-bo'nah

Saavedra Lamas, Sah-bay'thrah Lah'mahs
Sacsahuamán, Sock-sah-wah-mahn'
Salvatierra, Sahl-bah-teeay'rah
San Cristóbal, Sahn Krees-toe'bahl
Sandoval, Sahn-dough-bahl'
San Juan, Sahn Hwahn'
San Luís Rey, Sahn Loo-ees' Ray
San Mateo, Sahn Mah-tay'o
San Miguel, Sahn Mee-gail'
San Pedro, Sahn Pay'thro
Santa Cruz, Sahn'tah Kroos'
Santa Lucía, Sahn'tah Loo-see'ah
Santiago, Sahn-teeah'go
San Xavier del Bac, Sahn Hah-beeyair' theyl Bock
Simón Bolívar, Si-moam' Bo-lee'-bahr

Tabasco, Tah-bahs'ko
Tahuantinsuyo, Tah-wahn-teen-soo'yo
Talcahuano, Tahl-cah-wah'no
Tamarel, Tah-mah-rail'
Tarapacá, Tah-rah-pah-kah'
Tenochtitlán, Tay-noke-teet-lahn'
Texcoco, Tace-ko'ko
Thereza, Tay-ray'sah
Tiahuanaco, Teeah-wah-nah'ko
Titicaca, Tee-tee-kah'kah
Tlascala, Tlahs-kah'lah
Toledo, Toe-lay'tho
Tomás Estrada Palma, Toe-mahs' Ace-trah'thah Pahl'mah
Toussaint L'Ouverture, Too-sahn' Loo-vair-toor'
tradicionista, trah-thee-seeoh-nees'tah
Tucsón, Too-sahn'
Tucumán, Too-coo-mahn'

Valdivia, Bahl-dee'beeah
Valle-Inclán, Bah'yay Een-klan'
Valparaíso, Bahl-pah-rah-ee'so
Vargas Vila, Bahr'gahs Bee'lah
Viajes, Beeah'hace
Vicente Valverde, Bee-sain'tay Bahl-bare'they
vicuña, bee-coon'yah
Villa Rica de Vera Cruz, Bee'yah Ree'kah they Bay'rah Kroos'
Von Tschudi, Foan Tshoe'dee

Xavier, Hah-beeyair'

Yapeyú, Yah-pay-you'
Yaqui, Yah'key
Yucatán, You-kah-tahn'

Zapotec, Sah-po-take'

INDEX